Layout and Design by
Laurence Maillet
www.laurencemaillet.com

English translation by Carmella Abramowitz Moreau

English typesetting and cover design by Kayleigh Jankowski

First published in the United States of America in 2017 by
Rizzoli International Publications
300 Park Avenue South
New York, NY 10010
www.rizzoliusa.com

Originally published in French in 2015 as *Cacao* by
Éditions de La Martinière

www.editionsdelamartiniere.fr

2017 2018 2019 2020 / 10 9 8 7 6 5 4 3 2 1

ISBN: 978-0-8478-5928-3

Library of Congress Control Number: 2016945403

Printed in China

CHOCOLAT

From the Cocoa Bean to the Chocolate Bar

170 Recipes from Chocolatier

PIERRE MARCOLINI

Photographs by
MARIE PIERRE MOREL

Edited by
CHAE RIN VINCENT

New York · Paris · London · Milan

CHOCOLATE

Chocolate: a food often associated with our early childhood, our first emotions, and one that continues to hold a special place in our lives. And, of course, it evokes memories like a Proustian madeleine. Yet few of us know much about the true nature of chocolate.

With this book, I want to pay tribute to cacao and share with you what I have come to know of it. My aim is not to demystify cacao—chocolate will always retain some of its alchemy—but to make it more accessible.

As a young pastry chef, I was told time and time again that making chocolate on one's own was exceedingly complicated, and even impossible. The complexity of the process was described with a profusion of confusing technical terms. Added to the difficulty, good machines were hard to come by and expensive, quality beans were a challenge to source, and to top it off, it was unlikely that consumers would show any interest in a chocolatier who made couverture chocolate. I saw all this as an attempt to discourage me. But I think the real reason was that chocolate makers were used to buying their chocolate from two or three large producers. It was certainly easier that way, and a practice that should not be called into question.

As a naïve beginner, I couldn't help wondering where the real added value of the profession of chocolate maker lay if everyone used the same raw materials. And so, motivated by my passion—and spurred on by a certain recklessness—I spent many long years learning how to make my own chocolate. I am happy to share my knowledge with you.

I will never forget the feeling I had the first time I tasted chocolate that I had made. My search for the beans, the trips to the plantations to understand the role of each terroir, and then mastering the process to respect the notes and aromas and enhance the subtlest flavors of chocolate: at last, my dream had been realized.

This book celebrates the twentieth anniversary of the Maison Marcolini and it is my fervent hope that it will inspire you to create your own signature chocolate.

I wish you many happy discoveries as you explore the recipes.

Pierre Marcolini

CONTENTS

Pierre Marcolini,
100% Cacao

In 1964, when Pierre Marcolini's compatriot, Belgian singer and composer Jacques Brel, debuted his famous song entitled "Les Bonbons" {The Candies}, Marcolini uttered his first cry in the town of Charleroi, Belgium. History does not tell us if he was already attracted by the promise of sweet treats but what remains of this early period are the photos of a chubby-cheeked infant. By the age of fourteen, Marcolini had decided to embark on a career as a pastry chef, with chocolate-making as his ultimate goal. It was a choice he made without question, his true calling, and a journey that would be all-consuming.

By the age of nineteen he was head pastry chef in a kitchen brigade and soon garnered major awards: Best Apprentice in Belgium in 1988; *Meilleur Ouvrier de Belgique* {Best Craftsman in Belgium} in 1991; and runner-up in the world Pastry-Making Championships in Lyon, France, in both 1992 and 1993, before becoming World Champion in 1995. That year, he opened his first boutique with a small workshop in Kraainem, Belgium. A string of other boutiques—in New York, Tokyo, London, Brussels, Paris, Monaco, Kuwait City, and Taipei—followed to showcase the pastry creations of a chef totally smitten with chocolate.

Marcolini continued his mission to share with us his pleasure in everything sweet. In 1999, the small kitchen expanded to a 16,000-square-foot space in the Brussels suburb of Haren. Soon after, Marcolini's love of cacao was to draw him to the very roots of his passion.

His encounter with the late Maurice Bernachon, the Lyon specialist renowned for being one of France's first bean-to-bar chocolate makers, triggered his curiosity. At the turn of the twenty-first century, Marcolini, no longer content to work with the chocolate that was supplied to him, decided to undertake making bean-to-bar chocolate. It was as though he had a vision and he committed himself heart and soul to the enterprise. Like the first explorers, Marcolini set off on a quest for premium cacao beans. From that moment onward he has traveled ceaselessly to the finest cacao plantations over the globe, seeking out the rare beans that inspire his creations.

The year 2003 was decisive, a revolution for both the palate and the eye: Maison Marcolini's new creation, Carre2Chocolat, a perfect square comprising three rows of three squares that is signed, sealed, and delivered to happy customers the world over.

During this time, Marcolini's boutiques were flourishing around the world, and the space in Haren doubled in size. By 2009, Marcolini's entire production was made from beans he sourced himself. His endeavor of bean-to-bar production had reached fruition.

In 2013, Marcolini's television career was launched when he accepted a new challenge as member of the jury of France's TV competition for the best professional pastry chef. After all, it had not been long since Marcolini himself had collected a multitude of accolades and awards.

Marcolini has kept his passion burning as bright as when he first started traveling the world, encountering those who share his love for fine beans, a passion that continues to provide inspiration for all things delicious. *Vive le cacao*!

THE EPIC TALE
of Cacao

IN THE BEGINNING

The pre-Columbian peoples of Central America were the first to cultivate the cacao tree. The Maya and Aztecs dried, roasted, and ground the beans before mixing them in water and, sometimes, combining them with corn porridge. It was a tonic beverage, a foaming drink that the upper echelons of the society enjoyed with chili pepper, vanilla and other spices, honey, and floral aromas. The ancestor of the chocolate we know today was born. Cacao beans, which were attributed with godly powers, were also used as offerings for births, marriages, and funerals, and served as currency and tributes paid by their subjects.

CONQUEST

In 1519, Hernando Cortés, the Spanish conquistador, landed on the Tabasco coast at the southeast tip of Mexico. Montezuma, the Aztec emperor, offered him a large cup filled with "xocoatl." But the Spaniards were not immediately won over by the bitter drink, keeping their eyes only on the prize of gold. In 1528, when Cortés brought cacao beans and the utensils to make chocolate back to Spain, he told Charles V of the invigorating virtues of the drink. Sweetened with cane sugar and vanilla, it became immensely popular with rich Spaniards. In the New World, cacao production increased and Spain gained the monopoly of the cacao bean trade.

CHOCOLATE ON THE OLD CONTINENT

When Anne of Austria, the eldest daughter of Philip III of Spain, wed Louis XIII in 1615 and became Queen of France, she brought the craze for chocolate to the court. Later, Marie-Theresa of Austria, wife of Louis XIV, had a real passion for what Linneaus had by then named *Theobroma cacao*, the food of the gods. At the court of Versailles, it was fashionable to be fanatical about the drink that symbolized refinement, aristocracy, and even debauchery, because it was said to be an aphrodisiac.

In 1657, a Frenchman opened the first chocolate houses in London. In England, the drink was not exclusively reserved for the aristocracy; it spread and was enjoyed by ordinary people. Until then, chocolate was consumed only as a drink, but it was first sold in solid form in London in 1674, under the name of chocolate rolls "in the Spanish style."

GHANA
8.04.15

PIERRE
MARCOLINI
PIERRE
MARCOLINI

THE CREATION OF A CHOCOLATE INDUSTRY

IN 1732, Debuisson, a Frenchman, invents a table mill for grinding cacao beans. It is heated with coal and enables workers to remain standing, thus increasing their productivity.

AROUND 1760, Englishman Joseph Storrs Fry builds the first hydraulic press for cacao beans, enabling more significant volumes of beans to be crushed and ground and reducing production costs.

IN 1811 French engineer Poincelet invents the first cacao bean mixer, thereby increasing production speed and eliminating manual labor.

Cacao plantations increase in size, and the chocolate industry is born, benefiting from technical progress.

IN 1828, Coenraad van Houten, a Dutch chemist, invents the cacao pressing method. This results in the production of cacao powder, and enables the different components of the bean to be separated.

IN 1830, Charles-Amédée Kohler, a Swiss confectionary manufacturer, invents hazelnut chocolate.

IN 1847, the first chocolate bar is produced by the Fry company in England.

IN 1875, Daniel Peter, a Swiss chocolatier, creates milk chocolate, thanks to Henri Nestlé's invention of milk powder.

IN 1879 Rodolphe Lindt develops the technique of conching in Switzerland, making chocolate creamier and refining its taste.

DURING THE NINETEENTH CENTURY, vast fortunes are built thanks to chocolate. They include Poulain and Menier in France, Côte d'Or in Belgium, Suchard in Switzerland, and Van Houten in the Netherlands.

TWENTIETH AND TWENTY-FIRST CENTURIES

Chocolate becomes increasingly affordable to people of all walks of life thanks to industrialization, mass production, lower costs, and the development of advertising. Demand increases and with new colonies available, Europeans encourage the development of cacao plantations in Africa.

In 2000, under what is known as the Chocolate Directive, the European Union allows up to 5 percent of the finished product of vegetable fats other than cacao butter to be included in chocolate. This means that the inclusion of pure cacao butter has become a guarantee of quality. While the demand for cacao worldwide is increasing thanks to the rising consumption of chocolate, particularly in Asia, certain people fear a scarcity of what is sometimes called "brown gold."

In response to these alarmist preoccupations, others—mainly bean-to-bar artisans—are focusing on cacao beans. From the transformation of the cacao bean to the creation of the chocolate we eat, these devotees firmly intend to control every stage of the production chain.

Their ethic involves developing plantations and supporting farm workers, particularly with equitable pay, and seeking out the unique features of each terroir, as is done in winemaking. With this approach, signature creations take on their full meaning. Only the future will tell us if the bean-to-bar movement will leave a lasting mark on the history of cacao. Pierre Marcolini, for one, is 100 percent convinced it will.

MEXICO
CUBA
VENEZUELA
ECUADOR
PERU
BRAZIL
CAMEROON

Cacao-producing countries form what is known as the "cacao belt," an imaginary strip located between 10°N and 10°S of the Equator.

This map indicates only the countries where the grand crus presented in this book are grown.

From Bean to Bar

IN THE COUNTRY OF THE PLANTATIONS

HARVEST

Twice a year, in spring and in fall, the pods, the fruit of the cacao tree, are harvested by hand.

> *{Pierre Marcolini}*
> *I have wonderful memories of the end of a harvest in Brazil. For the first time, I tasted "cacao honey syrup," the juice of fresh beans that you can drink from the pods. It's a surprising taste, as fresh as lychee, and similar to, yet far-removed from, the aromas of cacao.*

BREAKING THE PODS

The pods are broken open with machetes. Inside, the cacao beans, which may be white or purple, are surrounded by a mucilaginous pulp.

FERMENTATION

Soon after the pods are opened, the beans, still enveloped in the pulp, are placed in fermentation bins covered with banana leaves to increase the temperature. The pulp is transformed into alcohol and the beans swell, developing the aromas that prefigure those of cacao. By the time the beans are fermented, they have turned a chocolate brown color.

> *The first time I smelled it, I was taken aback by the strong odor of acetic acid, very vinegary, that comes from the fermentation bins. When you dip your hand in, you feel an astonishing heat, between 104 and 140°F {40 to 60°C}.*

DRYING

The beans, which still contain 60 percent humidity, are spread out in the sun to reduce the water percentage to between 3 and 7 percent.

> *The drying surfaces resemble natural carpets in hues ranging from darkest brown to the most flamboyant red, suggesting contemporary marquetry work with textured effects.*

SORTING AND GRADING

Moldy beans, and those that are otherwise spoiled, are discarded, and the others are packed into sacks for transportation to chocolate-producing countries.

ESO NETO 60Kg
ESO BRUTO 60.7Kg
ALIDAD:CACAO A
OSECHA:2009
OTE:2
ECHA/PROD:

AT THE CHOCOLATIER

STORAGE

When the beans arrive at the Maison Pierre Marcolini, the chocolatier and the head of production test samples using an instrument that looks like a guillotine. The beans are arranged in a square frame with 50 holes. The box is closed and a blade is inserted, slicing the beans in two. A bean that is running with veins is a herald of rich aromas, to be confirmed by a tasting test.

ROASTING

Just like green coffee beans, cacao beans are roasted in a rotating machine for 20 to 30 minutes at a temperature that ranges between 212 and 300°F {100 and 150°C}, according to the type of cacao. Here, any remaining moisture is eliminated, thereby allowing the aromas to be amplified. It's a crucial stage of the process and one that is closely watched over.

The sleeping beauty is awoken when the aromas of the beans are revealed at this stage.

CRUSHING

After they are cooled by ventilators, the beans are coarsely crushed. A ventilation system separates the skins from the cacao nibs {the shards of the beans}.

The spirit of chocolate is like a rough diamond, and a joy to the taste buds.

GRINDING

The cacao nibs are crushed beneath various mills that grind them increasingly finely. Because of their high fat content—between 40 and 50 percent—they are transformed into cacao paste, also known as cacao liqueur. The objective here is to achieve a substance smaller than 25 microns. At the Maison Marcolini, it is smaller than 18 microns. At this stage, the human tongue cannot distinguish between the particles.

Watching the cacao paste that comes from the mills is like seeing chocolate waves surging out.

CONCHING

A conch is a tank in which rollers constantly move back and forth to ensure that the chocolate is creamy, velvety, and refined. During this part of the process, cacao paste, sugar, and cacao butter are added to make bittersweet chocolate. To make milk chocolate, milk powder is also added. White chocolate, on the other hand, comprises only cacao butter, sugar, and milk powder, which is why some people consider that it is not truly chocolate.

The most delicate stage:

TEMPERING

Before chocolate is molded, it is heated to a specific temperature, a process known as tempering, to give it a stable sheen: 82°F {28°C} for white and milk chocolate, and 90°F {32°C} for bittersweet chocolate.

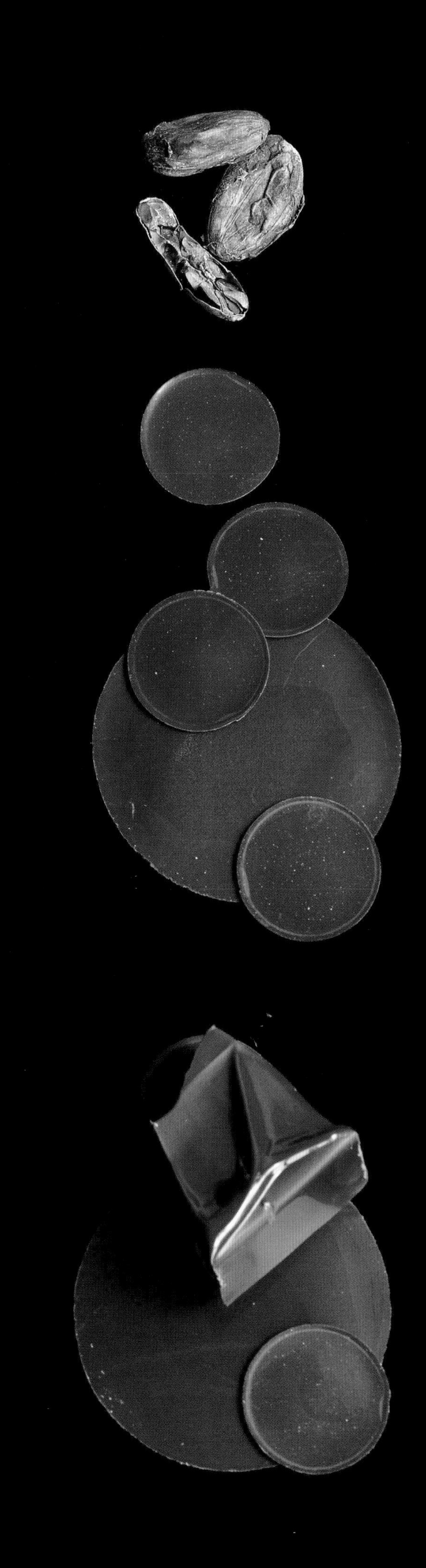

Bean to Bar at Home

Make your own bean to bar chocolate at home, using only basic equipment. Pierre Marcolini shares his secrets with you.

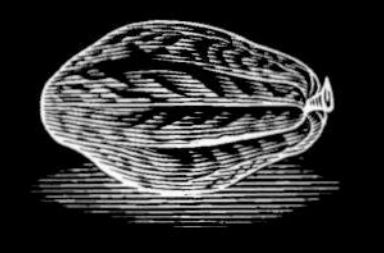

Roasted Cacao Beans with Cashew Nuts,

Salt & Sarawak Pepper

Serves 8 as a snack
Prep: 10 minutes
Cook: 20 minutes

INGREDIENTS

7 oz. {200 g} whole raw cacao beans
Fleur de sel
Freshly ground Sarawak pepper
3½ oz. {100 g} unsalted cashew nuts

Preheat the oven to 325°F {160°C}. Line a baking sheet with parchment paper. Spread the cacao beans over the prepared sheet and roast for 20 minutes. On removing them from the oven, peel them, taking care not to burn yourself, and season them generously with salt and Sarawak pepper. Combine with the cashew nuts and serve.

Chef's note

Vary the seasonings, for example by using a ground chili pepper of your choice instead of Sarawak pepper.

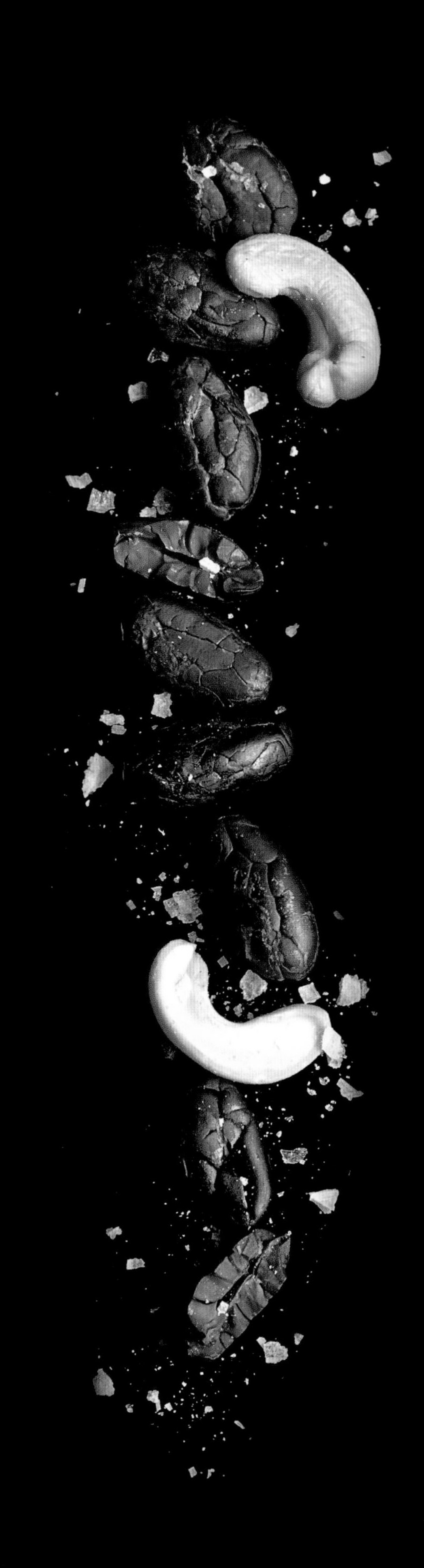

Natural Chocolate
with Raw Cacao Beans

Serves 6
Prep: 15 minutes
Cook: 1 hour

INGREDIENTS

7 oz. {200 g} cacao beans
2/3 oz. {20 g} cacao butter
1/3 cup {2 oz. / 60 g} granulated sugar

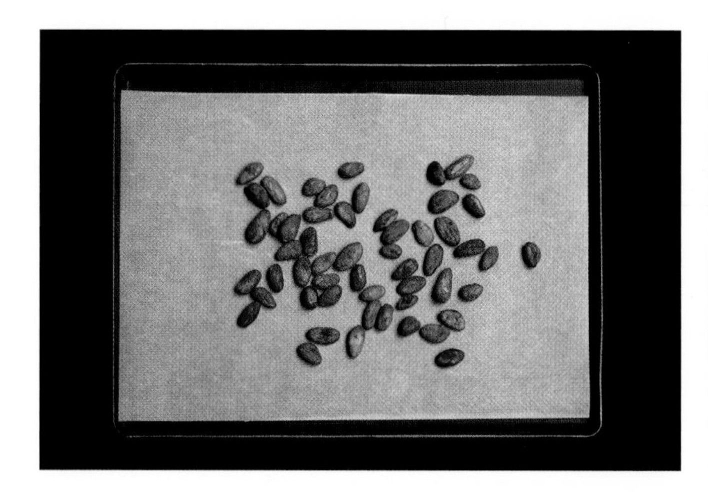

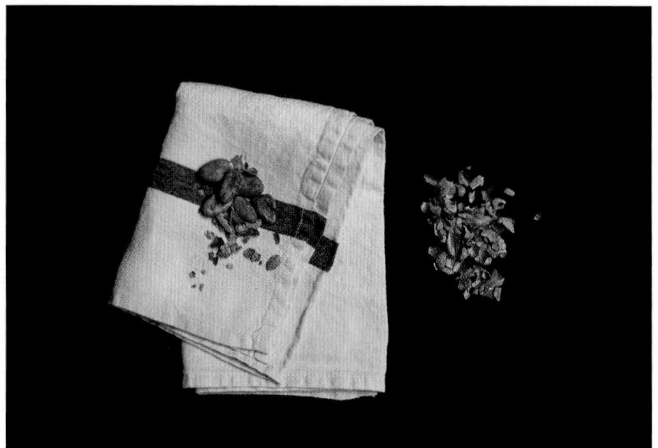

The aim of placing the beans in the oven is to dry them, not to roast them, and retain all their polyphenols. Ensure that your oven does not get any hotter than the recommended temperature.

Preheat the oven to 140°F {60°C}. Line a baking sheet with parchment paper.

Spread the cacao beans over the prepared sheet and dry for 1 hour in the oven. A few minutes before removing the cacao beans from the oven, heat the cacao butter over low heat—it must be very hot when added.

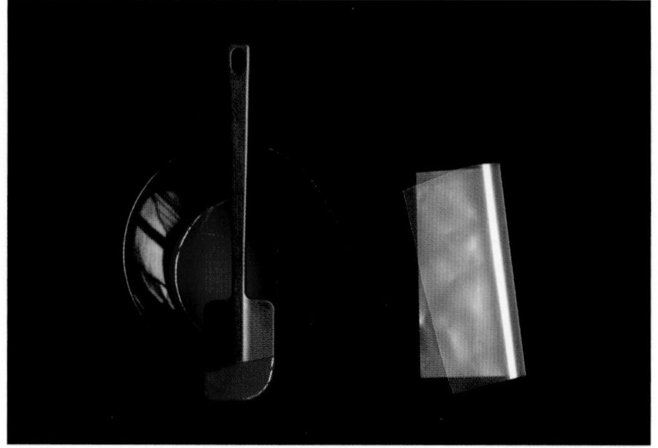

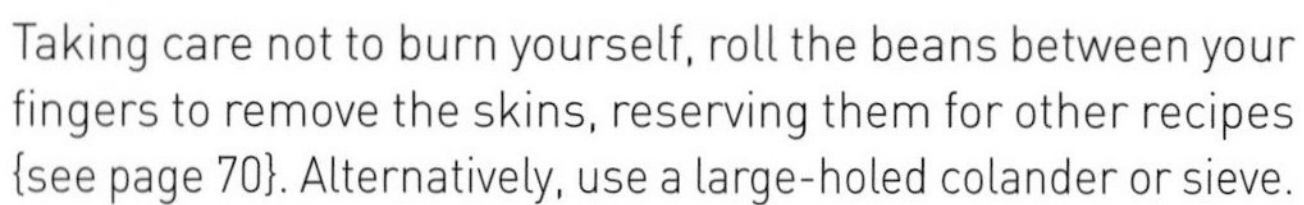

Taking care not to burn yourself, roll the beans between your fingers to remove the skins, reserving them for other recipes {see page 70}. Alternatively, use a large-holed colander or sieve.

In a blender, combine the cacao beans with the sugar. Pour in the hot cacao butter and blend for almost 5 minutes.

This makes raw natural chocolate. Pour it onto a sheet to cool. You can then enjoy it just like a traditional bar of chocolate, or use it in other chocolate recipes.

This recipe allows you to enjoy the taste of fresh cacao beans.

Natural Chocolate Bar

with Raw Cacao Beans

Makes one 10½-oz. {300-g} bar
Prep: 15 minutes

INGREDIENTS

10½ oz. {300 g} Natural Chocolate
{see recipe, page 34}
A few raw cacao beans

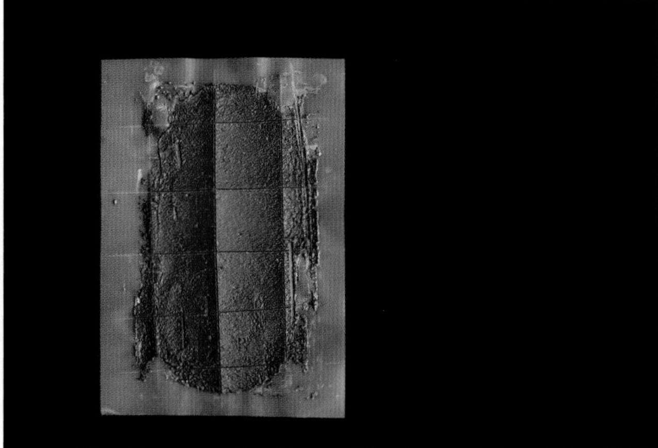

Place a sheet of food-safe acetate on a baking sheet. Chop the chocolate with a knife.

To ensure that your chocolate bar is glossy, temper it as follows:
- Over a hot water bath, heat the natural chocolate to 122°F {50°C}.
- Place over a cool water bath and cool to 82°F {28°C}.
- Reheat the chocolate to 90°F {32°C} over a hot water bath.

Spread the chocolate over the prepared baking sheet to the thickness you prefer. Allow to cool for about 10 minutes and sprinkle with shards of raw cacao beans to add some crunch.

Allow to set at room temperature, then wrap in foil.

MAR
COL
INI

MAR
COL
INI

Raw Cacao Bean Ganache

Serves 8
Prep: 15 minutes

INGREDIENTS

½ cup {120 ml} heavy cream {35% butterfat}
1½ tablespoons {20 g} granulated sugar
5½ oz. {160 g} Natural Chocolate
{see recipe, page 34}
3 tablespoons {40 g} unsalted butter, room temperature, diced

Heat the cream to 175°F {80°C}. Stir in the sugar until dissolved.

Chop the chocolate with a knife and place it in a mixing bowl.

Pour the hot cream in a steady stream over the chocolate, whisking constantly. The final texture should be very smooth, similar to that of mayonnaise. When the emulsion has formed, gently whisk in the butter.

The ganache is ready to be served.

Chef's note

This ganache is ideal for making small truffles.

Hot Chocolate

made with Raw Cacao Beans

Serves 6
Prep: 15 minutes

INGREDIENTS

3½ oz. {100 g} Natural Chocolate
{see recipe, page 34}
1 cup {240 ml} whole milk
¾ cup {200 ml} heavy cream {35% butterfat}
½ cup {120 ml} water
2½ teaspoons {10 g} granulated sugar

Chop the chocolate with a knife.

Pour the milk, cream, and water into a saucepan. Add the sugar and bring to a boil. Immediately remove from the heat and add the chocolate. With an immersion blender, process the mixture very briefly, until a light foam appears and the drink is creamy. Serve hot.

Chef's note

The small pieces of raw beans contained in the raw natural chocolate give a crunchy note to this hot chocolate drink.

Roasting Beans in the Oven

Serves 10
Prep: 10 minutes
Cook: 20 minutes

INGREDIENTS
7 oz. {200 g} finest-quality raw cacao beans

Preheat the oven to 325°F {160°C}. Line a baking sheet with parchment paper.

Spread the beans over the sheet and roast for 20 minutes.

On removing the beans from the oven, there are two methods to separate the beans from their skins.
-Taking care not to burn yourself, roll the beans between your fingers to remove the skins.
-Crush the beans and use a colander with large holes to sift them.

Be sure to reserve the skins; you will need them for other recipes {see page 70}.

The roasted, crushed cacao beans are known as **cacao nibs**.

The roasted beans may be eaten immediately.

Photo on following spread

Roasting Beans in a Skillet

Serves 10
Prep: 10 minutes
Cook: 10 minutes

INGREDIENTS

10½ oz. {300 g} finest-quality cacao beans

Spread the cacao beans in the skillet, ensuring that there is one layer only. If the skillet is not large enough, work in batches.

Place the skillet over high heat and roast the beans just as you would roast pine nuts, pistachios, or other nuts. Stir from time to time so that the beans color all over.

Remove from the heat and allow to cool to lukewarm.

There are two methods to separate the beans from their skins.
-Roll the beans between your fingers.
-Crush the beans and use a colander with large holes to sift them.

Be sure to reserve the skins; you will need them for other recipes {see page 70}.

The roasted, crushed cacao beans are known as **cacao nibs**.

Chef's note

As an accompaniment to your chocolate desserts, these roasted beans will accentuate their cacao flavor.

Adding a Personal Touch
to Roasted Beans

Serves 10
Prep {a day ahead}: 10 minutes
Cook: 20 minutes
Rest: 24 hours

INGREDIENTS

1 vanilla bean, preferably Madagascar vanilla
10½ oz. {300 g} finest-quality cacao beans
1 cinnamon stick
Freshly ground pepper of your choice, one or more varieties {Sarawak and Timut, for example}

Preheat the oven to 325°F {160°C}. Line a baking sheet with parchment paper.

Split the vanilla bean in half lengthwise and scrape out the seeds. In a mixing bowl, combine the vanilla bean and seeds with the cacao beans and the cinnamon stick. Transfer to the prepared baking sheet and grind the pepper over.

Roast for 20 minutes.

Transfer the hot beans with the cinnamon stick and vanilla bean to an airtight container. Allow to rest for 24 hours for the beans to absorb the flavors of the spices before you use them.

Chef's note

This recipe will enable you to make naturally flavored chocolate with a personal touch.

Smoking Beans
in Hay

Serves 10
Prep {a day ahead}: 10 minutes
Cook: 20 minutes
Rest: 24 hours

INGREDIENTS

2 oz. {50 g} fresh hay
10½ oz. {300 g} raw cacao beans

Preheat the oven to 325°F {160°C}. Spread the hay over a baking sheet and place it in the oven. Cook for 20 minutes.

Transfer the hay to a large mixing bowl. Place the cacao beans in a smaller mixing bowl and place it over the hay in the center of the larger bowl. Cover with plastic wrap, enclosing both the smaller and larger bowls.

Allow to rest for 24 hours. The cacao beans will absorb the flavors of the hay.

Chef's note

Beans prepared with this method are perfect for making natural smoked chocolate.

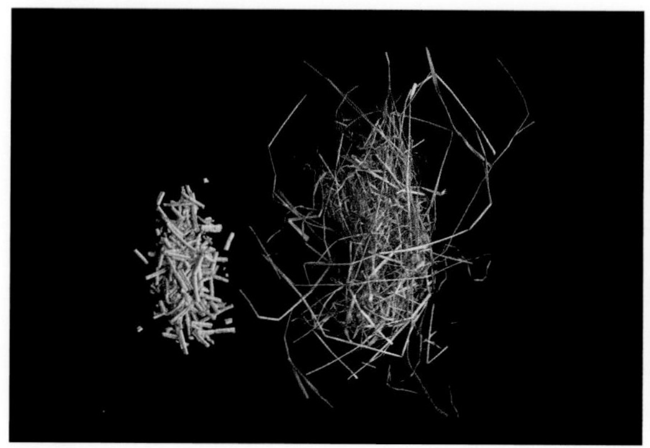

SMOKING BEANS
with Wood Chips

Serves 10
Prep {a few hours ahead}: 10 minutes
Cook: 10 minutes
Rest: 3 hours

INGREDIENTS

2 oz. {50 g} wood chips
10½ oz. {300 g} raw cacao beans

Begin burning the wood chips, preferably on a grill. When they are partially burnt but haven't turned to ash, transfer them carefully to a heatproof mixing bowl. Place the cacao beans in a smaller mixing bowl. Set this in the center of the hot wood chips. Cover with plastic wrap, enclosing both the smaller and larger bowls.

Allow to rest for 3 hours. The cacao beans will absorb the aromas of the wood chips.

Chef's note

Beans prepared with this method are perfect to make natural smoked chocolate. Select the type of wood according to the type of flavor you are aiming to achieve. Oak gives a very pronounced flavor, apple wood is milder and fruity, and ash wood results in a full-bodied flavor.

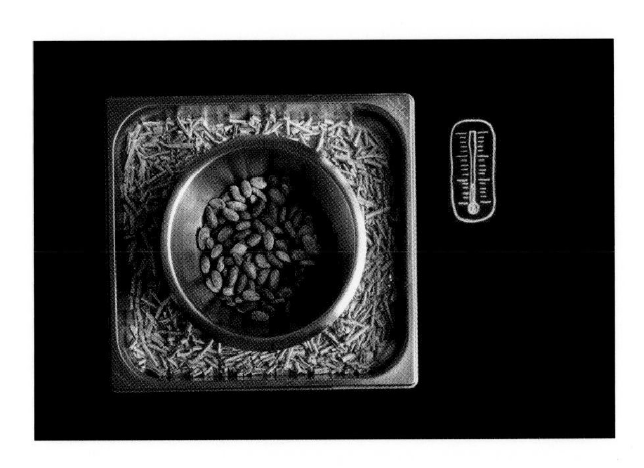

Cacao Nib Pepper

Prep: 10 minutes

INGREDIENTS

⅔ oz. {20 g} assorted black peppercorns,
such as Timut, Sarawak, or Voatsiperifery
3½ oz. {100 g} freshly roasted cacao nibs
{see recipe, page 44 or 45}

Using the flat side of a knife, lightly crush the peppercorns. Combine them well with the cacao nibs.

Chef's note

Use this flavored pepper on meat and fish.

Savory Cacao Spread

Makes the equivalent of one large jam jar
Prep: 15 minutes

INGREDIENTS

⅓ oz. {10 g} cacao butter
3½ oz. {100 g} freshly roasted cacao nibs
{see recipe, page 44 or 45}
7 oz. {200 g} black olive tapenade {see Notes}
Piment d'Espelette
Salt and freshly ground pepper

In a saucepan, heat the cacao butter to 160°F {70°C}. Blend or process the cacao butter with the cacao nibs until the mixture has the consistency of pesto.

Combine thoroughly with the tapenade. Season to taste with piment d'Espelette, salt, and freshly ground pepper.

Chef's notes

This savory spread keeps for up to two weeks, and makes an original condiment to serve with meat and fish.

Tapenade classically comprises olives, capers, and anchovies, all blended with olive oil, and sometimes lemon juice and garlic.

Raw Cacao Bean Spread

Makes the equivalent of two jam jars

Prep: 20 minutes

INGREDIENTS

9 oz. {250 g} Natural Chocolate
{see recipe, page 34}
1/3 cup {70 ml} whole milk
Scant 2/3 cup {4 oz. / 120 g} granulated sugar
1¾ sticks {7 oz. / 200 g} unsalted butter, diced
2 eggs

Chop the chocolate with a knife and place it in a mixing bowl.

Pour the milk into a saucepan. Add the sugar and butter and bring to a boil.

Pour the hot liquid over the chocolate, whisking constantly. When the mixture is smooth, whisk in the eggs.

With an immersion blender, process the mixture until it forms an emulsion.

Pour into the jars, allow to cool, and seal.

Chef's note

This spread keeps for up to two weeks stored in the refrigerator.

Sweet Chocolate Spread

Makes 2 small jars

Prep: 10 minutes
Chill: 12 hours

INGREDIENTS

2½ oz. {65 g} Natural Chocolate
{see recipe, page 34}
3½ tablespoons {1 oz. / 25 g} unsweetened cocoa powder
2/3 cup {160 g} whipping cream {35% butterfat}
3½ tablespoons {1½ oz. / 40 g} granulated sugar
2 tablespoons plus 1 teaspoon {2 oz. / 50 g} glucose syrup
¼ teaspoon {1 g} fleur de sel

Chop the chocolate with a knife and place it in a mixing bowl. Add the cocoa powder.

Pour the cream into a saucepan and add the sugar, glucose syrup, and fleur de sel. Bring to a boil and pour in a steady stream over the chocolate and cocoa powder, whisking constantly. When the mixture is smooth, process the mixture with an immersion blender.

Pour into the jars and refrigerate 12 hours before serving on bread.

COD FILLETS
with a Cacao Nib Crust

Serves 4
Prep: 10 minutes
Cook: 7 minutes

INGREDIENTS

2 oz. {50 g} cacao nibs
{see recipe, page 44 or 45}
Finely grated zest of 1 unwaxed orange
Finely grated zest of 1 unwaxed lemon
Freshly ground Sarawak pepper
Fleur de sel
1 lb. {500 g} fillet of cod, preferably the loin
4 leaves bear's garlic to serve

Preheat a steam oven to 320°F {160°C} and set the moisture to 25 percent {see Note}. Line a baking sheet with parchment paper.

Make the coating: Combine the cacao nibs, orange and lemon zest, pepper, and fleur de sel in a small bowl. Place the cod fillet on the prepared baking sheet and spread the coating over it.

Cook for 7 minutes.

Place a leaf of bear's garlic on each plate and set a portion of cod over it.

Chef's note

If you do not have a steam oven, simply place a clean, damp cloth under the fish fillet before cooking it at the same temperature for the same length of time.

Cacao Nibs
for Foie Gras

Serves 6
Prep: 10 minutes

INGREDIENTS

10 oz. {300 g} foie gras, cooked or semi-cooked
0.2 oz. {5 g} roasted cacao beans
{see recipe, page 44 or 45}
Freshly ground Timut pepper
Fleur de sel

Slice the foie gras into equal-sized servings.

In the center of each slice, place a few roasted cacao nibs. Season to taste with Timut pepper and fleur de sel.

Cacao Nib
Brittle

Makes 1¾ lb. {800 g} bars of brittle
Prep: 15 minutes
Cook: 12 minutes

INGREDIENTS

0.2 oz. {5 g} pectin
1 cup {7 oz. / 200 g} granulated sugar, divided
Scant ½ cup {100 ml} whole milk
Scant ⅓ cup {3½ oz. / 100 g} glucose syrup
10½ oz. {300 g} cacao nibs
{see recipe, page 44 or 45}
1 stick {4½ oz. / 125 g} unsalted butter, diced

Preheat the oven to 340°F {170°C}.

Combine the pectin with one-quarter cup of the sugar. In a saucepan, bring the milk, remaining sugar, and glucose syrup to a boil. Stir in the pectin-sugar mixture and heat to 217°F {103°C}. Stir in the cacao nibs and butter.

Spread the mixture between two sheets of parchment paper and roll with a rolling pin until it is as thin as possible. Place on a baking sheet and bake for 12 minutes.

Immediately transfer to a rack and allow to cool, unless you are making decorative shapes. In this case, use a knife or pastry cutter to cut your shapes before the brittle has cooled completely.

Chef's note

The brittle keeps for up to two weeks in an airtight container at room temperature.

Cacao Nib
Clusters

Makes 10 clusters
Prep: 15 minutes

INGREDIENTS

2½ oz. {70 g} Natural Chocolate
{see recipe, page 34}
⅓ oz. {10 g} cacao butter
3½ oz. {100 g} finely crushed cacao nibs
{see recipe, page 44 or 45}

Chop the chocolate with a knife. Over a hot water bath, melt the cacao butter with the chocolate. When it reaches 95°F {35°C}, stir in the cacao nibs.

With two teaspoons, shape small mounds on a sheet of parchment paper. Allow to cool to room temperature.

Serve these clusters with coffee.

Chef's note

These clusters keep for several weeks. If you wish, add nuts or dried fruit, such as raisins.

Recipe photo on following spread

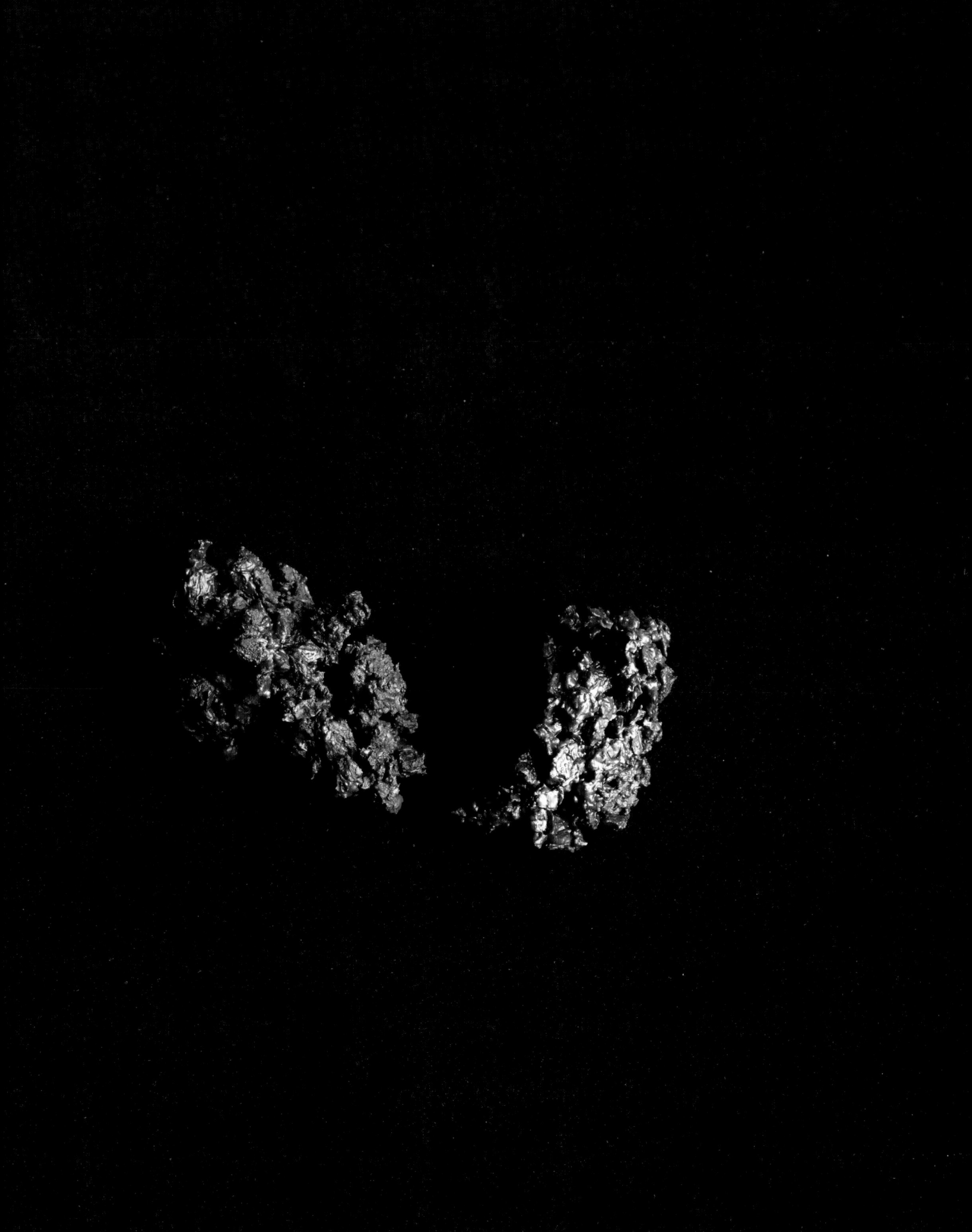

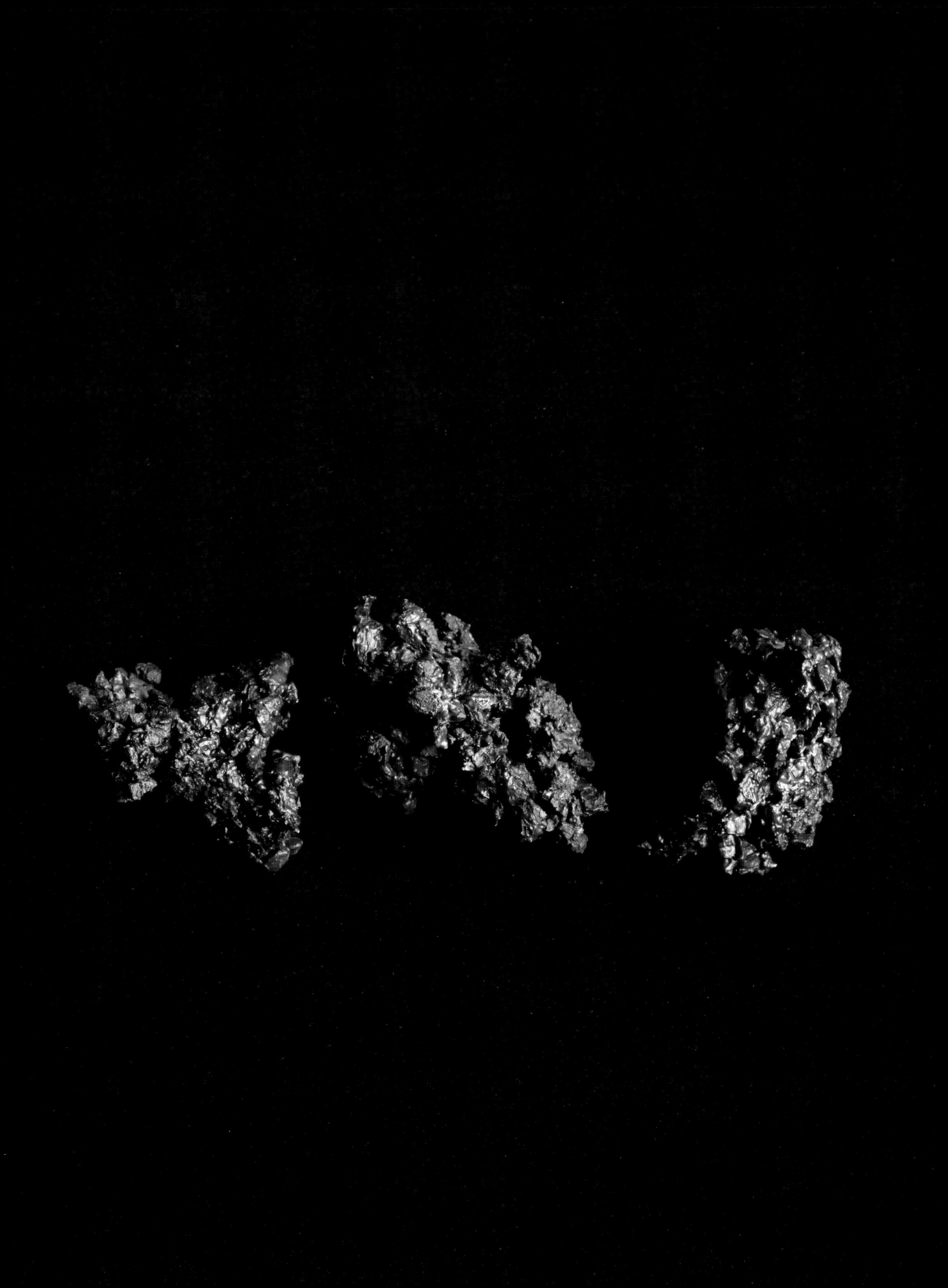

Caramel
with Cacao Nibs

Serves 4
Prep: 15 minutes

INGREDIENTS

1 cup {7 oz. / 200 g} granulated sugar
2 oz. {50 g} cacao nibs
{see recipe, page 44 or 45}

In a saucepan over low heat, begin heating the sugar. When it reaches 340°F {170°C}, at which point the color is a pronounced yellow color, stir in the cacao nibs.

Pour the caramel onto a silicone baking mat and allow to cool before using, unless you are making decorative shapes. In this case, grease a sharp knife to cut your shapes before the caramel has cooled completely.

Chef's note

This caramel is an excellent accompaniment for a chocolate cream dessert and can also be used as a base for other recipes.

Cacao Infusion

Gin-Tonic Style

{An original recipe by Matthieu at Chez Hortense in Brussels}

Serves 10
Prep: 15 minutes
Rest: 24 hours

INGREDIENTS

FLAVORED GIN
½ oz. {15 g} skins of roasted cacao beans {see recipe, page 44 or 45}, 2 cups {500 ml} gin

PER COCKTAIL
3 tablespoons plus 1 teaspoon {50 ml} flavored gin, 5 drops Black Walnut Bitters®, ½ cup {120 ml} sparkling tonic water, zest of a quarter unwaxed lemon, 1 slice unwaxed lemon

Soak the cacao bean skins in the gin for 24 hours, then strain.

Pour the flavored gin into a tall glass with the Black Walnut Bitters®. Add ice cubes. Then add the sparkling tonic water, lemon zest, and lemon slice. Serve chilled.

Chef's note: If you cannot find Black Walnut Bitters®, substitute Angostura®.

Cacao Infusion

Serves 4
Prep: 10 minutes

INGREDIENTS

1¼ cups {300 ml} water
½ oz. {15 g} skins of roasted cacao beans {see recipe, page 44 or 45},
2½ teaspoons {10 g} granulated sugar {optional}

Heat the water to 175°F {80°C}. Place the cacao bean skins in the water and infuse for 5 to 7 minutes. Stir in the sugar, if using. Strain and serve.

Cacao Foam Infusion

Serves 4
Prep: 10 minutes
Chill: 2 hours

INGREDIENTS

1 sheet gelatin, 1¼ cups {300 ml} water,
2½ teaspoons {10 g} granulated sugar
½ oz. {15 g} skins of roasted cacao beans
{see recipe, page 44 or 45}

Soften the gelatin in a bowl of very cold water for 10 minutes.

In a saucepan, heat the water and sugar to 175°F {80°C}. Add the cacao bean skins and infuse for 5 minutes.

Squeeze the water from the gelatin sheet and stir it in. When dissolved, pour the mixture into a whipping siphon. Insert 2 cartridges and close the siphon. Refrigerate for 2 hours.

Using the nozzle of your choice, dispense the foam into serving glasses.

Cacao Infusion

on the Rocks

Serves 4
Prep: 10 minutes

INGREDIENTS

2½ cups {600 ml} water
1 oz. {30 g} skins of roasted cacao beans
{see recipe, page 44 or 45}, zest of half an unwaxed lime,
zest of half an unwaxed lemon,
½ vanilla bean, split lengthwise and seeds scraped,
2½ teaspoons {10 g} granulated sugar

Heat the water to 175°F {80°C}. Place all the ingredients in the water and infuse for 5 to 7 minutes. If you wish, strain the liquid. Allow to cool and serve, well chilled, with ice cubes.

Jelled Cacao Infusion

Serves 4
Prep: 10 minutes
Chill: 3 hours

INGREDIENTS

2 sheets gelatin
1¼ cups {300 ml} water
2½ teaspoons {10 g} granulated sugar
½ oz. {15 g} skins of roasted cacao beans
{see recipe, page 44 or 45}
Assorted nuts and dried fruit of your choice
{dried apricots, cashew nuts, hazelnuts, etc.}
to line the base of the bowl

Soften the gelatin in a bowl of very cold water for 10 minutes.

Heat the water and sugar to 175°F {80°C}. Remove from the heat, add the skins of the cacao beans, and infuse for 5 minutes. Strain. Squeeze the water from the gelatin. Stir the gelatin into the sugar-water mixture and stir until completely dissolved. Allow to cool.

Place the nuts and dried fruit at the bottom of a wide, fairly shallow plastic mold or bowl.

Pour in the infusion and refrigerate for 3 hours, until set. Turn out of the mold, cut into cubes, and serve.

Chef's note

This jelled infusion is excellent with a chocolate dessert, providing a fresh note while still retaining the cacao notes. To enhance it with citrus flavors, add some zest to the infusion at the same time as the cacao bean skins.

Cacao Infusion

Granita

Serves 4
Prep: 15 minutes
Freeze: 8 hours minimum

INGREDIENTS

⅔ cup {150 ml} water
0.2 oz. {5 g} skins of roasted cacao beans
{see recipe, page 44 or 45}
Zest of half an unwaxed lime, in strips
2½ teaspoons {10 g} granulated sugar
A few cacao nibs {see recipe, page 44 or 45}
Fleur de sel

Heat the water to 175°F {80°C}. Add the cacao bean skins, lime zest, and sugar. Infuse for 5 minutes. Strain into a wide, fairly shallow bowl. Place the bowl in the freezer. After 1 hour, scrape the liquid well {it will just have started to freeze} with a fork, stirring it too. Repeat every hour, until the mixture resembles coarse crystals.

When the granita is frozen, shape it into oval scoops, place on dessert plates, and scatter with a few cacao nibs and fleur de sel.

Chef's note

To speed up the freezing process, place the bowl in the freezer 30 minutes before pouring the mixture into it.

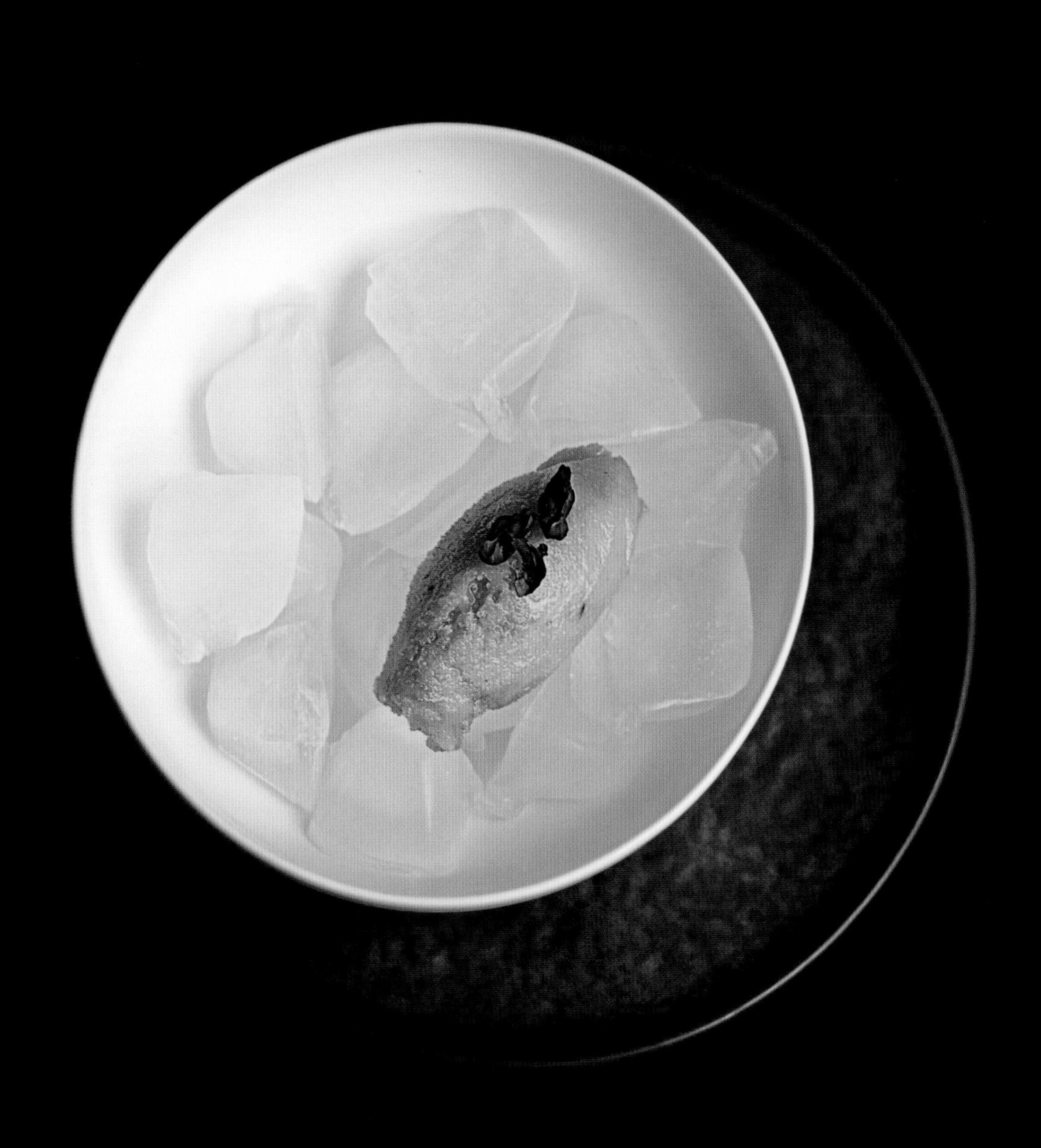

Natural Bittersweet Chocolate

Makes one 13-oz. {375-g} bar
Prep: 15 minutes
Rest: 1 hour

INGREDIENTS

0.9 oz. {25 g} cacao butter
9 oz. {250 g} cacao nibs, room temperature
{see recipe, page 44 or 45}
¾ cup {3½ oz. / 100 g} confectioners' sugar

In a small saucepan, heat the cacao butter to 160°F {70°C}. Place the cacao nibs and sugar in the bowl of a Thermomix® {see Note}. Set the time to 4 minutes and the temperature to 160°F {70°C}, using speed 4.

Pour in the hot cacao butter and process for approximately 4 minutes more, until the chocolate is as smooth as possible. Pour it into a silicone mold and allow to cool for 1 hour at room temperature.

Your homemade chocolate is ready!

Chef's note

If you do not have a Thermomix®, simply use a professional-grade blender. All that changes is that the cacao butter must be heated to 195°F {90°C}.

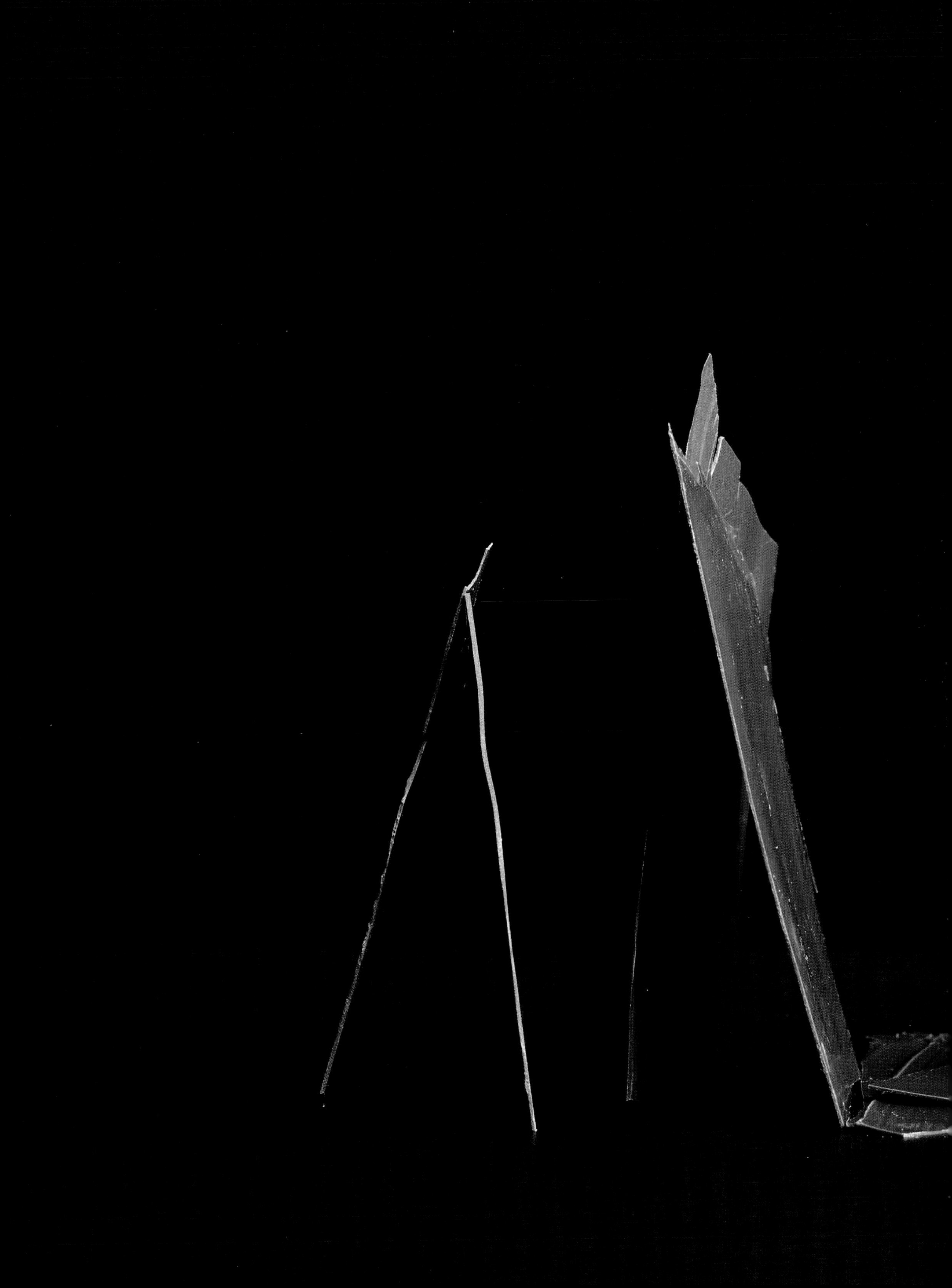

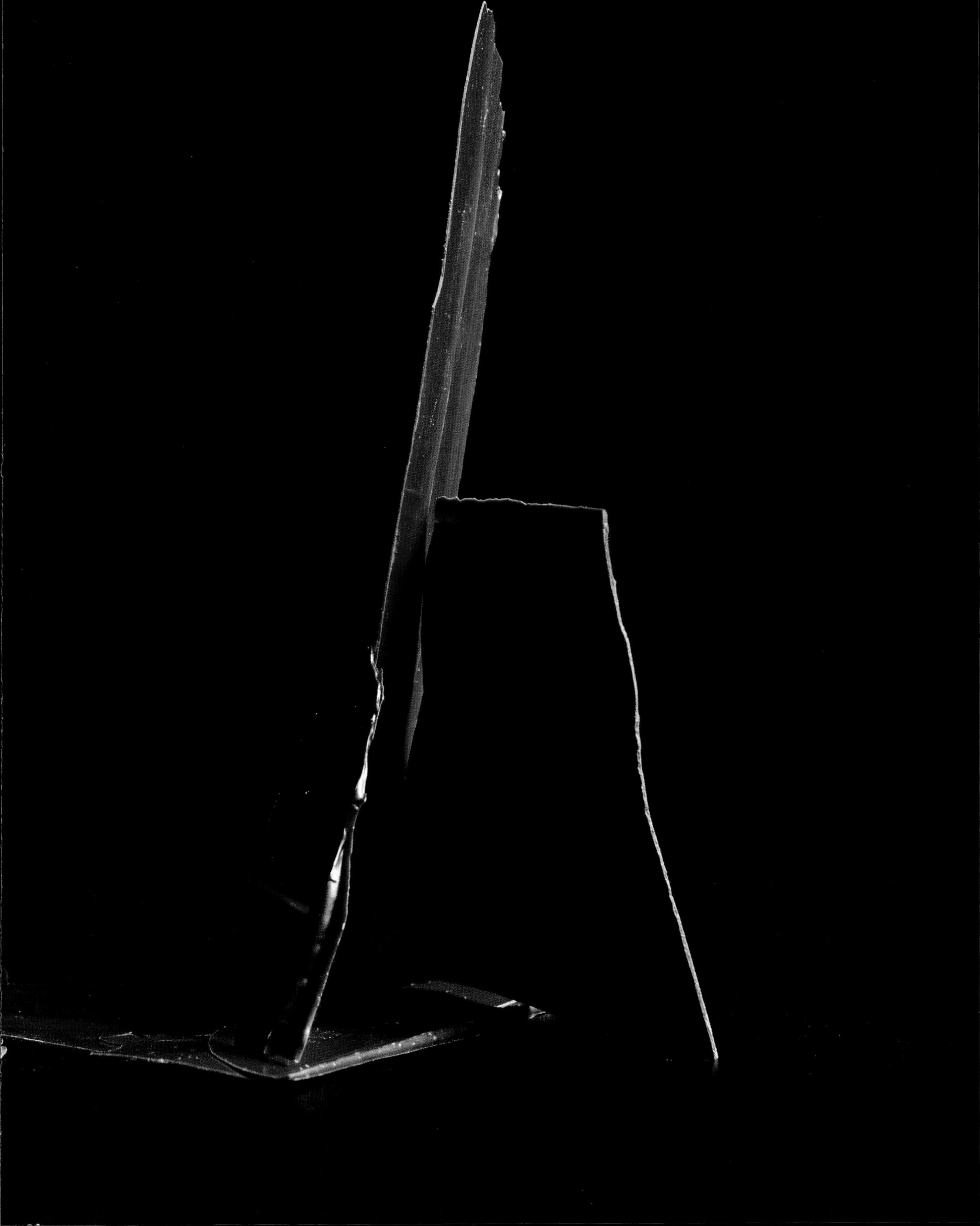

MAR
COL
INI

Natural Bittersweet Chocolate
with Coconut Sugar

Makes 1½ lbs. {750 g} bars of chocolate
Prep: 15 minutes
Rest: 1 hour

INGREDIENTS

1 lb. 2 oz. {500 g} cacao nibs
{see recipe, page 44 or 45}
7 oz. {200 g} coconut sugar {see Notes}
2 oz. {50 g} cacao butter

Place the cacao nibs and coconut sugar in the bowl of a Thermomix® {see Note}. Set the time to 4 minutes and the temperature to 160°F {70°C}, using speed 4.

In a small saucepan, heat the cacao butter to 160°F {70°C}.

Pour the hot cacao butter into the Thermomix® bowl and continue processing for about 4 minutes, until the chocolate is as smooth as possible. Pour it into a silicone mold and allow to cool for 1 hour at room temperature.

Your coconut chocolate is ready!

Chef's notes

If you do not have a Thermomix®, simply use a professional-grade blender. All that changes is that the cacao butter should be heated to 195°F {90°C}.

Coconut sugar comes from the sap of the cut flowers of the coconut palm and has the benefit of having a lower glycemic index than ordinary sugar. Its taste is similar to that of caramelized brown sugar.

Small Squares
of Natural Bittersweet Chocolate

Makes 30 squares
Prep: 15 minutes

INGREDIENTS

10½ oz. {300 g} Natural Bittersweet Chocolate {see recipe, page 78}

Chop the chocolate with a knife.

To ensure that your squares are glossy, temper the chocolate as follows:

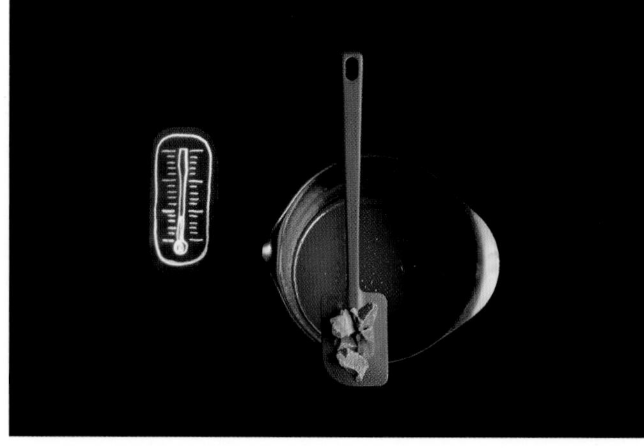

- Over a hot water bath, heat the chocolate to 122°F {50°C}.
- Place over a cool water bath and cool to 82°F {28°C}.
- Return to the hot water bath and reheat the chocolate to 90°F {32°C}.

Using a spatula, spread the melted chocolate over a sheet of parchment paper to a thickness of just under ¼ inch {5 mm}.

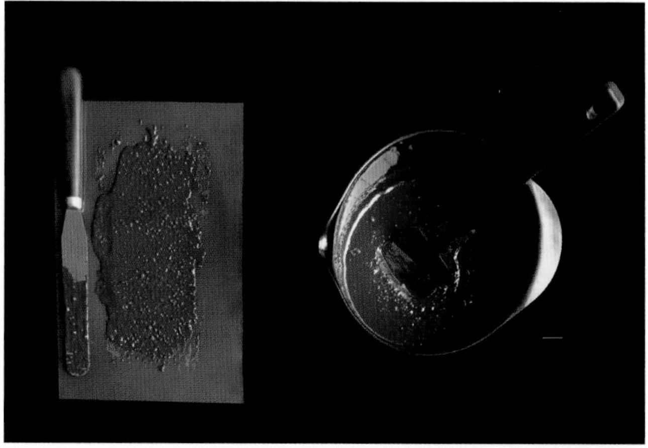

When it begins to set {approximately 10 minutes}, use a sharp knife to cut out squares. Then brush the surface with a metal brush to create a textured effect.

Natural Bittersweet Chocolate Truffles

Makes 40 truffles
Prep: 20 minutes
Chill: 12 hours

INGREDIENTS

5½ oz. {160 g} Natural Bittersweet Chocolate
{see recipe, page 78}
Scant ½ cup {100 ml} whole milk
5 tablespoons {2½ oz. / 70 g} unsalted butter, diced
⅓ cup {2 oz. / 60 g} granulated sugar
Scant ½ cup {100 ml} whipping cream {35% butterfat}
6 tablespoons {1½ oz. / 40 g} unsweetened cocoa powder

Chop the chocolate with a knife.

In a saucepan over low heat, melt the chocolate with the milk, stirring until smooth. Add the butter and stir well. Remove from the heat and stir in the sugar and cream. When smooth, pour into a shallow dish.

Allow to cool, cover with plastic wrap, and refrigerate for 12 hours.

Using the palms of your hands, shape teaspoonfuls of ganache into small balls. Roll them in the cocoa powder.

Chef's note

The truffles keep for up to 2 weeks in an airtight container at room temperature.

Hot Natural Chocolate

Makes 1 large serving
Prep: 10 minutes

INGREDIENTS

2 oz. {60 g} Natural Bittersweet Chocolate {see recipe, page 78}
Scant ½ cup {100 ml} whole milk
2 tablespoons {30 ml} whipping cream {35% butterfat}
Scant ½ cup {100 ml} water

Chop the chocolate with a knife. Bring the milk, cream, and water to a boil.

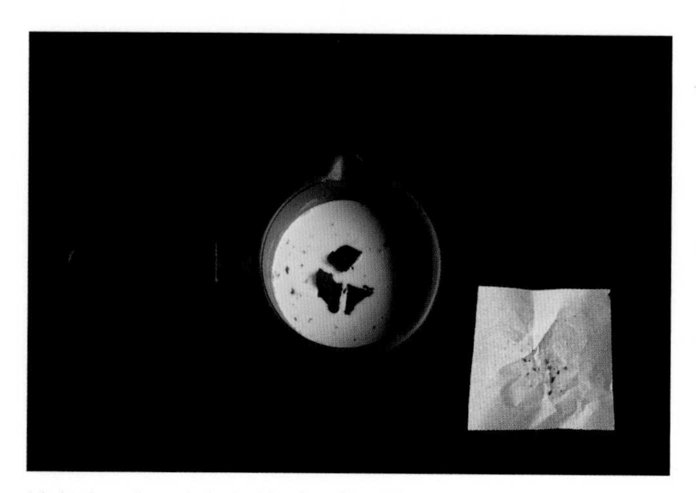

Melt the chocolate in the hot liquid.

Process the mixture with an immersion blender.

If you prefer a drink that is smooth, strain the mixture.

Natural Chocolate Pastry Cream

Serves 6
Prep: 15 minutes

INGREDIENTS

⅔ oz. {20 g} Natural Bittersweet Chocolate
{see recipe, page 78}
1 cup {250 ml} whole milk
2 egg yolks
1 heaping tablespoon {½ oz. / 15 g} granulated sugar
2 tablespoons {⅔ oz. / 20 g} flour

Chop the chocolate with a knife.

In a saucepan, bring the milk to a boil. In the bowl of a mixer fitted with the whisk, beat the egg yolks with the sugar until pale. Incorporate the flour.

Gradually pour in a little of the milk, whisking constantly. Whisk in the remaining milk.

Return the mixture to the saucepan and bring to a boil. Stir in the chocolate.

When fully blended, press a sheet of plastic wrap over the entire surface {this prevents a skin from forming} and place in the refrigerator to cool.

Chef's note

This pastry cream is ideal for filling chocolate éclairs, and can also be used as a base if you are making a Diplomat Cream {see recipe, page 179}.

Natural Bittersweet Chocolate Mousse

Serves 4
Prep: 30 minutes
Chill: 3 hours

INGREDIENTS

7 oz. {200 g} Natural Bittersweet Chocolate
{see recipe, page 78}
3 tablespoons {2 oz. / 50 g} unsalted butter, diced
5 egg yolks
⅓ cup {2 oz. / 60 g} granulated sugar, divided
¾ cup {180 ml} whipping cream {35% butterfat}
10 egg whites

Chop the chocolate with a knife and melt it over a hot water bath.

Add the butter and stir until smooth.

In the bowl of a mixer fitted with the whisk, combine the egg yolks with half of the sugar. Whisk until pale.

Pour the egg yolk–sugar mixture over the melted chocolate and stir well.

Whisk the cream until it holds soft peaks and fold it carefully into the chocolate mixture.

Whisk the egg whites with the remaining sugar until they hold firm peaks. Gradually fold the egg whites into the chocolate mixture, taking care not to deflate the mixture.

Pour the chocolate mousse into a large serving bowl and refrigerate for 3 hours, until set, before serving.

Natural Milk Chocolate

Prep: 15 minutes

INGREDIENTS

2⅓ cups {10 oz. / 300 g} confectioners' sugar
5¾ oz. {165 g} cacao nibs {see recipe, page 44 or 45}
1½ cups {6¼ oz. / 176 g} powdered skim milk
½ teaspoon {3 g} fine salt
1 Madagascar vanilla bean, split, seeds scraped
7½ oz. {215 g} cacao butter

Place the confectioners' sugar, cacao nibs, powdered skim milk, salt, and vanilla seeds in the bowl of a Thermomix® {see Note} fitted with the mixing knife.

Set the time to 4 minutes and the temperature to 160°F {70°C}, using speed 4.

In a saucepan, bring the cacao butter to a boil. Immediately pour it into the Thermomix®. Process for a further 3 minutes at the same speed and temperature.

Pour the chocolate into a silicone mold and allow to cool for 1 hour at room temperature.

Your homemade milk chocolate is ready!

Chef's note

If you do not have a Thermomix®, simply use a professional-grade blender. All that changes is that the cacao butter should be heated to 195°F {90°C}.

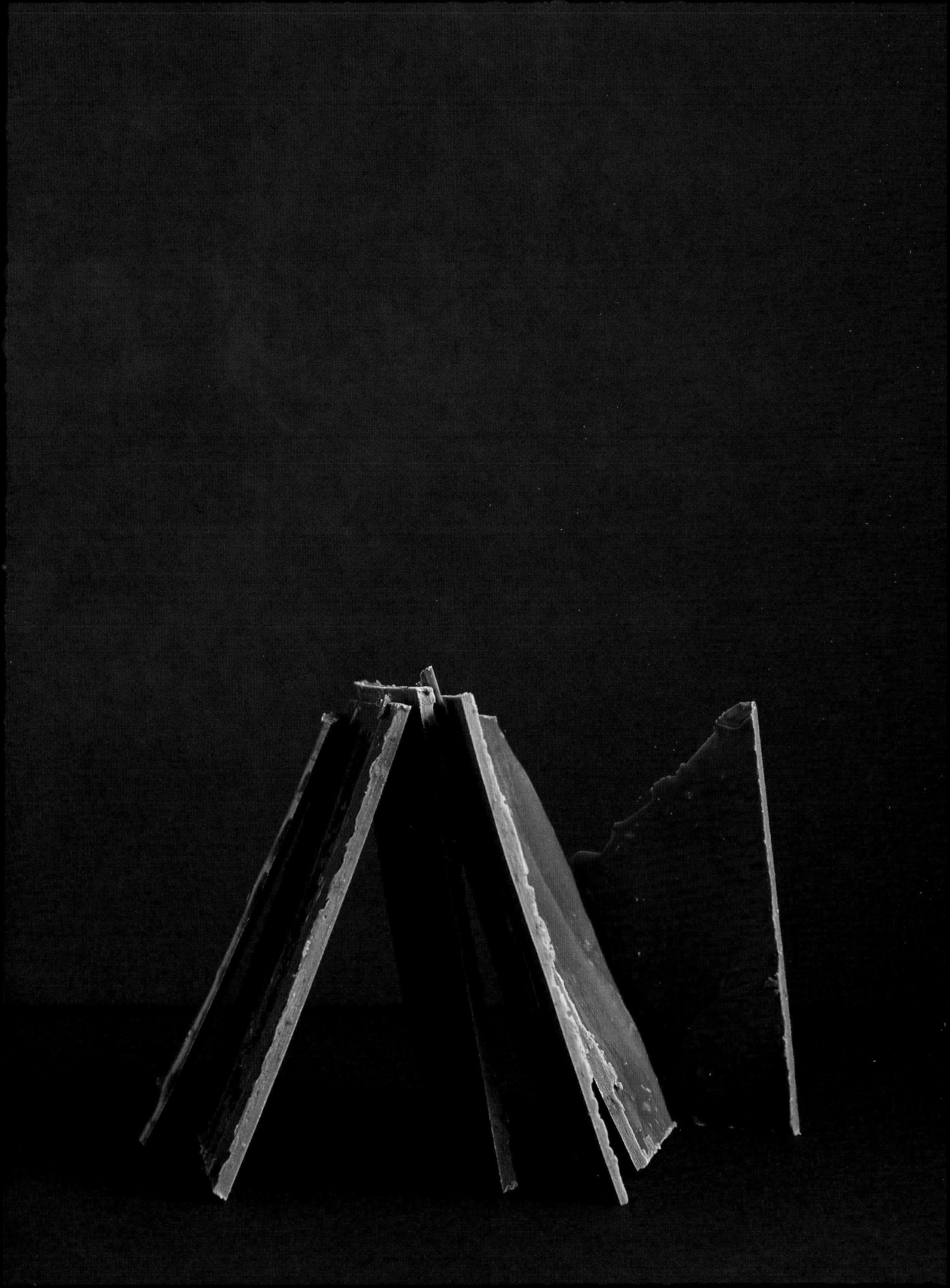

Natural Milk Chocolate Squares

Makes 10 squares
Prep: 20 minutes

INGREDIENTS

10½ oz. {300 g} Natural Milk Chocolate
{see recipe, page 94}
Fleur de sel

Chop the chocolate with a knife.

To ensure that your squares are glossy, temper the chocolate as follows:
- Over a hot water bath, heat the chocolate to 104°F {40°C}.
- Place over a cool water bath and cool to 79°F {26°C}.
- Return to the hot water bath and reheat the chocolate to 82°F {28°C}.

Using a spatula, spread the chocolate over a sheet of parchment paper to a thickness of just under ¼ inch {5 mm}.

When the chocolate begins to set {after about 10 minutes}, use a sharp knife to cut 1½-inch {4-cm} squares.

Before the chocolate has set completely, sprinkle it with a little fleur de sel.

Caramel-topped Milk Chocolate Squares

Makes 20 squares
Prep: 40 minutes
Chill: 12 hours

INGREDIENTS

3 tablespoons {50 ml} whipping cream {35% butterfat}
1 pinch fleur de sel
¼ vanilla bean, split lengthwise, seeds scraped
½ cup {3½ oz. / 100 g} granulated sugar
3 tablespoons {2 oz. / 50 g} unsalted butter, diced
10½ oz. {300 g} Natural Milk Chocolate
{see recipe, page 94}

A day ahead {or 12 hours ahead}, make a butter caramel.

Warm the cream with the fleur de sel, vanilla bean, and seeds in a small saucepan.

In another saucepan, heat the sugar without adding any water until it is a light caramel color. Pour in the cream and stir to deglaze. Refrigerate the caramel for 12 hours.

Add the diced butter and process with an immersion blender until smooth.

Using a knife, chop the chocolate.

To ensure that your squares are glossy, temper the chocolate as follows:
- Over a hot water bath, heat the chocolate to 104°F {40°C}.
- Place over a cool water bath and cool to 79°F {26°C}.
- Return to the hot water bath and reheat the chocolate to 82°F {28°C}.

Using a spatula, spread the chocolate over a sheet of parchment paper to a thickness of just under ¼ inch {5 mm}.

When the chocolate begins to set {after about 10 minutes}, use a sharp knife to cut 1¼-inch {3-cm} squares.

With a pastry bag fitted with a plain ¼-inch {6-mm} tip, pipe the caramel over the center of the chocolate squares.

Milk Chocolate Hazelnut Tuiles

Makes 10 cookies
Prep: 25 minutes
Cook: 15 minutes
Rest: 30 minutes

INGREDIENTS

2 oz. {50 g} peeled, unsalted hazelnuts
2 teaspoons {10 ml} water
2 tablespoons {1 oz. / 25 g} granulated sugar
9 oz. {250 g} Natural Milk chocolate
{see recipe, page 94}

Preheat the oven to 350°F {170°C}.

Spread the hazelnuts on a baking sheet and roast them for 15 minutes.

Begin heating the water and sugar in a small saucepan. When the temperature reaches 240°F {115°C} pour in the hazelnuts and stir until they are completely coated in caramel.

Spread the caramelized hazelnuts on a silicone baking sheet and allow to cool. Chop finely. Chop the chocolate with a knife.

To ensure that your squares are glossy, temper the chocolate as follows:
- Over a hot water bath, heat the chocolate to 104°F {40°C}.
- Place over a cool water bath and cool to 79°F {26°C}.
- Return to the hot water bath and reheat the chocolate to 82°F {28°C}.

Line a baking sheet with parchment paper. Drop a teaspoonful of tempered chocolate on the sheet, pressing down with the teaspoon to flatten it as much as possible. Repeat until all the chocolate has been used up. Before it sets {after about 5 minutes}, scatter with the chopped caramelized hazelnuts.

Allow to set for 30 minutes. Carefully lift the tuiles from the parchment paper and store in an airtight container until serving.

Chef's notes

If you prefer curved tuile cookies {the name comes from the curved roof tiles they resemble}, allow the chocolate to set in the base of a curved mold or use a special tuile pan. {You can also drape the cookies over clean bottles or a rolling pin as you remove them from the oven.}

For a quicker version of the recipe, replace the chopped, caramelized hazelnuts with readymade candied peanuts.

Milk Chocolate Twists
with Dried Fruit

Makes 15 twists
Prep: 15 minutes

INGREDIENTS

5 oz. {150 g} assorted dried fruit and nuts, such as apricots, hazelnuts, pistachios, and almonds
10½ oz. {300 g} Natural Milk Chocolate {see recipe, page 94}

Chop the dried fruit and nuts with a knife.

Chop the chocolate with a knife.

To ensure that your twists are glossy, temper the chocolate as follows:
- Over a hot water bath, heat the chocolate to 104°F {40°C}.
- Place over a cool water bath and cool to 79°F {26°C}.
- Return to the hot water bath and reheat the chocolate to 82°F {28°}.

Line a baking sheet with parchment paper. Using a pastry bag fitted with a plain ¼-inch {6-mm} tip, pipe out the twisted shapes.

Before the chocolate sets, sprinkle it with the chopped dried fruit and nuts. Serve with coffee.

Chef's note

Store these *mignardises* in an airtight container in a cool place for up to 3 months.

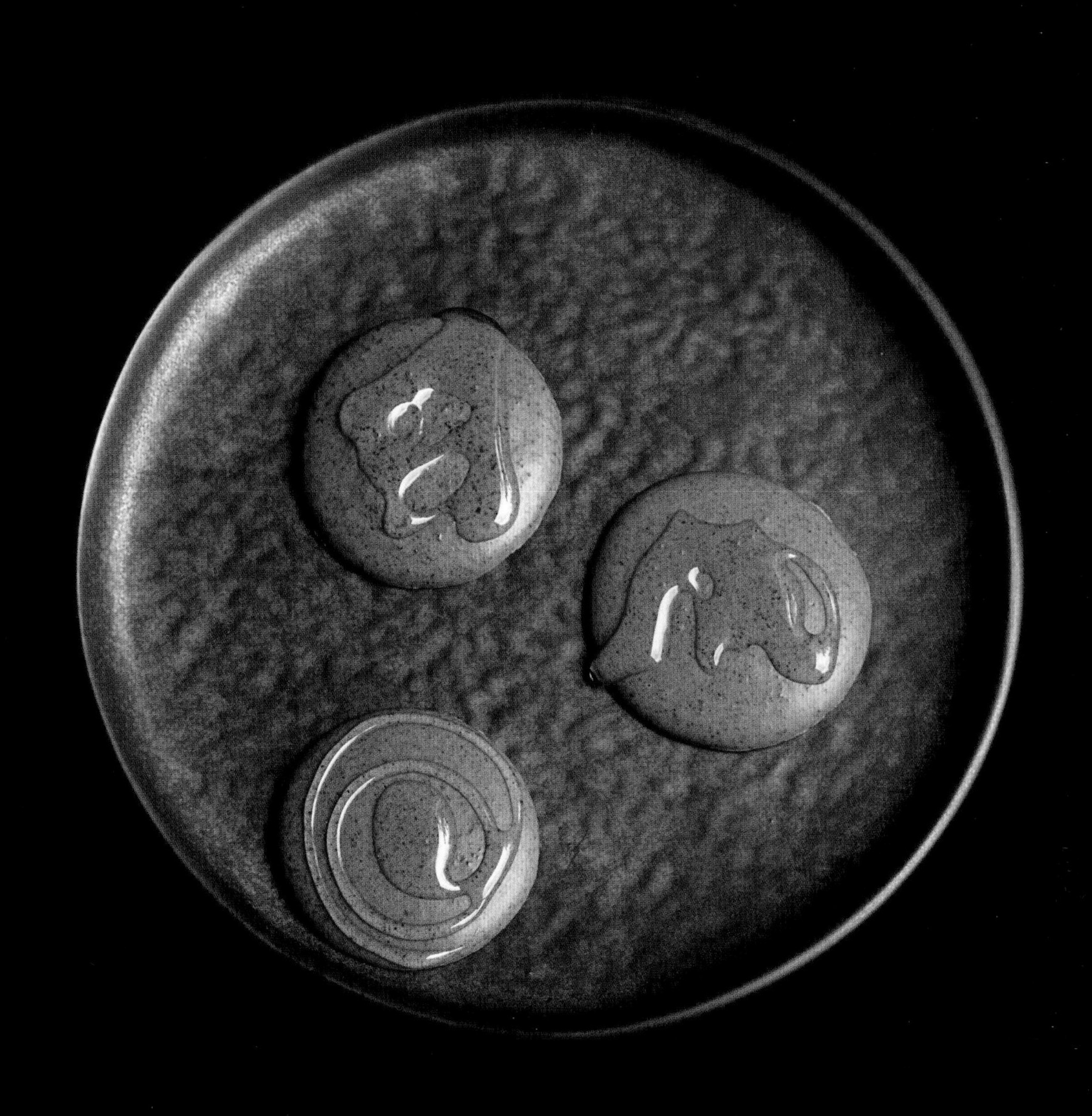

Delicate Honey-Flavored Milk Chocolate Disks

Makes 15 chocolates
Prep: 25 minutes
Chill: 1 hour

INGREDIENTS

7 oz. {200 g} Natural Milk Chocolate
{see recipe, page 94}
1 tablespoon {20 g} acacia honey {or multi-floral honey}

Chop the chocolate with a knife.

To ensure that your chocolates are glossy, temper the chocolate as follows:
- Over a hot water bath, heat the chocolate to 104°F {40°C}.
- Place over a cool water bath and cool to 79°F {26°C}.
- Return to the hot water bath and reheat the chocolate to 82°F {28°C}.

Line a baking sheet with parchment paper. Using a pastry bag fitted with a plain ⅛-inch {4-mm} tip, pipe disks of chocolate. Before the chocolate sets completely, spin spirals of honey over the tops. Refrigerate until set, about 1 hour.

Chantilly Cream

with Milk Chocolate

Serves 8
Prep: 10 minutes
Chill: 12 hours

INGREDIENTS

7½ oz. {210 g} Natural Milk Chocolate
{see recipe, page 94}
1¼ cups {300 ml} heavy cream {35% butterfat}

A day ahead {or 12 hours}: Chop the chocolate with a knife and place it in a bowl. Pour the cream into a saucepan and heat to 175°F {80°C}. Pour it over the chocolate and stir until smooth. Press plastic wrap on surface to prevent skin from forming and refrigerate for 12 hours.

Transfer the cream-chocolate mixture to the bowl of a stand mixer fitted with a whisk. Whisk at medium speed until the mixture holds between the loops of the whisk {Chantilly texture}.

Recipe photographs on following spread

Natural White Chocolate

Prep: 20 minutes

INGREDIENTS
1 lb. 2 oz. {500 g} cacao butter, divided
2½ cups {10½ oz. / 300 g} powdered skim milk
2⅔ cups {12 oz. / 350 g} confectioners' sugar

Heat 8 oz. {225 g} of the cacao butter to 140°F {60°C}. Place the powdered milk and confectioners' sugar in the bowl of a Thermomix® fitted with the mixing knife. Add the melted butter. Set the temperature to 140°F {60°C}. Process for 3 minutes at speed 5.

In a saucepan, heat the remaining cacao butter to between 140 and 160°F {60 to 70°C}. Pour it over the mixture in the Thermomix® and process for 3 minutes at 140°F {60°C}, speed 5.

Chef's note

If you do not have a Thermomix®, simply use a professional-grade blender. All that changes is that the cacao butter should be heated to 195°F {90°C}.

Natural White Chocolate Squares

Makes 20 squares
Prep: 20 minutes

INGREDIENTS
7 oz. {200 g} Natural White Chocolate
{see recipe, page 108}

Chop the chocolate with a knife.

To ensure that your chocolate squares are glossy, temper the chocolate as follows:
- Over a hot water bath, heat the chocolate to 104°F {40°C}.
- Place over a cool water bath and cool to 79°F {26°C}.
- Return to the hot water bath and reheat the chocolate to 82°F {28°C}.

With a spatula, spread the chocolate on a sheet of parchment paper to a thickness of just under ¼ inch {5 mm}. After approximately 10 minutes, when it is beginning to set, cut 2½-inch {6-cm} squares with a sharp knife.

Recipe photos on following spreads

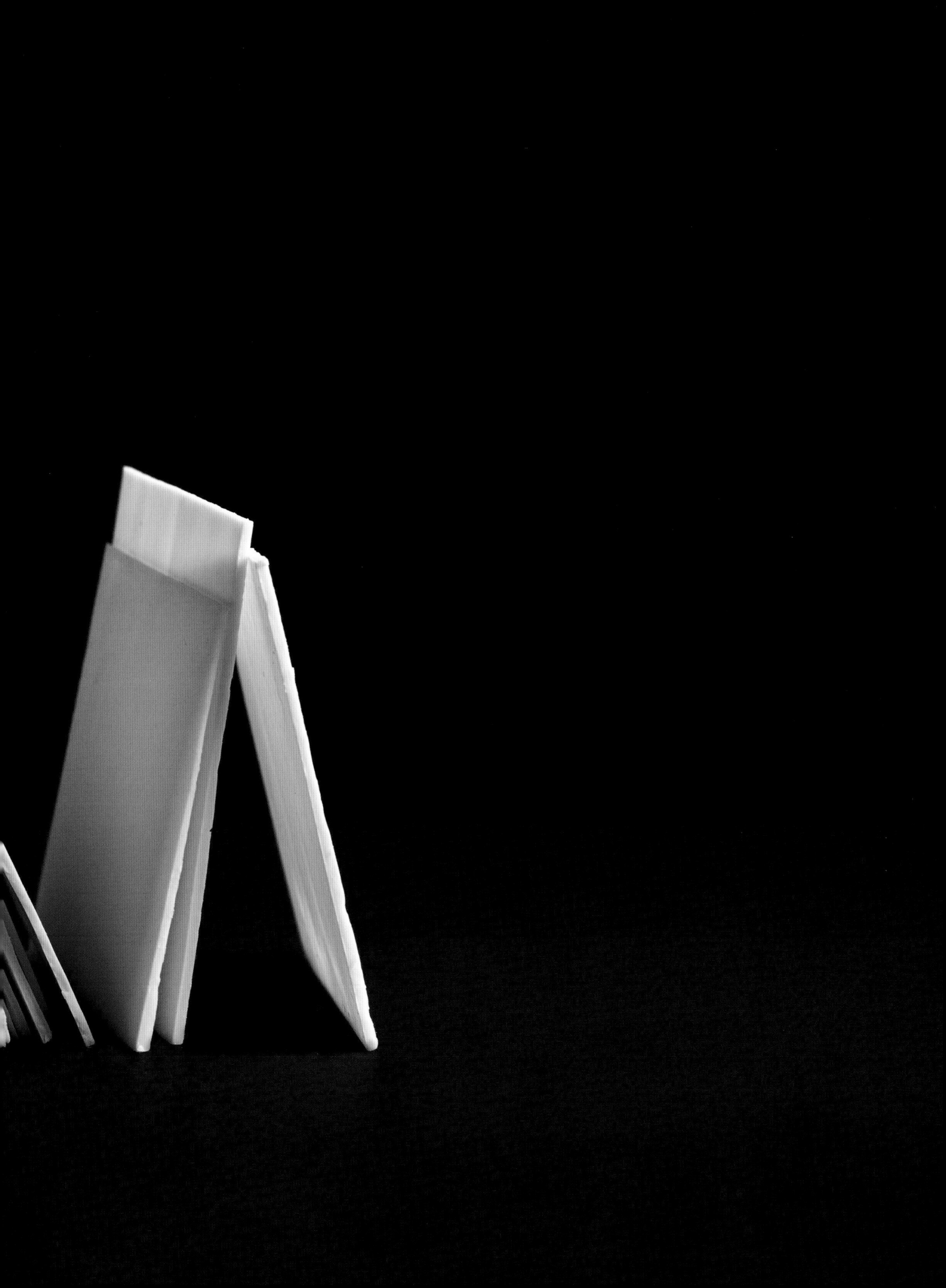

White Chocolate Disks

with Pepper, Fleur de Sel & Vanilla

Makes 20 chocolates
Prep: 20 minutes
Chill: 1 hour

INGREDIENTS
7 oz. {200 g} Natural White Chocolate
{see recipe, page 108}
Voatsiperifery pepper
Fleur de sel
½ Tahitian vanilla bean, split, seeds scraped

Chop the chocolate with a knife. Cut squares of parchment paper the size you intend to make the chocolate.

To ensure that your chocolate disks are glossy, temper the chocolate as follows:
- Over a hot water bath, heat the chocolate with the pepper, fleur de sel, and vanilla seeds to 104°F {40°C}.
- Place over a cool water bath and cool to 79°F {26°C}.
- Return to the hot water bath and reheat the chocolate, with the pepper, fleur del sel, and vanilla seeds, to 82°F {28°C}.

Spoon the tempered chocolate into a pastry bag fitted with a plain ¼-inch {6-mm} tip and pipe a ball of chocolate onto a sheet of parchment paper. Then press a square of parchment paper over each dollop to shape round chocolates. Refrigerate until set, about 1 hour.

Chef's note

White chocolate pairs well with any number of spices, so use your imagination to create your own taste combination.

Natural White Chocolate Sesame-Topped Disks

{Mendiants}

Makes 20 disks
Prep: 20 minutes
Chill: 1 hour

INGREDIENTS

1 tablespoon {1/3 oz. / 10 g} sesame seeds
9 oz. {250 g} Natural White Chocolate
{see recipe, page 108}
5 kumquats
1 coffee spoon matcha powder

Heat a small skillet and toast the sesame seeds over high heat for 1 minute, stirring constantly.

Chop the chocolate with a knife.

To ensure that your chocolate disks are glossy, temper the chocolate as follows:
- Over a hot water bath, heat the chocolate to 104°F {40°C}.
- Place over a cool water bath and cool to 79°F {26°C}.
- Return to the hot water bath and reheat the chocolate to 82°F {28°C}.

Pour the chocolate into a silicone mold with shallow round cavities. Smooth the chocolate with an angled spatula.

Finely slice the kumquats and arrange them over the chocolate disks. Sift a light dusting of matcha powder through a fine-mesh sieve and sprinkle with a few sesame seeds. Refrigerate for 1 hour.

Thyme-infused Chantilly Cream

Serves 8
Prep: 15 minutes
Chill: 12 hours

INGREDIENTS
5 oz. {150 g} Natural White Chocolate
{see recipe, page 108}
2 cups {500 ml} heavy cream {35% butterfat}
A few leaves of fresh thyme

Chop the chocolate with a knife and place in a bowl.

Pour the cream into a saucepan and bring to a boil. Remove from the heat and stir in the thyme leaves. Cover with a lid, infuse for 5 minutes, and strain.

Pour the hot cream over the white chocolate and stir well. When smooth, refrigerate for 12 hours to set.

Place the chilled cream-chocolate mixture in the bowl of a mixer fitted with the whisk. Whisk at medium speed until it holds between the loops of the whisk. Your thyme-infused Chantilly cream is ready to be used.

Chef's note

A dollop of this Chantilly cream on a meringue is truly wonderful!

Thick Saffron-scented White Chocolate Slab

Makes one 1-lb {450-g} slab
Prep: 20 minutes
Cook: 15 minutes

INGREDIENTS

3½ oz. {100 g} peeled hazelnuts
2 oz. {50 g} peeled pistachios
10½ oz. {300 g} Natural White Chocolate {see recipe, page 108}
A few threads of saffron

Preheat the oven to 325°F {160°C}. Spread the hazelnuts and pistachios over a baking sheet lined with parchment paper. Roast for 15 minutes.

Chop the chocolate with a knife.

To ensure that your chocolate bar is glossy, temper the chocolate as follows:
- Over a hot water bath, heat the chocolate to 104°F {40°C}.
- Place over a cool water bath and cool to 79°F {26°C}.
- Return to the hot water bath and reheat the chocolate to 82°F {28°C}.

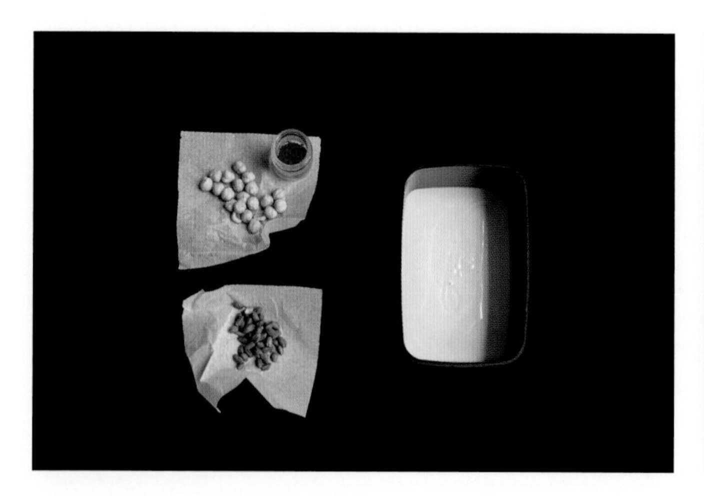

Stir in the hazelnuts and pistachios. When evenly distributed, pour into a silicone mold. Allow to set at room temperature.

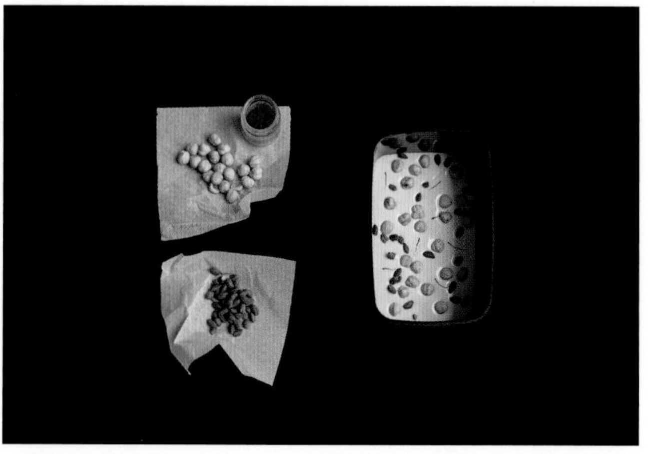

After about 45 minutes, before it is completely set, sprinkle with the saffron threads and allow to finish setting at room temperature.

Unmold the chocolate. It is ready to be eaten.

Chef's note: To speed up the setting process, refrigerate the chocolate for about 10 minutes.

Hazelnut Praline

Serves 8
Prep: 15 minutes
Cook: 15 minutes

INGREDIENTS

3½ oz. {100 g} peeled hazelnuts
1 cup {7 oz. / 200 g} granulated sugar

Preheat the oven to 325°F {160°C}. Spread the hazelnuts on a baking sheet lined with parchment paper. Roast for 15 minutes.

In a saucepan over low heat, melt the sugar. When it reaches 340°F {170°C}, at which stage the color is a pronounced yellow color, add the hazelnuts and stir well to coat them with caramel.

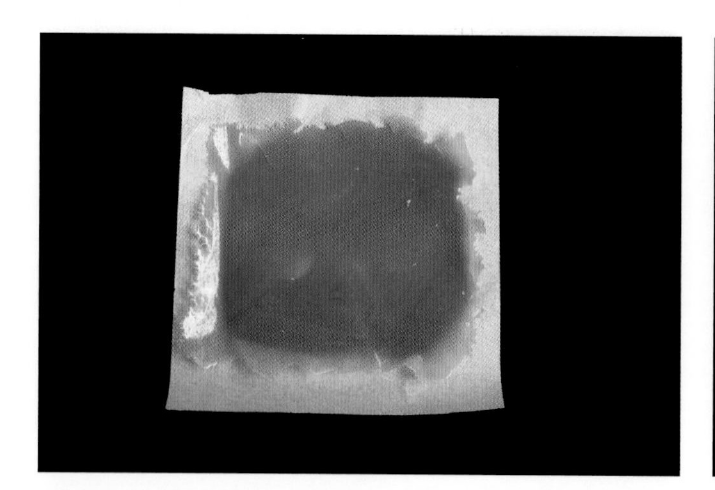

Pour the contents of the saucepan over a silicone mat and allow to cool for about 40 minutes. The above photograph shows what the caramel should look like when firm and ready to process in a professional-grade blender.

Transfer the caramel to a blender in pieces and process. If you prefer your praline to be chunky, process for only a few minutes. Increase the time for a well-ground blend.

Chef's note: This hazelnut praline is ideal to use for the classic Paris-Brest cake, a choux pastry cake filled with hazelnut cream. It is also delicious over chocolate mousse.

Praline, before it is ground.

Crisp Milk Chocolate-Praline Clusters

Serves 8
Prep: 15 minutes
Chill: 20 minutes

INGREDIENTS
2 oz. {50 g} crisp Gavottes® cookies {see Note}
1¼ oz. {35 g} Natural White Chocolate {see recipe, page 94}
⅔ oz. {20 g} cacao butter
3½ oz. {100 g} ground Hazelnut Praline {see recipe, page 122}

Crush the cookies roughly.

Chop the chocolate with a knife. Melt the chocolate and cacao butter over a hot water bath.

Stir in the crushed cookies, and then stir in the hazelnut praline.

Using two teaspoons, shape small mounds on a baking sheet lined with parchment paper. Refrigerate for 20 minutes, until set.

Chef's note

Crisp lace crêpes are cookies from Brittany. Extremely fine and crumbly, they are easy to crush.

Hazelnut Praline Spread

Makes the equivalent of one jam jar
Prep: 10 minutes

INGREDIENTS
3 tablespoons {40 g} unsalted butter
5 oz. {150 g} ground Hazelnut Praline {see recipe, page 122}
2½ teaspoons {6 g} unsweetened cocoa powder
1 egg
2 tablespoons {30 ml} hot water

Melt the butter and pour it over the hazelnut praline. Add the cocoa powder and egg.

Process together in a professional-grade blender, pouring in the water in a steady stream.

This spread keeps at room temperature for up to 10 days in an airtight jar.

Hazelnut Cream

Serves 6
Prep: 15 minutes

INGREDIENTS

⅓ oz. {10 g} peeled hazelnuts
2 sheets gelatin
1 cup {250 g} heavy cream {35% butterfat}
3 egg yolks
1 heaping tablespoon {½ oz. / 15 g} granulated sugar
5 oz. {150 g} ground Hazelnut Praline
{see recipe, page 122}
Chopped, roasted hazelnuts for decoration

Heat a skillet over high heat. Roast the hazelnuts for 1 minute, stirring constantly.

When they are cool enough to handle, chop them finely with a knife.

Soften the gelatin in a bowl of very cold water for 10 minutes.

Make a custard: Bring the cream to a boil. In the bowl of a stand mixer fitted with the whisk, beat the egg yolks with the sugar until pale. Pour a little of the hot cream over the yolk-sugar mixture to warm it slightly; whisk briefly. Then pour in the remaining hot liquid, whisking constantly until blended.

Transfer to a saucepan and, stirring constantly, heat to 180°F {82°C}, at which stage it has thickened and coats the back of a spoon.

Squeeze the water from the gelatin sheets and add them along with the chopped hazelnuts to the custard. In a blender, process together. Divide the hazelnut cream among small bowls and sprinkle with a few chopped hazelnuts.

A suggested presentation

Pistachio Praline

Serves 8
Prep: 15 minutes
Cook: 15 minutes

INGREDIENTS
3½ oz. {100 g} unsalted peeled pistachios
1 generous pinch fine salt
1 cup {7 oz. / 200 g} granulated sugar
A small drizzle of grape-seed oil

Preheat the oven to 325°F {160°C}. Spread the pistachios on a baking sheet and roast for 15 minutes. As soon as you remove the pistachios from the oven, sprinkle them lightly with salt.

In a saucepan over low heat, melt the sugar. When it reaches 340°F {170°C}, at which point it is a pronounced yellow color, add the pistachios and stir to coat them in the caramel.

Pour the contents of the saucepan over a silicone mat and allow to cool for about 40 minutes.

When the pistachio caramel is firm, transfer it to a professional-grade blender and process. If you prefer your praline to be chunky, process for only a few minutes. Increase the time for a well-ground blend.

Chef's note

If you have a very smooth praline paste, use it as a coulis over creamy chocolate desserts.

Praline, before it is ground

Pistachio-flavored Almond Paste Petit Fours

{Mignardises}

Makes 20 petit fours
Prep: 15 minutes

INGREDIENTS
5 oz. {150 g} almond paste
½ oz. {15 g} ground Pistachio Praline
{see recipe, page 131}
2 teaspoons {10 ml} sake
1 teaspoon matcha powder

In the bowl of a stand mixer fitted with the paddle, combine the almond paste with the pistachio praline. Incorporate the sake.

Using the palms of your hands, shape teaspoonfuls of the paste into small balls. Roll them in the matcha powder.

Crème Brûlée
with Pistachio Praline

Serves 6
Prep: 15 minutes
Cook: 1 hour
Chill: several hours

INGREDIENTS

1¼ cups {300 ml} heavy cream {35% butterfat}
6 egg yolks
½ cup plus 3 tablespoons {5 oz. / 135 g} granulated sugar, divided
1 oz. {30 g} ground Pistachio Praline
{see recipe, page 131}

Preheat the oven to 250°F {120°C}. Bring the cream to a boil.

In the bowl of a mixer fitted with the whisk, combine the egg yolks with ⅓ cup {2 oz. / 60 g} of the sugar. When the mixture is pale, pour a little of the hot cream over it to warm it. Whisk briefly, then pour in the remaining cream and the pistachio praline. Whisk until just incorporated.

Transfer to a saucepan and, stirring constantly, heat to 180°F {82°C}, at which stage it has thickened and coats the back of a spoon.

Divide among 6 ramekins, place in a baking dish, add water to come halfway up the sides of the ramekins, and bake for 1 hour.

Allow to cool, and refrigerate for several hours.

Just before serving, sprinkle the tops with the remaining sugar {about 1 tablespoon per ramekin} and caramelize with a kitchen torch, or under the broiler in the oven. The crème brûlées are ready to serve.

Chef's note

If you have a Thermomix®, place all the ingredients in the bowl. Using the whisk, process for 10 minutes at speed 4, temperature 180°F {82°C}.

Savory Pistachio Praline Sauce

Serves 8
Prep: 15 minutes

INGREDIENTS
2 oz. {50 g} ground Pistachio Praline
{see recipe, page 131}
Scant ½ cup {100 ml} hot chicken stock
1 pinch fleur de sel
Freshly ground black pepper
1 pinch piment d'Espelette
1 pinch cinnamon
1 pinch ground yuzu
{or the zest of a fresh yuzu}

Using an immersion blender, process the pistachio praline with the chicken stock. Season with the fleur de sel, pepper, piment d'Espelette, cinnamon, and ground yuzu. Serve hot.

Chef's note

This sauce is excellent with rice and Moroccan-inspired dishes, such as tagines. It can be stored in the refrigerator for up to two days.

Black Sesame Seed Praline

Serves 8
Prep: 25 minutes
Cook: 15 minutes

INGREDIENTS

3½ oz. {100 g} black sesame seeds {just under ⅔ cup}
1 cup {7 oz. / 200 g} granulated sugar
3 tablespoons {50 ml} grape-seed oil

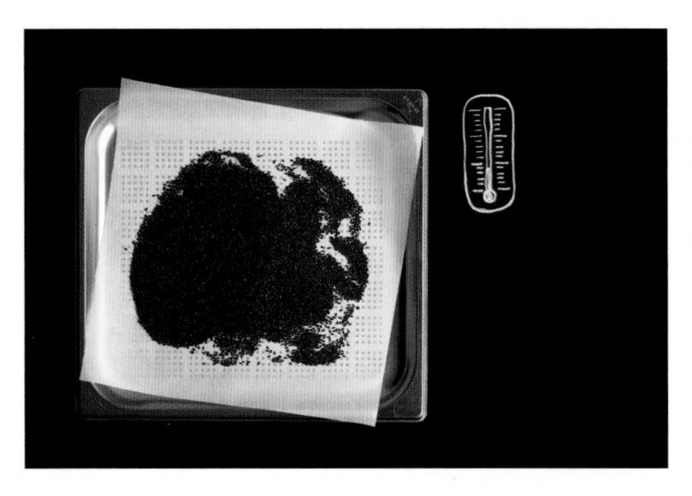

Preheat the oven to 325°F {160°C}. Line a baking sheet with parchment paper and spread the sesame seeds over it. Roast for 15 minutes.

In a saucepan over low heat, melt the sugar. When it reaches 340°F {170°C}, at which point the color is a pronounced yellow color, pour it over a silicone baking mat and allow to cool for

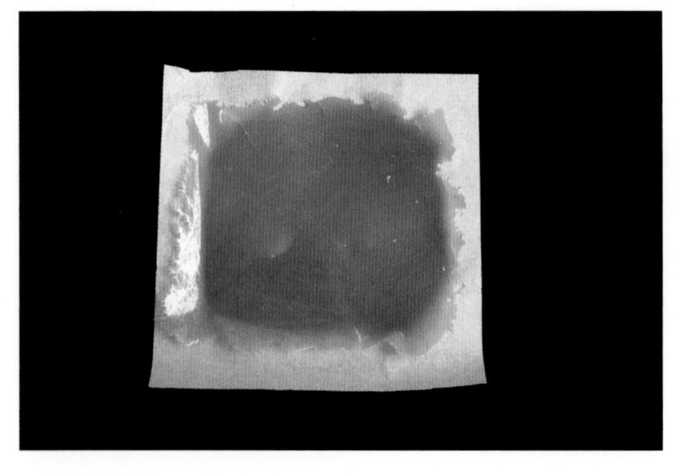

approximately 40 minutes. When it is firm, break up the caramel, place it in a blender, and process to the texture you desire.

Add the roasted black sesame seeds and grape-seed oil. Process for a few minutes to make a praline that has some pieces remaining, or longer if you prefer a very smooth paste.

Chef's note: This praline is perfect as a base for making ice cream {see recipe, page 142}, and is delicious poured into the base of bowls of creamy chocolate desserts.

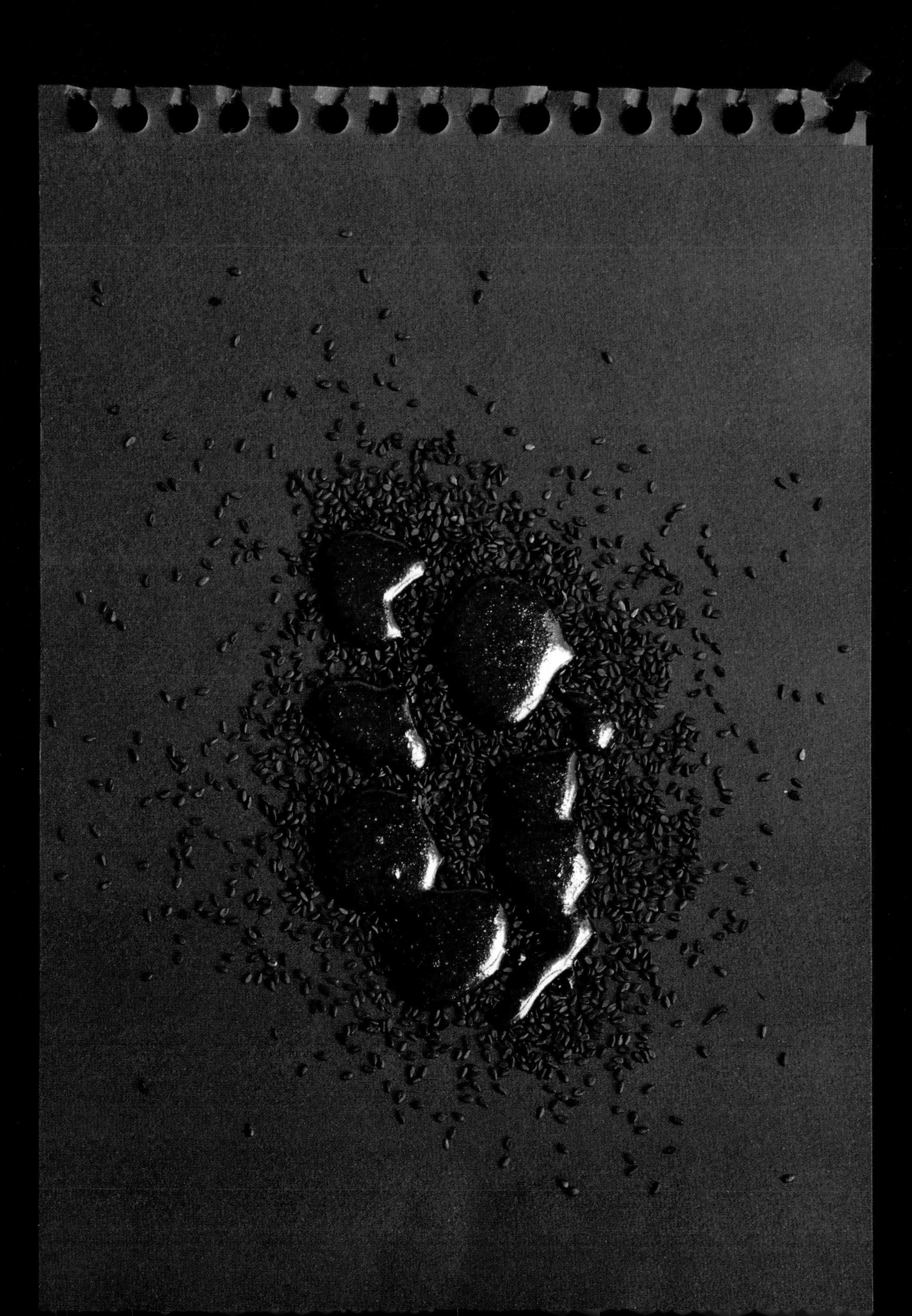

Savory Black Sesame Praline Sauce

Serves 8
Prep: 15 minutes

INGREDIENTS
3½ oz. {100 g} ground Black Sesame Seed Praline
{see recipe, page 138}
Scant ½ cup {100 ml} hot chicken stock
Grated zest of a yuzu {or lime}
1 tablespoon sake
1 pinch cacao nibs
{see recipe, page 44 or 45}
Salt and freshly ground pepper

Stir the sesame seed praline into the hot chicken stock. Add the yuzu zest and sake. Season with the cacao nibs, salt, and pepper. Process with an immersion blender. Serve hot.

Chef's note

This sauce is excellent to accompany Nobashi prawns cooked tempura-style.

Photo on the preceding pages

Ice Cream with Black Sesame Seed Praline

Serves 8
Prep: 20 minutes

INGREDIENTS
2 cups {500 ml} whole milk
Scant ½ cup {100 ml} heavy cream {35% butterfat}
4 egg yolks
2½ tablespoons {1 oz. / 30 g} granulated sugar
3½ oz. {100 g} ground Black Sesame Seed Praline
{see recipe, page 138}

Bring the milk and cream to a boil in a saucepan. In the bowl of a stand mixer fitted with the whisk, beat the egg yolks and sugar until the mixture is pale yellow. Pour in a little of the hot milk-cream mixture to warm it up, whisk briefly, then pour in the remaining liquid, whisking to combine.

Return to the saucepan and heat to 185°F {85°C}, stirring constantly.

Remove from the heat and cool rapidly over a large bowl with ice cubes. Stir in the sesame seed praline. The ice cream is now ready to be processed in the ice cream maker according to the manufacturer's instructions.

Chef's note

This ice cream is outstanding with chocolate sauce!

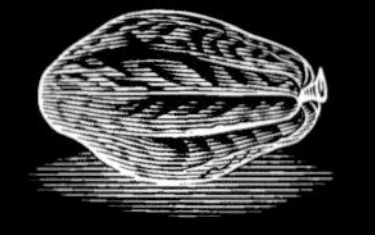

Cacaos

Four Main Varieties and Their Terroirs

With over 300 aromatic components, cacao has an extremely wide range of tastes, a fact that is often forgotten. Just like the world of wine with its appellations and varieties, cacao is full of single-origin grand crus grown from specific varieties on different terroirs. Climate, soil composition, and farming practices all have a significant influence on the flavors of the chocolate that will be made from the cacao plants.

The ten grand crus selected by Pierre Marcolini come from the four principal varieties of cacao:

Forastero

Origin: Amazonia, 80% of world production

Forastero is the most widely cultivated variety of cacao trees, as well as the most robust. Its dark purple or garnet-colored beans are less aromatic than others, but very hardy. This variety has been extensively planted in Africa.

Criollo

Origin: Central America, 1% of world production

An exceptional cacao notable for its highly aromatic white seeds.

Trinitario

Origin: Trinidad, 18% of world production

A natural hybrid of a Criollo and a Forastero, this variety produces variably colored beans: light purple, dark purple, or white, and makes for a fine cacao.

Ecuador Nacional

Origin: Ecuador, 1% of world production

Cultivated exclusively in Ecuador, the dark beans are highly prized for their excellent floral aromas, known as "arriba."

**The following recipes call for a specific grand cru, but you may substitute a dark chocolate of a similar percentage as indicated.*

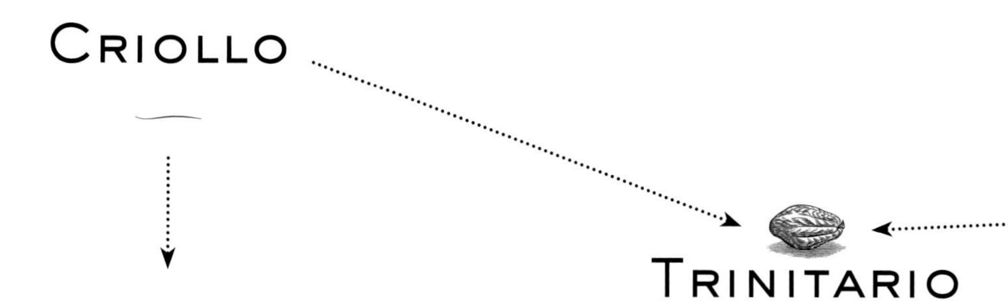

{Mexico, Tabasco State – Finca La Joya Plantation}

Variety: exceptional white Criollo Blanco similar to a Porcelana
Primary tastes: surprisingly strong acidity with a slight bitterness
Flavors: very lemony and invigorating, with hints of nuts
Other information: A light-colored chocolate from Carmelo Criollo beans, which are white, though some have narrow pink stripes. In comparison to a dark Forastero bar from Brazil, one might even take it for a bar of milk chocolate.

{Indonesia, Java – State Plantation of Kendeng Lembu}

Variety: old Criollo, light-colored pod
Primary taste: Marked acidity
Flavors: pepper and other spices, fruit, a smoky note that is typical of this variety
Other information: An isolated terroir between the mountains and the sea, accessible only by boat. This variety of rare cacaos has remained untouched over the centuries.

{Venezuala, Aragua – Chuao Terroir}

Variety: natural Criollo
Primary tastes: Balanced acidity and bitterness
Flavors: exceptional cacao with delicate mouthfeel, subtle violet freshness, strong cacao
Other information: An isolated terroir between the mountains and the sea, accessible only by boat. This variety of rare cacaos has remained untouched over the centuries.

{Peru, Alto Piura – Las Pampas Plantation}

Variety: Criollo Blanco
Primary taste: Balanced
Flavors: elegant, citrus, cacao, and fermented tastes
Other information: Piura, the terroir where most of Peru's Criollos grow.

{Brazil, Bahia – Fazenda Leonida Farm}

Variety: Trinitario
Primary tastes: balanced acidity with a little bitterness
Flavors: tropical fruits {passion fruit and bananas} and nuts {walnuts}
Other information: A model farm, thanks to the perfectionism of its owner.

{Cuba, Oriente – Terruno de Baracoa}

Variety: heirloom Trinitario from the Caribbeans
Primary tastes: pronounced but not excessive bitterness
Flavors: notes of dry wood, dried hazelnuts; full-bodied with a hint of tobacco
Other information: Extremely powerful nose. When it is roasted, the smells of this cacao fill the surrounding streets.

{Vietnam, Mekong Delta – Ben Tre Island Cooperative}

Variety: Trinitario
Primary tastes: fine balance between bitterness and acidity
Flavors: red wine, nuts, cacao
Other information: The cacao grown in Vietnam reflects recent updated and very promising farming methods.

{Madagascar, Sambirano – Domaine of Ambanja – Somia Plantation}

Variety: Trinitario
Primary taste: Fine acidity
Flavors: cinnamon, red and yellow berries, floral notes thanks to the ylang-ylang planted close by on same property
Other information: The Sambirano Valley is known for its varieties of rare cacaos, Criollo and Trinitario, an exception among the African cacaos.

Forastero

{Cameroon, Upper Penja – Dark Mungo Plantation}

Variety: Forastero
Primary tastes: barely acidic with a pronounced bitterness
Flavors: citrus, earthy, basil
Other information: A small experimental farm exclusively reserved for the Maison Marcolini. The volcanic terroir is rich and gives a distinctive identity to the beans.

Nacional

{Ecuador, Los Rios – Hacienda Puerto Romero}

Variety: Nacional
Primary tastes: fine balance between bitterness and acidity
Flavors: jasmine and orange flower {a taste the locals call "arriba"}, walnuts, red wine
Other information: A bean with a sensitivity closer to that of Criollo than to Forastero; dark purple.

Los Rios
Hacienda
Puerto Romero

Grand cru Arriba Nacional Ecuadorian

{Ecuador}

A fine, rare cacao with dark purple beans that produce a deep black-brown chocolate.

Outstanding floral aromas.

A fine balance between bitterness and acidity.

Flavors: jasmine, orange flower, walnuts, and red wine

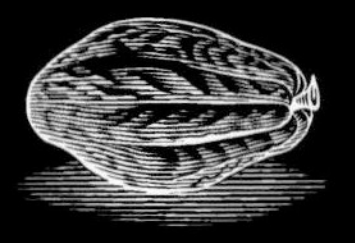

Chocolate-Hazelnut Meringue Cakes

{Dacquoises aux Chocolat}

Makes 15 small sponge cakes
Prep: 25 minutes
Cook: 20 minutes

INGREDIENTS

1½ cups {4½ oz. / 130 g} ground hazelnuts
1 cup {4½ oz. / 130 g} confectioners' sugar
5 egg whites
¼ cup {2 oz. / 50 g} granulated sugar
3½ oz. {100 g} dark chocolate {78% cacao}, preferably Arriba Nacional Ecuadorian grand cru chocolate, plus shavings for decoration

Preheat the oven to 300°F {150°C}.

Spread the ground hazelnuts on a baking sheet lined with parchment paper and roast for 10 minutes. Allow to cool.

Preheat the oven to 350°F {180°C}. Line a baking sheet with parchment paper.

Combine the confectioners' sugar with the ground hazelnuts. Whisk the egg whites until they hold soft peaks. Incorporate the granulated sugar in three additions, whisking until the texture is that of a soft, glossy meringue. Pour in the confectioners' sugar–hazelnut mixture, folding it in carefully with a flexible spatula.

Scoop the batter into a pastry bag fitted with a plain ⅓-inch {7-mm} tip. Pipe 2¾-inch {7-cm} diameter mounds about 2 inches {4 to 5 cm} high onto the prepared baking sheet. Bake for 10 minutes, then cool on a rack.

Chop the chocolate with a knife and melt it over a hot water bath. When the hazelnut meringue cakes have cooled, dip the top of each one in the melted chocolate. Allow to set and sprinkle with chocolate shavings.

Chef's note

An easy way to make attractive chocolate shavings is to rub the flat surface of a bar of chocolate with the palm of your hand, and then use a knife {with a flexible blade} to gently scrape it off.

Individual Genovese Sponges

Makes 15 Genovese sponges
Prep: 25 minutes
Cook: 15 minutes

INGREDIENTS

4 tablespoons {2¼ oz. / 65 g} unsalted butter
7 oz. {200 g} almond paste, 50% almonds, at room temperature
Grated zest of 4 unwaxed lemons
½ cup {4½ oz. / 130 g} egg yolks {6 to 7}
⅓ cup {2½ oz. / 75 g} egg whites {2 to 3}
1½ tablespoons {20 g} granulated sugar

GARNISH

5½ oz. {160 g} dark chocolate {78% cacao}, preferably Arriba Nacional Ecuadorian grand cru chocolate
½ cup {110 ml} heavy cream {35% butterfat}
3 tablespoons {40 g} unsalted butter, diced

DECORATION

Unsalted pistachios
Zest of an unwaxed lime
Small Squares of Bittersweet Chocolate {see recipe, page 84}

EQUIPMENT

2½-inch {6-cm} diameter silicone molds

Preheat the oven to 325°F {165°C}.

Melt the butter in a large saucepan over medium heat. When it begins to brown and has the fragrance of roasted hazelnuts, remove from the heat and pour it into a bowl to prevent it from cooking any further.

Soften the almond paste in the microwave oven at 600W for 45 seconds, or leave it at room temperature until softened. In a food processor, thoroughly combine the almond paste with the lemon zest. Add the egg yolks, one by one, continuing until thoroughly blended.

Whisk the egg whites until they hold soft peaks, then whisk in the sugar. Stir a little of the egg whites into the melted butter, then stir the butter–egg white mixture into the almond paste mixture.

With a flexible spatula, carefully fold in the remaining egg whites. Pour the batter into the silicone molds and bake for 15 minutes. Allow to cool on a rack.

Chop the chocolate with a knife and place it in a bowl. Heat the cream in a small saucepan to 175°F {80°C}. Pour it over the chocolate in a steady stream, whisking constantly. This makes a ganache with a texture similar to that of mayonnaise. When the mixture is completely emulsified, gently whisk in the butter. Allow to cool.

Spoon the ganache into a pastry bag fitted with a fluted ⅓-inch {8-mm} tip. Pipe attractive rosettes over the Genovese sponge cakes.

Scatter pistachios and grated lime zest over the ganache and decorate with a few bits of bittersweet chocolate squares.

Chef's note

The Genovese sponge is a cake that keeps and even travels well {in French, it's called a *gateau de voyage*}–but without the ganache, of course!

Chocolate Soufflés

Serves 8
Prep: 20 minutes
Cook: 16 minutes

INGREDIENTS

1½ oz. {40 g} dark chocolate {78% cacao}, preferably Arriba Nacional Ecuadorian grand cru chocolate
1¼ cups {300 ml} whole milk
Scant ¼ cup {2 oz. / 60 g} egg yolks {3 yolks}
Scant ½ cup {3oz./80 g} granulated sugar
2 tablespoons {⅔ oz. / 20 g} cornstarch
Scant cup {7 oz. / 200 g} egg whites {6 to 7 whites}
3 tablespoons {2 oz. / 50 g} unsalted butter for the ramekins

Preheat the oven to 375°F {190°C}. Grease 8 ramekins with butter.

Make a chocolate pastry cream: Chop the chocolate with a knife and place in a mixing bowl. Bring the milk to a boil in a saucepan. While it is heating, beat the egg yolks with the sugar in the bowl of a stand mixer fitted with a whisk until the mixture is pale. Incorporate the cornstarch. Pour one-third of the boiling milk over the yolk-sugar mixture to heat it. Whisk well and pour in the remaining milk and whisk to combine. Return the liquid to the saucepan and bring to a boil. Remove from the heat. Stir in the chocolate until thoroughly combined. Allow to cool to room temperature.

Whisk the egg whites. With a flexible spatula, carefully fold them into the pastry cream. Divide the soufflé batter among the prepared ramekins and bake for 16 minutes.

Chef's note

Serve the chocolate soufflés with a scoop of ice cream.

Chocolate Foam

with Salted Butter Caramel

Serves 6
Prep: 30 minutes

INGREDIENTS

4 oz. {110 g} dark chocolate {78% cacao}, preferably Arriba Nacional Ecuadorian grand cru chocolate
½ cup {125 ml} heavy cream {35% butterfat}
Scant ⅔ cup {4½ oz. / 135 g} egg whites {4 to 5 whites}

SALTED BUTTER CARAMEL

3 tablespoons {50 ml} heavy cream {35% butterfat}
½ cup {3½ oz. / 100 g} granulated sugar
2 tablespoons {1 oz. / 30 g} unsalted butter, diced
1 generous pinch fleur de sel

EQUIPMENT

Siphon
1 gas cartridge

Chop the chocolate with a knife and place it in a mixing bowl.

In a saucepan, bring the cream to a boil. Pour it over the chocolate and stir well to combine.

Lightly beat the egg whites and stir them into the chocolate-cream mixture until smooth.

Strain through a fine-mesh sieve.

Fill a siphon with the mixture and install a gas cartridge. Place the siphon in a 140°F {60°C} hot water bath.

Make the salted butter caramel: Warm the cream in a small saucepan. In another saucepan, cook the sugar without adding any water until it is a light yellow color. Deglaze the caramel with the cream, stirring as you pour it in. Incorporate the butter and fleur de sel.

Just before serving, pour the caramel into the bottom of the serving bowls. Dispense the chocolate mixture from the siphon over the caramel.

Chef's note

If you prefer, serve the chocolate foam with salted caramel ice cream, just like in the original recipe.

Original recipe by Laurent and Vincent Folmer of Couvert Couvert, *Heverlee, Belgium*

Hot Chocolate

with Darjeeling Tea

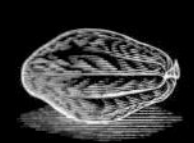

Serves 2
Prep: 5 minutes
Rest: 1 hour 10 minutes

INGREDIENTS

3 oz. {90 g} dark chocolate {78% cacao}, preferably Arriba Nacional Ecuadorian grand cru chocolate
¾ cup {200 ml} water
Scant ½ cup {100 ml} whole milk
2 mousseline bags Darjeeling tea
⅓ oz. {10 g} ground Hazelnut Praline {see recipe, page 122}

Chop the chocolate with a knife. Combine the water and milk. Place the mousseline bags in the cold liquid and infuse for one hour.

Heat the liquid with the mousseline bags to 175°F {80°C}, take off the heat, and infuse for a further 10 minutes. Remove the bags. Meanwhile chop the chocolate and place it in a bowl with the hazelnut praline.

Pour the liquid over the chocolate and praline. With an immersion blender, process for 2 minutes, until the texture is foamy and creamy.

Chef's note

The note of coffee in Arriba Nacional Ecuadorian is sublime when combined with the taste of hazelnuts.

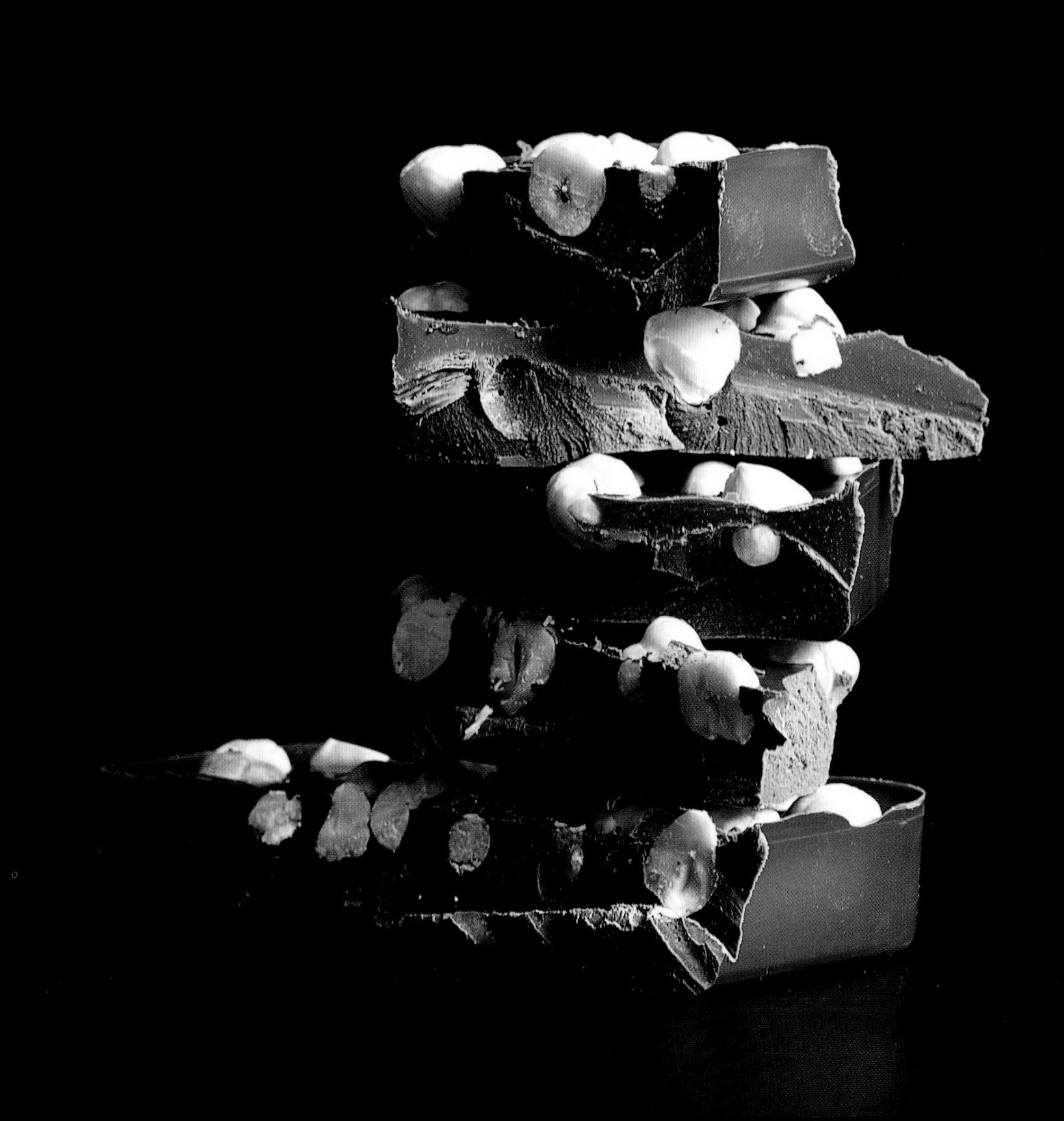

Grand Cru Chocolate Bar

with Hazelnuts

Makes one 14-oz. {400-g} bar
Prep: 10 minutes
Cook: 15 minutes
Chill: 30 to 60 minutes

INGREDIENTS

3½ oz. {100 g} peeled hazelnuts
10½ oz. {300 g} dark chocolate {78% cacao}, preferably Arriba Nacional Ecuadorian grand cru chocolate

Preheat the oven to 325°F {160°C}. Spread the hazelnuts over a baking sheet and roast for 15 minutes. Cool to room temperature.

Chop the chocolate with a knife.

To ensure that your chocolate bar is glossy, temper it as follows:
- Over a hot water bath, heat the chocolate to 122°F {50°C}.
- Place over a cool water bath and cool to 82°F {28°C}.
- Reheat the chocolate to 90°F {32°C} over a hot water bath.

Stir the roasted hazelnuts into the chocolate and pour into a silicone mold. Refrigerate only until set, from 30 minutes to one hour, depending on the thickness of the bar, and turn out of the mold.

Chef's note

Vary the taste by adding other nuts.

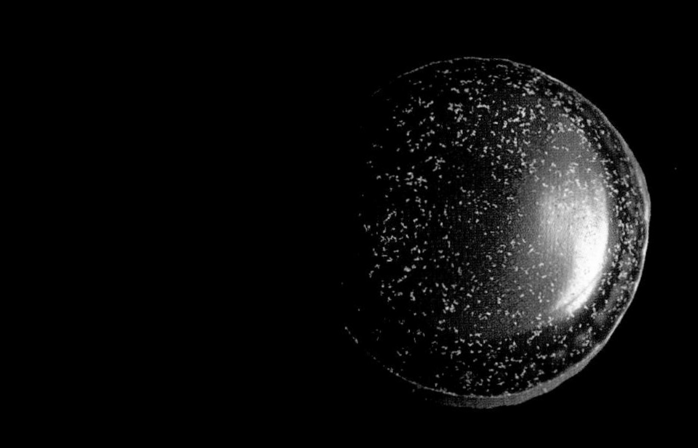

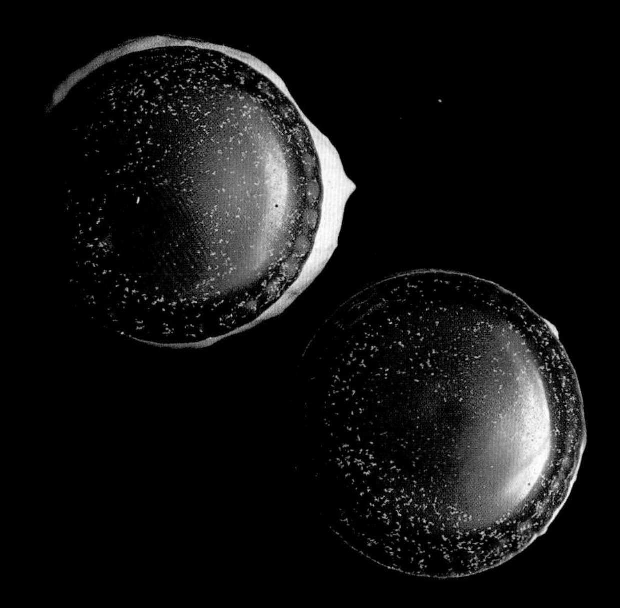

Ganache-filled Chocolate Cookies

Makes 10 filled cookies/chocolates
Prep: 30 minutes
Rest: 2 hours plus 15 minutes

INGREDIENTS

12½ oz. {360 g} dark chocolate {78% cacao}, preferably Arriba Nacional Ecuadorian grand cru chocolate, divided
½ cup {110 ml} heavy cream {35% butterfat}
3 tablespoons {40 g} unsalted butter, diced

EQUIPMENT

Plastic or silicone shell-shaped macaron molds

Chop 5½ oz. {160 g} of the chocolate with a knife and place it in a mixing bowl. Heat the cream to 175°F {80°C}. Pour it over the chocolate in a steady stream, whisking constantly. This makes a ganache with a texture similar to that of mayonnaise. When the mixture is completely emulsified, gently whisk in the butter. Press a sheet of plastic wrap directly over the surface and refrigerate for two hours.

Chop the remaining 7 oz. {200 g} chocolate with a knife. To ensure that your chocolate cookies have a lovely sheen, temper the chocolate as follows:
- Over a hot water bath, heat the chocolate to 122°F {50°C}.
- Place over a cool water bath and cool to 82°F {28°C}.
- Over a hot water bath, reheat the chocolate to 90°F {32°C}.

Pour the chocolate into the molds; you will need 20 filled. Refrigerate only until the chocolate has set, about 15 minutes, and turn out of the molds.

Pour the ganache into a pastry bag fitted with a plain ⅓-inch {8 mm} tip. Pipe ganache over half of the chocolate shells and top with the remaining shells.

Candied Kumquats
with Chocolate Sauce

Makes 10 candied kumquats
Prep: 20 minutes

INGREDIENTS
10 kumquats

SYRUP
1⅔ cups {400 ml} water
2 cups {14 oz. / 400 g} granulated sugar, divided

CHOCOLATE SAUCE
3½ oz. {100 g} dark chocolate {78% cacao}, preferably Arriba Nacional Ecuadorian grand cru chocolate, divided

Bring a saucepan of water to a boil. Place the kumquats in it and leave for 2 minutes to blanche, then drain.

Make the syrup: Bring the water to a boil with 1 cup {7 oz. / 200 g} of the sugar. Allow to simmer for 3 minutes.

Place the kumquats in the syrup and allow to boil for 30 minutes. Remove the kumquats from the water and add ¼ cup {1¾ oz. / 50 g} of the sugar to the water. Return the kumquats to the water and boil for 3 minutes.

Repeat the procedure three times, adding ¼ cup {1¾ oz. / 50 g} of the sugar each time, until the kumquats are softened and candied. Allow them to cool.

Chop the chocolate with a knife and melt it over a hot water bath. Pour the chocolate sauce over the candied kumquats.

Chef's note

You can also make this recipe with another citrus fruit of your choice, although cooking times may vary.

Chocolate Tart
with Fresh Figs

Serves 6
Prep: 40 minutes
Chill: 1 hour
Cook: 22 minutes

INGREDIENTS

7 oz. {200 g} Chocolate Streusel dough {see page 304}
Half-recipe Chocolate Soufflés {see page 154}
¼ cup {2 oz. / 50 g} granulated sugar
2 tablespoons {30 g} unsalted butter
4 fresh figs

On a lightly floured work surface, roll the streusel dough with a rolling pin. Grease a 6-inch {16-cm} tart pan with butter and line it with the streusel dough to a height of just under ½ inch {1 cm}. Refrigerate for one hour.

Preheat the oven to 325°F {160°C}. Place a sheet of parchment paper over the streusel dough and cover with baking beans. Bake for 10 minutes and allow to cool on a rack. {You will need the oven to be at the same temperature for the next step.}

Make the Chocolate Soufflé mixture and pour it over the streusel dough. Bake for 12 minutes.

In a skillet over low heat, melt the sugar with the butter to make a caramel. Cut the figs into halves and sauté them in the skillet. Allow to caramelize for 2 to 3 minutes. Serve warm slices of the chocolate tart with the figs.

Chef's note

Instead of lining the tart with the streusel dough, chill it well and grate it into the base of the ring. Moisten with a little water and press in the dough. Bake blind according to the instructions above.

Arriba

Serves 6
Prep: 10 minutes

INGREDIENTS

3 Genovese Sponges {see recipe, page 153}
Chocolate Foam {see recipe, page 156}
18 Candied Kumquats {see recipe, page 164}
3 oz. {90 g} Hot Chocolate with Darjeeling Tea {see recipe, page 159}

To Plate

Break the Genovese loaf cakes into small pieces—but not too small. Dispense the chocolate foam from the siphon into the center of each serving plate. Scatter the broken loaf cakes over the plate and arrange the candied kumquats attractively around. Pour a little hot chocolate on the side.

Chef's note

An arrangement of all these components makes for a simple, very tasty dessert. If you prefer, replace the chocolate foam with another creamy dessert of your choice.

Tabasco
Finca La Joya

Criollo Carmelo Tabasco Grand Cru

{Mexico}

A unique cacao.

White Porcelana beans with thin pink stripes
that produce a light brown chocolate.
Surprisingly strong acidity
with a slight bitterness.
Flavors: lemony and invigorating, with hints of nuts

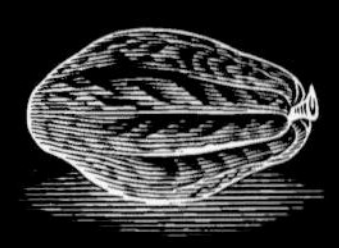

Cookies
with Chocolate Chips

Makes 60 cookies
Prep: 20 minutes
Chill: 1 hour
Cook: 10 minutes

INGREDIENTS

6 oz. {180 g} dark chocolate {78% cacao}, preferably Criollo Blanco grand cru chocolate {Mexico}
2 sticks plus 1 tablespoon {9 oz. / 260 g} unsalted butter, room temperature
4 tablespoons {2 oz. / 60 g} butter with sea salt crystals, room temperature
1¼ cups {5½ oz. / 160 g} confectioners' sugar
1 egg yolk
3¼ cups {14 oz. / 400 g} all-purpose flour, sifted

Coarsely chop the chocolate with a knife to make large chips.

In the bowl of a mixer fitted with the paddle, beat the two types of butter until very creamy. Beat in the confectioners' sugar and egg yolk. When combined, add the flour, and lastly, the chocolate chips.

Cover in plastic wrap and refrigerate for 1 hour.

Preheat the oven to 325°F {160°F}. Line a baking sheet with parchment paper or a silicone baking mat.

Using your hands, shape small balls the size of a walnut. Place them on the prepared baking sheet, taking care to leave enough space between them for the cookies to spread. With the palm of your hand, flatten the balls slightly.

Bake for 10 minutes and transfer to a rack to cool.

Chef's note

This cookie dough keeps very well in the freezer and can also be used as a tart crust.

Brownies
with Caramel Sauce & Nuts

Serves 10
Prep: 20 minutes
Cook: 40 minutes

INGREDIENTS

7 oz. {200 g} shelled pistachios {about 1½ cups}
1 oz. {30 g} peeled hazelnuts {about ¼ cup}
1 oz. {30 g} blanched almonds {about ¼ cup}
6 oz. {180 g} dark chocolate {78% cacao}, preferably Criollo Blanco grand cru chocolate {Mexico}
2 sticks {8½ oz. / 240 g} butter, diced, plus extra for the brownie pan
5 eggs
2 cups {14 oz. / 400 g} granulated sugar
1 cup {4 oz. / 120 g} all-purpose flour

CARAMEL

3 tablespoons {50 ml} whipping cream {35% butterfat}
1 cup {7 oz. / 200 g} granulated sugar
3 tablespoons {2 oz. / 50 g} unsalted butter, diced
1 generous pinch fleur de sel

Preheat the oven to 325°F {160°C}. Grease a brownie pan with butter.

Spread the pistachios, hazelnuts, and almonds on a baking sheet and roast for 15 minutes.

Make and bake the brownies:
Chop the chocolate with a knife. Melt it over a hot water bath with the butter and allow to cool to lukewarm.

Whisk the eggs with the sugar, then whisk in the melted chocolate and butter. Incorporate the flour.

Pour the batter into the prepared pan and bake for 40 minutes. Allow to cool slightly in the pan and turn out.

Make the caramel:
Warm the cream in a saucepan. In another saucepan, cook the sugar over medium heat until it is a light caramel color. Deglaze with the warm cream, stirring constantly, and stir in the butter and fleur de sel.

Stir in the roasted nuts and allow to cool to lukewarm. Drizzle the still-warm brownie with the caramel sauce with nuts.

Chocolate Crème Brûlée

Serves 6
Prep: 20 minutes
Cook: 20 minutes

INGREDIENTS

4 oz. {120 g} dark chocolate {78% cacao}, preferably Criollo Blanco grand cru chocolate {Mexico}
1 cup {250 ml} whipping cream {35% butterfat}
1 cup {250 ml} whole milk
4 egg yolks
3½ tablespoons {1½ oz. / 40 g} granulated sugar
Fine chocolate shavings for decoration

Preheat the oven to 210°F {100°C}.

Chop the chocolate with a knife and place in a bowl. In a saucepan, bring the cream and milk to a boil.

In the bowl of a mixer fitted with the whisk, beat the egg yolks with the sugar until pale. Pour a little of the hot cream-milk mixture over the yolk-sugar mixture, beating constantly, to warm it slightly. Then pour in the remaining hot liquid, still beating.

Transfer to a saucepan and, stirring constantly, heat to 180°F {82°C}, at which stage it has thickened and coats the back of a spoon. Pour it over the chocolate and process with an immersion blender until completely emulsified.

Divide among six ramekins and place in a larger baking pan. Pour some water into the pan and bake for 20 minutes. The crème brûlées should still be wobbly when you remove them from the oven. Allow to cool and scatter with fine chocolate shavings.

Chef's note

Heating the mixture to 180°F {82°C} before baking the desserts means you have more control over the texture than if the crème brûlées were only baked in the oven.

Diplomat Cream

Serves 6
Prep: 20 minutes
Set: 2 hours
Chill: 1 hour

INGREDIENTS

2½ oz. {70 g} dark chocolate {78% cacao}, preferably Criollo Blanco grand cru chocolate {Mexico}
1 cup {250 ml} whole milk
2 egg yolks
3½ tablespoons {1½ oz. / 40 g} granulated sugar
2 tablespoons plus 1 teaspoon {22 g} cornstarch
⅔ cup {150 ml} whipping cream {35% butterfat}, well chilled
2 oz. {50 g} chocolate shavings

Make a chocolate pastry cream:
Chop the chocolate with a knife and place it in a bowl. Bring the milk to a boil in a saucepan.

In the bowl of a mixer fitted with the whisk, beat the egg yolks with the sugar until pale. Incorporate the cornstarch. Pour a little of the hot milk over the yolk-sugar mixture to warm it, beating constantly. Pour in the remaining milk, still beating. Return the mixture to the saucepan and bring to a boil.

Pour the hot pastry cream over the chocolate and stir to combine. Allow to cool for 2 hours at room temperature. As soon as it is cool, process with an immersion blender for 1 minute.

Whisk the cream until it holds very soft peaks. With a flexible spatula, carefully fold the whipped cream into the chocolate mixture. Pour into the containers of your choice and refrigerate for 1 hour. Just before serving, scatter with chocolate shavings.

Chef's note

Processing the pastry cream with an immersion blender ensures that it is smooth and soft.

Light Chocolate
& Passion Fruit Sauce

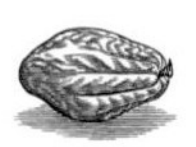

Serves 8 as an accompaniment to a dessert
Prep: 5 minutes

INGREDIENTS

4½ oz. {125 g} dark chocolate {78% cacao}, preferably Criollo Blanco grand cru chocolate {Mexico}
⅔ cup {150 ml} whole milk
⅔ cup {150 ml} passion fruit juice
2½ tablespoons {2 oz. / 50 g} glucose syrup

Chop the chocolate with a knife and place it in a bowl. In a saucepan, bring the milk to a boil with the passion fruit juice and glucose. Pour it over the chocolate. Process with an immersion blender for a few minutes until the sauce is perfectly smooth.

This sauce keeps for up to three days in the refrigerator.

Chef's note

Glucose syrup gives the sauce a lovely sheen. You can also make this recipe with mango juice.

TRUFFLES
with Black Sesame Seeds & Sake

Makes 50 truffles
Prep {a day ahead}: 20 minutes
Chill: 12 hours
Rest: 1 to 2 hours

INGREDIENTS

9 oz. {250 g} dark chocolate {78% cacao}, preferably Criollo Blanco grand cru chocolate {Mexico}
⅔ cup {150 ml} whipping cream {35% butterfat}
2½ tablespoons {1 oz. / 30 g} granulated sugar
3 tablespoons {1½ oz. / 45 g} unsalted butter, diced
1 tablespoon plus 1 teaspoon {20 ml} sake
2 oz. {50 g} black sesame seeds {about 5 tablespoons}
Shiso leaves to serve {found at Asian grocery stores}

A day {or 12 hours} ahead, make a classic ganache: Chop the chocolate with a knife and place it in a mixing bowl. Bring the cream and sugar to a boil in a saucepan. Pour the hot liquid in a steady stream over the chocolate, whisking constantly. To ensure that the emulsion is complete, process with an immersion blender. Allow to cool slightly, then add the butter and sake. Process again with the immersion blender.

Line a deep dish with plastic wrap and pour in the ganache. Press a sheet of plastic wrap over the surface and refrigerate for 12 hours.

Preheat the oven to 325°F {160°C}. Spread the sesame seeds on a baking sheet and roast for 10 minutes, then allow to cool.

To shape the truffles, cut small rectangles in the ganache. Sprinkle with the black sesame seeds and return to the refrigerator.

Serve the truffles on shiso leaves–they make edible plates!

Chef's notes

It is best to make the ganache 12 hours ahead so that it can set well.

Carefully sealed in an airtight container, these truffles keep for up to two weeks in the vegetable crisper of the refrigerator.

Before serving, leave them at room temperature {68°F / 20°C} for one to two hours.

Nama
CHOCOLATES

Makes 10 chocolates
Prep: 15 minutes
Chill: 2 hours

INGREDIENTS

9 oz. {250 g} dark chocolate {78% cacao}, preferably Criollo Blanco grand cru chocolate {Mexico}
¾ cup {190 ml} whipping cream {35% butterfat}
2½ tablespoons {1 oz. / 30 g} granulated sugar
1 Madagascar vanilla bean, split, seeds scraped
2 tablespoons {35 g} unsalted butter, diced
Matcha powder for dusting

Make a classic ganache:
Chop the chocolate with a knife and place it in a mixing bowl. Bring the cream, sugar, and vanilla seeds and bean to a boil in a saucepan. Remove the vanilla bean. Pour the hot liquid in a steady stream over the chocolate, whisking constantly. To ensure that the emulsion is complete, process with an immersion blender. Allow to cool slightly, then add the butter. Process again with the immersion blender.

Line a deep dish with plastic wrap and pour in the ganache. Press the plastic wrap on the surface and refrigerate for 2 hours.

With a 1¾-inch {4-cm} cookie cutter, cut out disks. Dust lightly with matcha powder.

Chef's note

Nama in Japanese means "fresh," just like the cream that is used in this unctuous recipe. Well wrapped, the nama chocolates keep for up to one week in the refrigerator.

Candied Lemon Peel
Dipped in Chocolate

Makes 20 pieces
Prep: 20 minutes

INGREDIENTS

2 large unwaxed Meyer lemons
1¼ cups {300 ml} water
1¾ cups {12 oz. / 350 g} granulated sugar, divided
3½ oz. {100 g} dark chocolate {78% cacao}, preferably Criollo Blanco grand cru chocolate {Mexico}

Wash and dry the lemons. With a small, sharp knife, remove the peel from the lemons and cut it into strips.

Bring the water and ¾ cup {5 oz. / 150 g} of the sugar to a boil. Allow to simmer for 3 minutes.

Place the lemon peel strips in the syrup and allow to boil for 3 minutes, then remove them from the syrup and drain.

Add ¼ cup {1¾ oz. / 50 g} of the sugar to the syrup. Return the strips to the saucepan and boil for 3 minutes.

Repeat the procedure three times, adding ¼ cup {1¾ oz. / 50 g} of the sugar each time, until the lemon peel strips are candied. They should be soft but retain some firmness. Drain and allow them to cool on a sheet of parchment paper.

Chop the chocolate with a knife. To ensure that the chocolate coating is glossy, temper it as follows:
- Over a hot water bath, heat the chocolate to 122°F {50°C}.
- Place over a cool water bath and cool to 82°F {28°C}.
- Reheat the chocolate to 90°F {32°C} over a hot water bath.

Dip each strip of lemon peel into the chocolate, coating three quarters of it. As you work, place each one on a plate lined with parchment paper and allow to cool.

Chef's note

Meyer lemons have a thin skin that is almost an orange hue when ripe. The flesh has little acidity and the flavor is delicate. All in all, it's a variety that is ideal for this recipe.

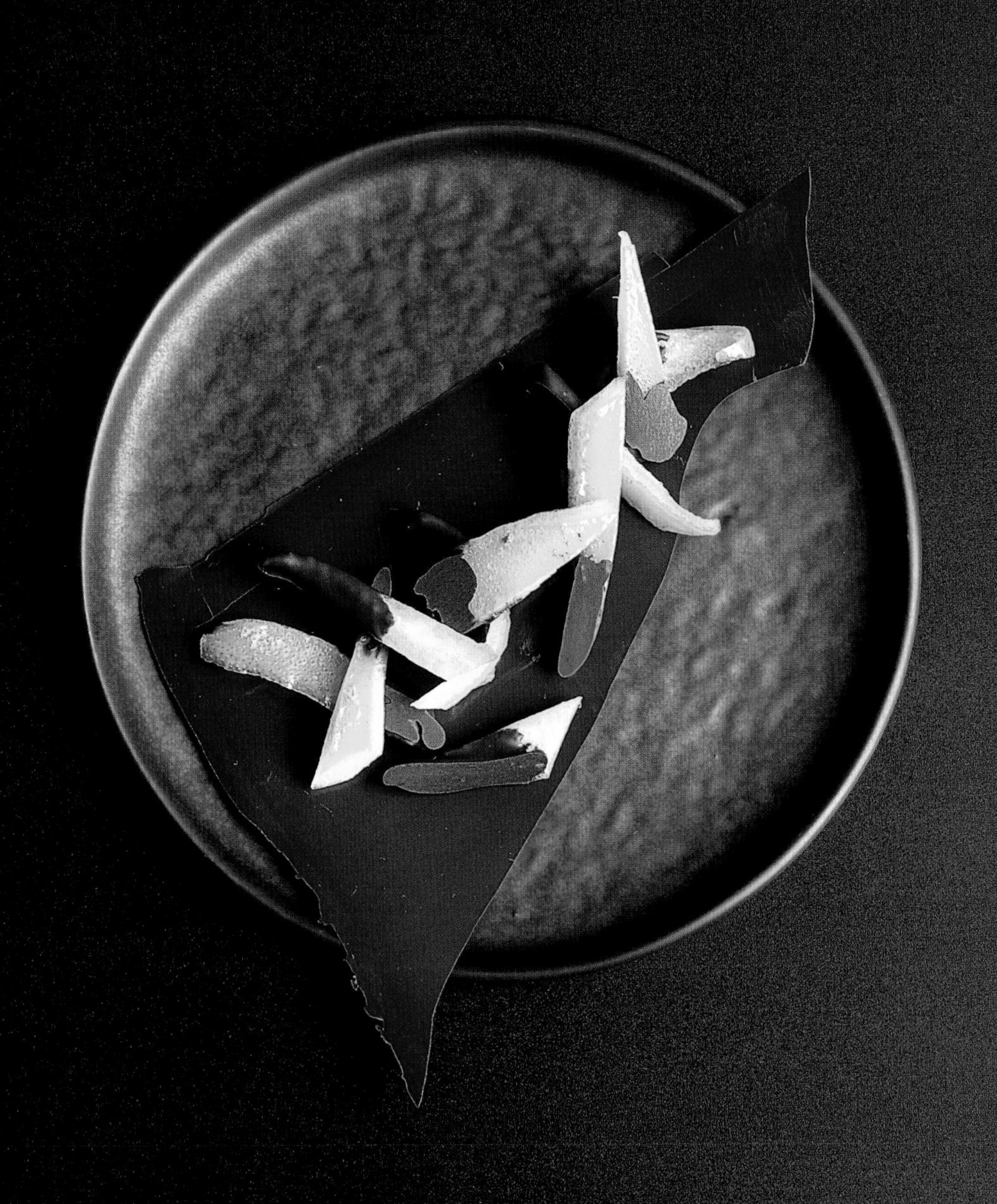

Chocolate Éclairs

Makes 10 éclairs
Prep: 40 minutes
Chill: 2 hours
Cook: 25 minutes

INGREDIENTS

PASTRY CREAM

2½ oz. {70 g} dark chocolate {78% cacao}, preferably Criollo Blanco grand cru chocolate {Mexico}
1 cup {250 ml} whole milk
2 egg yolks
3½ tablespoons {1½ oz. / 40 g} granulated sugar
2 tablespoons plus 1 teaspoon {22 g} cornstarch
1 pinch fleur de sel
2 tablespoons {25 g} unsalted butter, diced

CHOUX PASTRY

1 cup {250 ml} whole milk
1 stick {4 oz. / 120 g} unsalted butter, diced
1 pinch granulated sugar
1 pinch salt
1 cup plus 1 tablespoon {5 oz. / 140 g} all-purpose flour
1 cup {8½ oz. / 240 g} eggs {4 to 5 eggs}

EGG WASH

1 egg yolk
1 tablespoon water
1 pinch salt {to heighten the color}

GLAZE

7 oz. {200 g} white fondant icing
1½ oz. {40 g} dark chocolate {78% cacao}, preferably Criollo Blanco grand cru chocolate {Mexico}
1 pinch fat-soluble red food coloring

Make the chocolate pastry cream:
Chop the chocolate with a knife and place it in a bowl. Bring the milk to a boil in a saucepan.

In the bowl of a mixer fitted with the whisk, beat the egg yolks with the sugar until pale. Incorporate the cornstarch. Pour one-third of the hot milk over the yolk-sugar mixture to warm it, beating constantly. Pour in the remaining milk with the fleur de sel, still beating. Return the mixture to the saucepan and bring to a boil.

Pour the hot pastry cream over the chocolate and stir to combine. When the pastry cream has cooled to lukewarm, add the butter and process with an immersion blender to emulsify the mixture. Press a sheet of plastic wrap over the surface and refrigerate for 2 hours.

Make the choux pastry:
Preheat the oven to 375°F {190°C} {see Notes}. Line a baking sheet with parchment paper or a silicone baking mat.

Bring the milk to a boil in a saucepan with the butter, sugar, and salt. Remove from the heat and pour in all of the flour at once. Stir in to combine, then return to the heat, stirring until the dough pulls away from the sides of the saucepan.

Transfer the batter to the bowl of a mixer fitted with the paddle. Add the eggs, one by one, beating until the dough is perfectly smooth. Spoon the dough into a pastry bag fitted with a plain ⅓-inch {7-mm} tip. Pipe 5-inch- {12-cm-} long éclairs onto the prepared baking sheet.

Combine the ingredients for the egg wash and brush the tops of the éclairs to ensure they rise more evenly. Draw the tines of a fork along the top of each éclair lightly to ensure that they rise evenly.

Bake for about 25 minutes; do not open the oven. Transfer to a rack and allow to cool.

Garnish the éclairs:
When the pastry cream and the choux pastries are completely cool, process the pastry cream with the immersion blender for 2 minutes so that it is perfectly smooth. Spoon the pastry cream into a pastry bag fitted with a plain ⅛-inch {4-mm} tip. Pierce a small hole at each end of all the éclairs with the tip and pipe the pastry cream in to fill them.

Make the glaze:
Melt the fondant icing and chocolate over a hot water bath. When the mixture reaches 86°F {30°C}, add the food coloring. Stir until the glaze is smooth. Carefully dip the top of each éclair into the glaze.

Chef's notes

To ensure that the choux pastry rises evenly, preheat the oven to 475°F {250°C}, then switch it off. Place the éclairs in the oven for 15 minutes. Adjust the temperature control to 350°F {180°C} and bake the éclairs for 25 minutes.

For a different presentation, glaze the éclairs before filling them. Use a serrated knife to cut them just below the glaze and pipe in the pastry cream using a pastry bag fitted with a fluted tip. This way, the filling is no longer hidden!

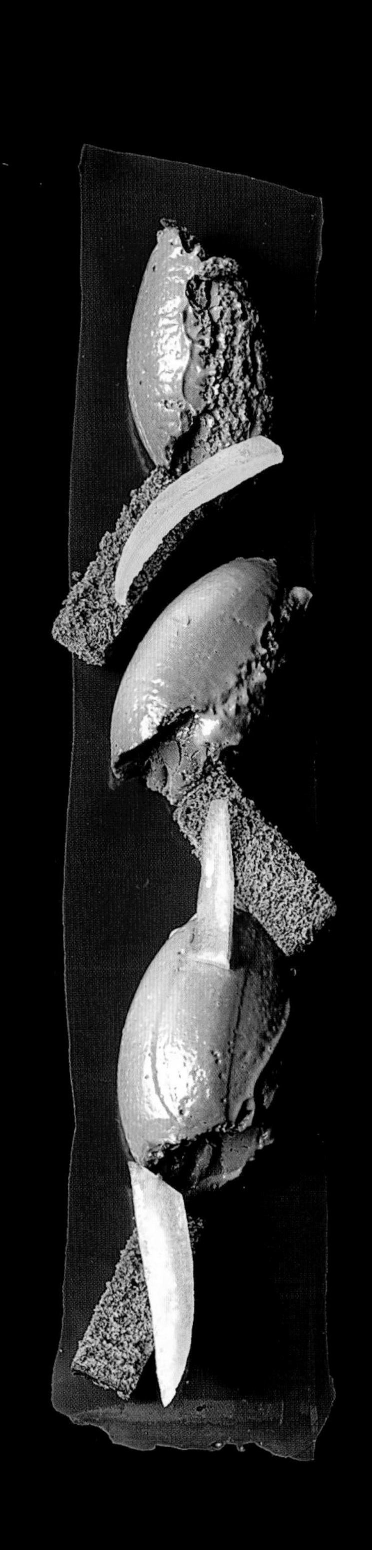

Carmelo

Serves 6
Prep: 30 minutes
Chill: 20 minutes

INGREDIENTS

3½ oz. {100 g} dark chocolate {78% cacao}, preferably Criollo Blanco grand cru chocolate {Mexico}
9 oz. {250 g} Diplomat Cream {see recipe, page 179}, to make a day ahead
5 oz. {150 g} Brownies with Caramel Sauce and Nuts {see recipe, page 174}
3½ oz. {100 g} Candied Lemon Peel, uncoated {see recipe, page 186}

Make thin rectangles of chocolate:
Chop the chocolate with a knife. To ensure that the chocolate leaves are glossy, temper it as follows:
- Over a hot water bath, heat the chocolate to 122°F {50°C}.
- Place over a cool water bath and cool to 82°F {28°C}.
- Reheat the chocolate to 90°F {32°C} over a hot water bath.

Pour the chocolate over a sheet of food-safe acetate and spread another sheet over the chocolate. With a rolling pin, roll it out very thinly. Cut 1½ by 4-inch {4 by 10-cm} rectangles and refrigerate them for 20 minutes. Remove the acetate.

Place three oval scoops of Diplomat Cream on each chocolate rectangle. Garnish with small rectangles of brownie and three strips of candied lemon peel.

Chef's note

If you wish, replace the candied lemon peel with other candied citrus peel.

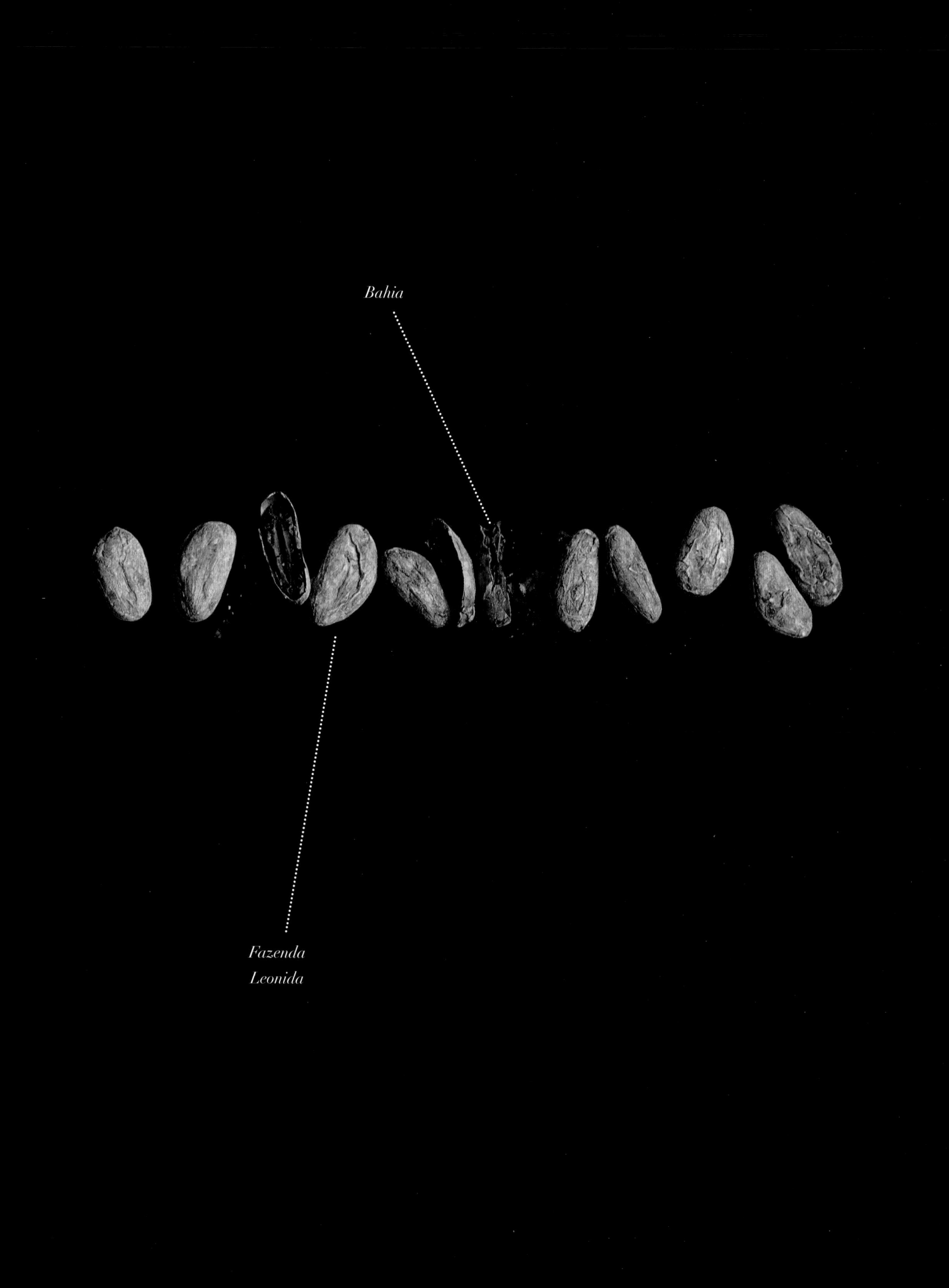

Bahia

Fazenda Leonida

Trinitario Bahia Grand Cru

{Brazil}

From the Bahia region, a grand cru
grown at the Fazenda Leonida.
Its acidity is balanced, and it has a subtle bitterness.
Flavors: tropical fruits {passion fruit, banana}
and nuts {walnuts}

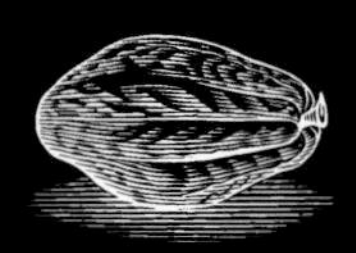

Chocolate Madeleines

Makes 20 madeleines
Prep: 20 minutes
Chill: 2 hours
Cook: 10 minutes

INGREDIENTS

1 cup plus 1 tablespoon {4½ oz. / 135 g} all-purpose flour, plus extra for pans
2¾ teaspoons {10 g} baking powder
1¼ sticks {5 oz. / 150 g} unsalted butter, plus extra for pans
⅓ oz. {10 g} dark chocolate (78% cacao), preferably Trinitario Scavina grand cru chocolate {Brazil}
4 eggs plus 3 egg yolks
½ cup {3½ oz. / 100 g} granulated sugar
1½ tablespoons {1 oz. / 30 g} acacia honey, or multi-floral honey
1 teaspoon {5 g} salt
A few drops of orange flower water

Sift the flour and the baking powder together.

Melt the butter and chocolate over a hot water bath.

In a mixing bowl, whisk the eggs, egg yolks, and sugar together. Whisk in the honey. Add the sifted dry ingredients, salt, and orange flower water and stir to combine. Lastly, add the melted chocolate and butter. Cover the bowl with plastic wrap and allow to rest for 2 hours at room temperature.

Preheat the oven to 400°F {210°C}. Grease a madeleine pan with butter and dust it lightly with flour.

Fill the cavities three-quarters full with the batter. Bake for 10 minutes, until nicely colored and a cake tester inserted into the center of one comes out dry. Turn out of the pan and allow to cool on a rack.

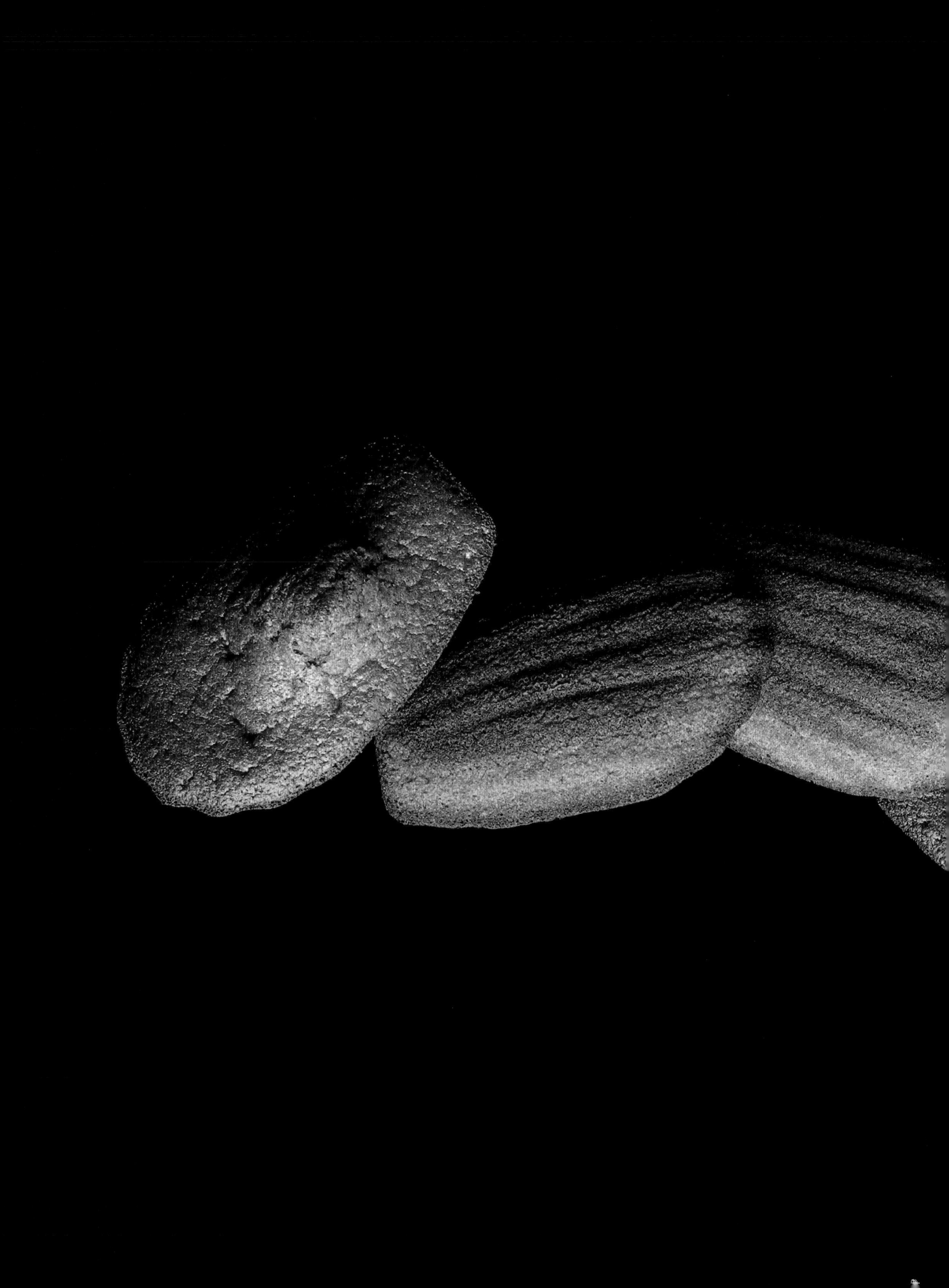

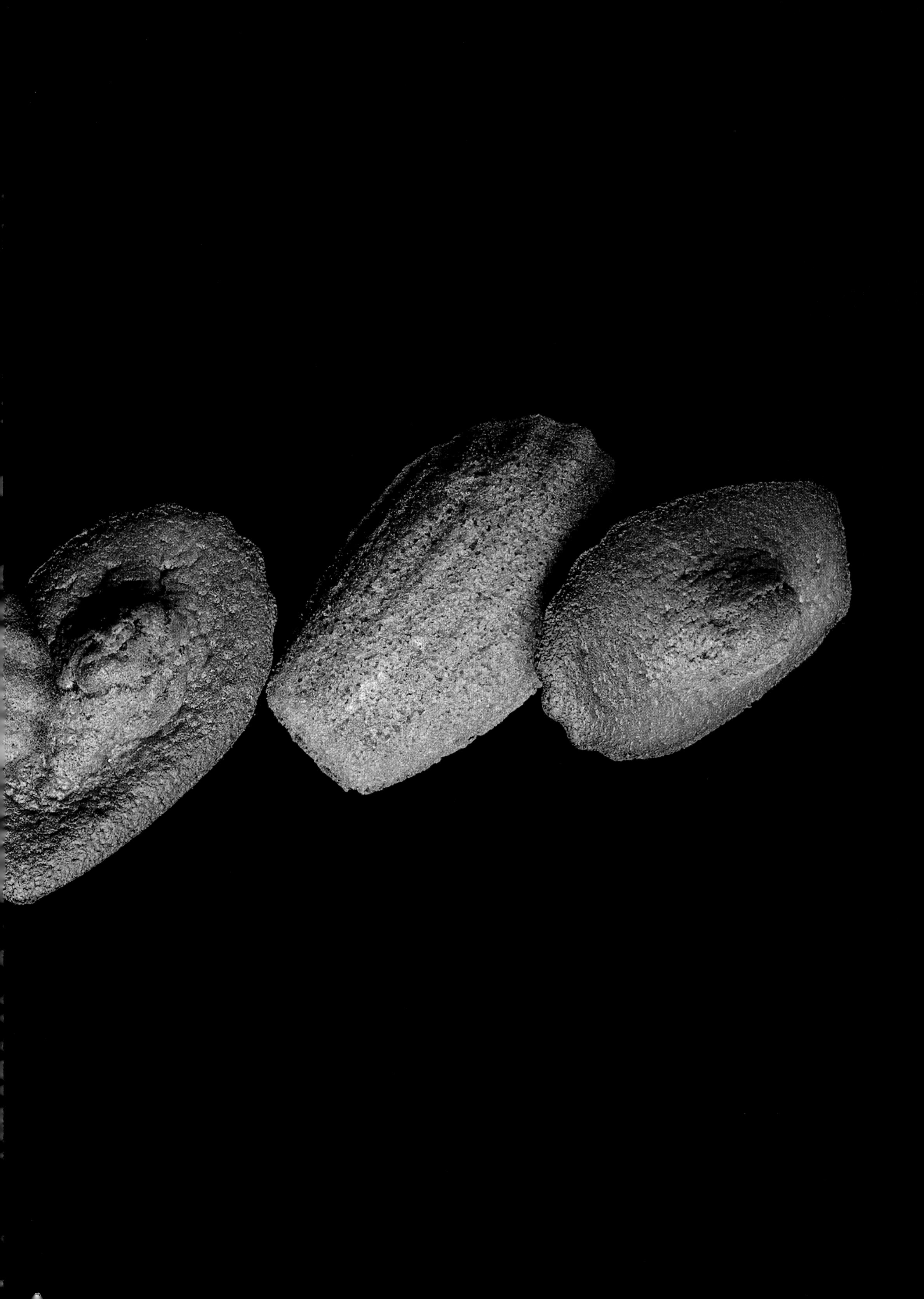

Mini Almond Loaves
with Chocolate

Makes 30 small loaves
Prep: 20 minutes
Cook: 15 minutes

INGREDIENTS

2 sticks {9 oz. / 250 g} unsalted butter, plus extra for pans
7 oz. {200 g} dark chocolate (78% cacao), preferably Trinitario Scavina grand cru chocolate {Brazil}, divided
⅓ cup {2½ oz. / 45 g} chestnut flour
1 cup plus 1 scant cup {9 oz. / 250 g} confectioners' sugar
3 cups {9 oz. / 250 g} ground almonds
1 cup plus 2 tablespoons {9 oz. / 250 g} egg whites {8 to 9 whites}

Place the butter in a saucepan over medium heat and cook until it browns and smells like hazelnuts {this is called *beurre noisette*, hazelnut butter}. Strain and allow to cool to lukewarm.

Chop 3½ oz. {100 g} of the chocolate with a knife and melt it over a hot water bath.

Sift the flour, confectioners' sugar, and ground almonds together.

Stir in the egg whites, then the browned butter, and lastly, the melted chocolate.

Preheat the oven to 350°F {180°C}. Grease financier pans with butter.

Pour the batter into the pans, filling them two-thirds full. Bake for 15 minutes, until nicely risen and a cake tester inserted into the center of one of them comes out dry.

Turn the mini loaves out of the pans and allow to cool on a rack.

Before serving, chop the remaining chocolate with a knife and melt it over a hot water bath. Dip the loaves in the melted chocolate to cover the top and half of the sides.

Chocolate Ice Cream

Makes 4 cups {1 liter} ice cream
Prep: 20 minutes
Chill: 12 hours

INGREDIENTS

4 oz. {110 g} dark chocolate (78% cacao), preferably Trinitario Scavina grand cru chocolate {Brazil}
¾ cup {200 ml} heavy cream {35% butterfat}
2 cups {500 ml} whole milk
¼ cup plus 1½ teaspoons {1 oz. / 33 g} skim milk powder
2 tablespoons {1½ oz. / 45 g} invert sugar {at specialized stores; see Note}
2 egg yolks
¾ cup {5 oz. / 140 g} granulated sugar

Chop the chocolate with a knife and place it in a mixing bowl. Bring the cream to a boil with the milk, skim milk powder, and invert sugar.

In the bowl of a mixer fitted with the whisk, beat the egg yolks and sugar until pale. Pour in a little of the hot liquid to warm up the yolk-sugar mixture, beating constantly. Beat in the remaining hot liquid.

Return the mixture to the saucepan, and, stirring constantly, heat to 180°F {82°C}, at which stage it is thickened and coats the back of a spoon. Pour it over the chocolate and process with an immersion blender.

Refrigerate for 12 hours. The next day, place in an ice cream maker and proceed according to the manufacturer's directions.

Chef's note

You can replace the invert sugar with acacia honey {or multi-floral honey}.

Chocolate Soup

& Floating Islands

Serves 6
Prep: 20 minutes

INGREDIENTS

CHOCOLATE SOUP

9 oz. {250 g} dark chocolate (78% cacao), preferably Trinitario Scavina grand cru chocolate {Brazil}
4 cups {1 liter} whole milk

FLOATING ISLANDS

¾ cup {200 ml} whole milk
¾ cup {200 ml} water
2 egg whites
1 heaping tablespoon {15 g} granulated sugar

Make the chocolate soup:
Chop the chocolate with a knife and place it in a mixing bowl. Bring the milk to a boil and pour it over the chocolate. Process with an immersion blender for 2 minutes.

Make the floating islands:
Bring the milk and water to a boil. Whisk the egg whites and sugar until the mixture holds soft peaks. Shape into ovals and poach in the boiling liquid for 1 minute.

Pour the hot chocolate soup into a soup plate and place a floating island in the center.

Chef's note

A garnish of a few raspberries or other red berries will give a tangy note to this dessert.

Soft Chocolate Caramel Candies

Makes 20 candies
Prep: 20 minutes
Rest: 24 hours

INGREDIENTS

2½ oz. {75 g} dark chocolate (78% cacao), preferably
Trinitario Scavina grand cru chocolate {Brazil}
½ cup plus 1 tablespoon {140 ml} heavy cream {35% butterfat}
⅓ cup {2½ oz. / 75 g} granulated sugar
¼ cup {3 oz. / 90 g} glucose syrup
1¾ teaspoons {12 g} chestnut honey
{or other strongly flavored honey}
A little grape-seed oil for the confectionery frame

EQUIPMENT

A confectionery frame or brownie pan

A recipe by my friend, pastry chef Philippe Conticini

Chop the chocolate with a knife.

Bring the cream to a boil with the sugar. Stir in the glucose syrup and honey and heat to 237°F {114°C}.

Stir in the chocolate and heat the mixture to 237°F {114°C} again. Oil a confectionary frame set over a baking pan with the grape-seed oil.

Pour in the chocolate-caramel mixture and allow to set at room temperature for 24 hours.

Turn out and cut into squares.

Wrap the caramel candies in cellophane.

Chef's note

These candies keep for up to two weeks.

Chocolate Eggs

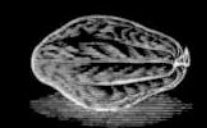

Makes 5 eggs
Prep: 30 minutes
Set and chill: 1 hour

INGREDIENTS

10½ oz. {300 g} dark chocolate {78% cacao}, preferably Trinitario Scavina grand cru chocolate {Brazil}

EQUIPMENT

Five egg-shaped silicone molds

Chop the chocolate with a knife.

To ensure that the chocolate coating is glossy, temper it as follows:
- Over a hot water bath, heat the chocolate to 122°F {50°C}.
- Place over a cool water bath and cool to 82°F {28°C}.
- Reheat the chocolate to 90°F {32°C} over a hot water bath.

Make a first coating in the molds: Pour in the chocolate and then turn them upside down over the bowl containing the tempered chocolate. Tap the molds gently to remove any air bubbles. When most of the chocolate has dripped off, place the molds over a rack and allow to drain for 15 minutes. With a spatula, scrape off the chocolate from around the molds.

Repeat the procedure once more. Refrigerate until set, about 30 minutes.

Remove from the refrigerator and immediately turn out of the molds, taking care not to break the eggs.

Using a slightly heated baking sheet, briefly melt the edges of each side of the egg shells and glue them together.

Chef's note

It's a fun idea to fill the eggs with surprise edible treats.

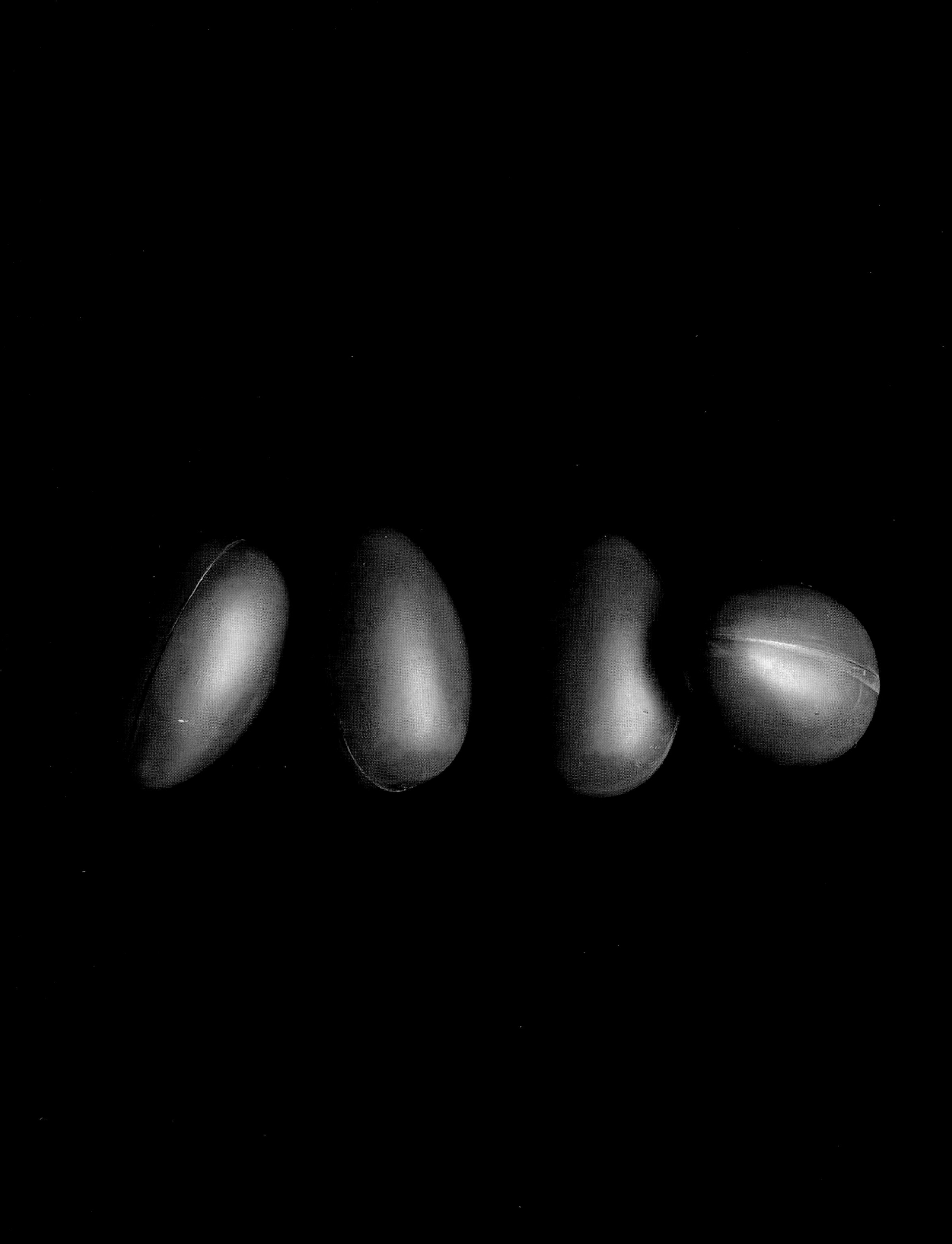

Passion Fruit Chocolate Truffles

Makes 40 truffles
Prep: 20 minutes
Chill: 12 hours

INGREDIENTS

4 oz. {110 g} dark chocolate (78% cacao), preferably Trinitario Scavina grand cru chocolate {Brazil}
7 oz. {200 g} milk chocolate {not too sweet, with more than 40% cacao content}
9 oz. {250 g} strained passion fruit
1¼ oz. {35 g} invert sugar
5 tablespoons {2½ oz. / 75 g} unsalted butter, diced
Thin shavings of fresh coconut, for decoration

Chop the chocolates with a knife and place them in a bowl. Bring the strained passion fruit and invert sugar to a boil. Remove from heat. Add the chocolate and process with an immersion blender. {This makes a ganache.}

When the ganache begins to cool, stir in the butter. Process again briefly with the immersion blender.

Pour the ganache into a rimmed baking pan lined with parchment paper and refrigerate for 12 hours.

Cut the ganache into small rectangles and place them on the fresh coconut shavings.

Chef's note

If you are not a fan of passion fruit, simply substitute mango.

LAYERED MERINGUE
& Chocolate Ganache Pastries

Makes 6 pastries
Prep: 30 minutes
Cook: 2 hours
Chill: 3 hours

INGREDIENTS

MERINGUE

¾ cup {3½ oz. / 100 g} confectioners' sugar
1 tablespoon plus 2 teaspoons {12 g} unsweetened cocoa powder
Scant ½ cup {3½ oz. / 100 g} egg whites {3 to 4 whites}
½ cup {3½ oz. / 100 g} granulated sugar

WHIPPED CHOCOLATE CREAM

3½ oz. {100 g} dark chocolate {78% cacao}, preferably Trinitario Scavina grand cru chocolate {Brazil}
1¾ cups {400 ml} heavy cream {35% butterfat}

Shavings of dark chocolate {78% cacao}, preferably Trinitario Scavina grand cru chocolate {Brazil} for decoration

Make the meringue:
Sift the confectioners' sugar with the cocoa powder.

Preheat the oven to 200°F {100°C}. Line a baking sheet with parchment paper.

Whisk the egg whites, gradually incorporating the granulated sugar, until they hold soft peaks. With a flexible spatula, fold in the sifted dry ingredients.

Spoon the meringue mixture into a pastry bag fitted with a plain ⅓-inch {7-mm} tip and pipe 1¼ by 5-inch {3 by 12-cm} rectangles on the prepared baking sheet. Bake for 2 hours and transfer to a rack to cool.

Make the whipped chocolate cream:
While the meringue layers are baking, chop the chocolate with a knife and place in a bowl. Bring the cream to a boil and pour it over the chocolate. Process with an immersion blender to make an emulsion. Refrigerate for 3 hours, then transfer to the bowl of a mixer fitted with the whisk and whisk until very light and airy.

With a pastry bag fitted with a plain ⅓-inch {7-mm} tip, pipe the chocolate cream over the meringue bases. Decorate with chocolate shavings.

Chef's note

I would advise you to bake the meringues a day ahead and leave them in the oven, once it is switched off, overnight. This ensures that they will be very crisp. For a variation, stir ½ oz. {15 g} cacao nibs {see page 44 or 45} into the meringue batter before baking.

Bahia

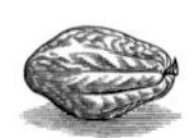

Serves 6
Prep: 20 minutes
Cook: 15 minutes

INGREDIENTS

1 oz. {30 g} unsalted pistachios {about ¼ cup}
4 oz. {120 g} Chocolate Soup, chilled
{see recipe, page 202}
30 orange segments
6 Chocolate Madeleines
{see recipe, page 194}

Preheat the oven to 325°F {160°C}. Spread the pistachios on a baking sheet and roast for 15 minutes, then allow to cool.

Process the chocolate soup with an immersion blender.

Place 5 orange segments on each of 6 soup plates {or other deep plates}. Pour in the chilled chocolate soup and scatter with a few pistachios. At the edge of each plate, place a slightly warm madeleine.

Chef's note

Instead of the orange segments, you could use poached apricots.

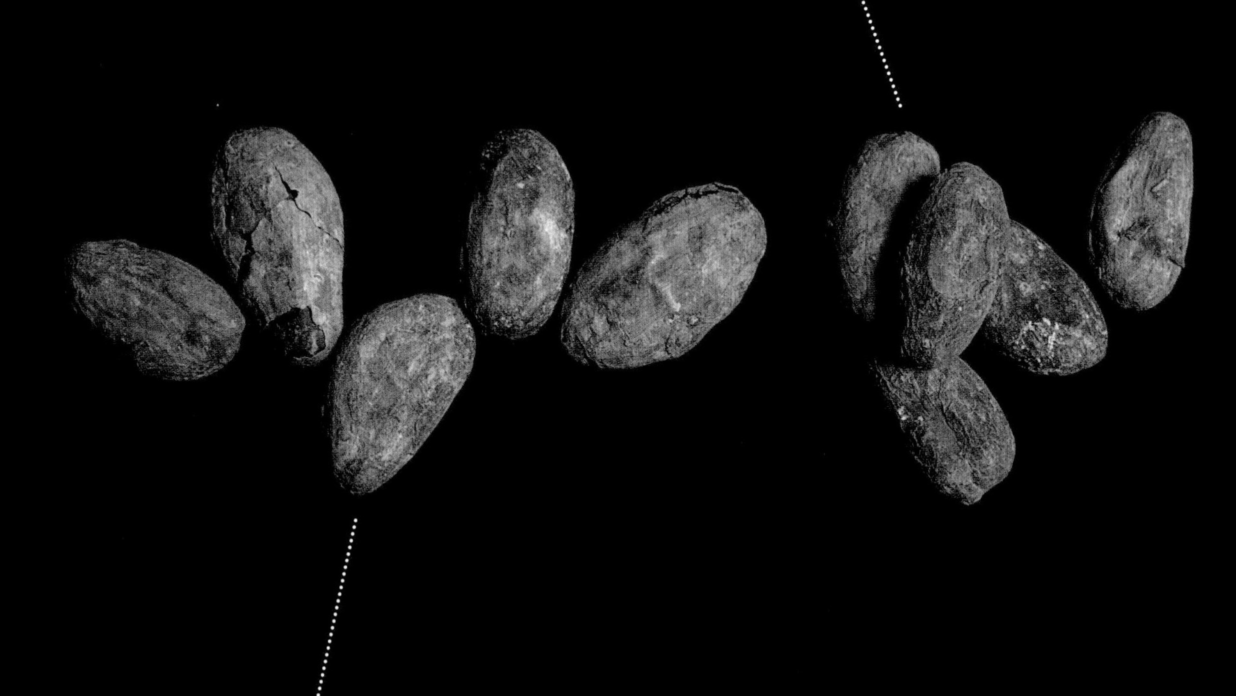
Oriente
Terruño de Baracoa

Trinitario Terruño de Baracoa Grand Cru

{Cuba}

Heirloom Trinitario from the Caribbean
A mixture of white and purple beans.
Extraordinary nose.

Pronounced bitterness.

Flavors: notes of dried wood, hazelnuts, full-bodied.

Billows of tobacco smoke.

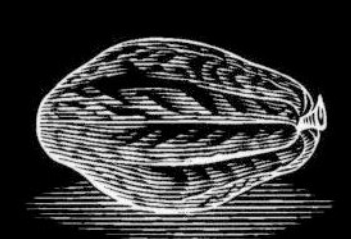

Flour-free Chocolate Sponge Cake

Makes one 5-inch- {12-cm-} diameter cake
Prep: 25 minutes
Cook: 15 minutes

INGREDIENTS

3 oz. {80 g} dark chocolate {78% cacao}, preferably Trinitario grand cru chocolate {Cuba}
1 cup plus 3 tablespoons {3½ oz. / 100 g} ground almonds
½ cup {2 oz. / 65 g} confectioners' sugar
5 eggs, separated, plus 1 yolk
⅓ cup {2 oz. / 65 g} granulated sugar

EQUIPMENT

A 5-inch- {12-cm-} diameter cake ring {or pan}, 1¾ inches {4 cm} high

Preheat the oven to 350°F {170°C}.

Chop the chocolate and place it in a bowl.

Sift the ground almonds and confectioners' sugar together. Add the egg yolks and whisk briskly for 2 to 3 minutes.

Over a hot water bath, heat the chocolate to 113°F {45°C}. Whisk the egg whites, gradually adding the sugar, until they hold soft peaks. Take care not to over-beat or they will become grainy!

In several additions, alternately fold in the egg whites and melted chocolate to the almond–egg yolk mixture, taking care not to deflate it, and ending with the melted chocolate.

Pour the batter into the prepared cake ring and bake for 15 minutes.

Allow to cool to lukewarm, remove the ring, and allow to cool completely on a rack.

Chef's note

This recipe is an ideal gluten-free option.

Sacher Cake

with Japanese Medlar Fruit

Makes one 5½-inch {14-cm} cake
Prep: 25 minutes
Cook: 30 minutes

INGREDIENTS

10 oz. {290 g} almond paste {50% almonds}
⅔ cup {3 oz. / 80 g} confectioners' sugar
6 eggs, separated, plus 1 egg yolk
2 oz. {50 g} dark chocolate {78% cacao}, preferably Trinitario grand cru chocolate {Cuba}, chopped
Scant ½ cup {3 oz. / 85 g} granulated sugar
½ cup {2 oz. / 65 g} all-purpose flour, sifted
6 Japanese medlar fruits {loquats}

EQUIPMENT

A 5½-inch- {14-cm-} diameter cake ring {or pan}, 1¾ inches {4 cm} high

Preheat the oven to 340°F {170°C}. If you are using a cake ring, line a baking sheet with parchment paper or a silicone baking mat. Lightly grease the ring {or cake pan, if using} with butter.

Place the almond paste and confectioners' sugar in a blender. Begin processing, adding one egg yolk at a time. Add the next egg yolk only when the mixture is perfectly smooth. Continue blending until the mixture is pale.

Melt the chocolate over a hot water bath and allow to cool to lukewarm.

Whisk the egg whites, gradually adding the sugar, until they hold soft peaks.

Fold the flour into the almond paste–egg yolk mixture. Carefully fold in the whisked egg whites. Lastly, fold in the melted chocolate. Pour the batter into the prepared cake ring.

Remove the pits of the medlar fruit and cut them into slices. Arrange them over the top of the batter.

Bake for 30 minutes until a cake tester comes out clean. Allow to cool slightly and remove the ring. Allow to cool completely on a rack.

Chef's note

You can pour a neutral glaze over the top of the cake when it is removed from the oven.

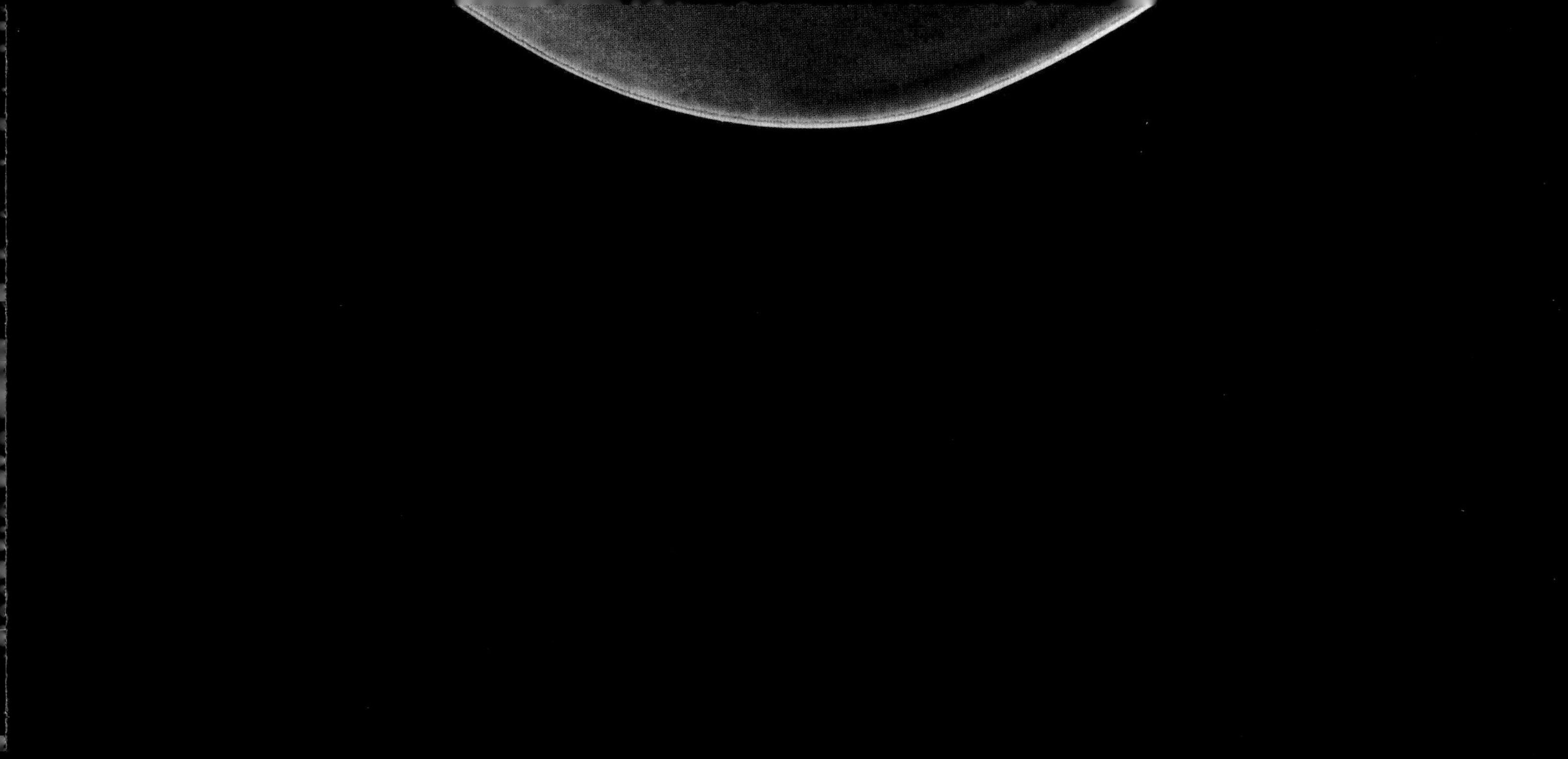

Chocolate Pastry Cream

Serves 6
Prep: 20 minutes
Chill: 2 hours

INGREDIENTS

1¼ oz. {35 g} dark chocolate {78% cacao}, preferably Trinitario grand cru chocolate {Cuba}
1 cup {250 ml} whole milk
2 egg yolks
3½ tablespoons {1½ oz. / 40 g} granulated sugar
1 tablespoon plus 2½ teaspoons {17 g} cornstarch
2 tablespoons {25 g} unsalted butter, diced
¼ teaspoon {1 g} fleur de sel

Chop the chocolate with a knife and place it in a mixing bowl.

Bring the milk to a boil. While it is heating, whisk the egg yolks with the sugar in the bowl of a stand mixer fitted with the whisk. Continue until pale, then incorporate the cornstarch.

Pour one-third of the boiling milk over the egg yolk–sugar mixture to heat it up. Beat, then pour in the remaining milk, beating constantly. Return the mixture to the saucepan and bring to a boil, stirring constantly. Pour over the chocolate, stirring until smooth. Stir in the butter and fleur de sel. Process with an immersion blender until perfectly smooth. Refrigerate for 2 hours.

Pastry cream is a pastry-making basic: use it in tarts as a bed for fruit, or between layers of delicate puff pastry to make a napoleon.

Chef's note

Before you use the chilled pastry cream, process it for 2 minutes with an immersion blender to ensure that it is smooth and light.

Airy Chocolate Cream Dessert

Makes 10 to 12 portions
Prep {a day ahead}: 30 minutes
Chill: 24 hours

INGREDIENTS

POURING CUSTARD

2½ oz. {70 g} dark chocolate {78% cacao}, preferably Trinitario grand cru chocolate {Cuba}
3½ sticks {14 oz. / 400 g} unsalted butter
1 cup {250 ml} whole milk
6 egg yolks
2½ teaspoons {10 g} granulated sugar

SWISS MERINGUE

4 egg whites
1 scant cup {6 oz. / 180 g} granulated sugar

Melt the chocolate over a hot water bath. Place the butter in a large bowl. Bring the milk to a boil.

In the bowl of a stand mixer fitted with the whisk, beat the egg yolks with the sugar until pale.

Pour one-third of the boiling milk over the egg yolk–sugar mixture to heat it up. Beat, then pour in the remaining milk, beating constantly. Return the mixture to the saucepan. Stirring constantly, heat it to 180°F {82°C}, at which stage it will have thickened. Pour it over the butter. Then pour in the melted chocolate. Process with an immersion blender and allow to cool to lukewarm.

While it is cooling, make the Swiss meringue: In a heatproof mixing bowl over a hot water bath, whisk the egg whites and sugar until thick. Continue until the temperature reaches 130° to 140°F {55 to 60°C}. Remove from the heat and continue to whisk until the mixture has cooled to room temperature.

Carefully fold the Swiss meringue into the chocolate cream. Refrigerate for 24 hours before serving.

Herby Chocolate Drink

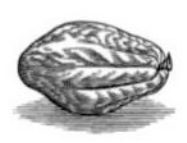

Serves 8 as a dessert or 2 as a drink
Prep: 10 minutes
Infuse: 10 minutes

INGREDIENTS

1½ oz. {40 g} dark chocolate {78% cacao}, preferably Trinitario grand cru chocolate {Cuba}
1 cup {250 ml} water
A few leaves of mint, sage, and thyme
1½ tablespoons {10 g} unsweetened cocoa powder

Chop the chocolate with a knife and place it in a bowl.

Bring the water to a boil. Place the herbs in it and infuse for about 10 minutes off the heat.

Strain over the chocolate, stirring in the cocoa powder. Process with an immersion blender for 2 minutes.

Chef's note

There is no added sugar in this drink, which can also complement a dessert.

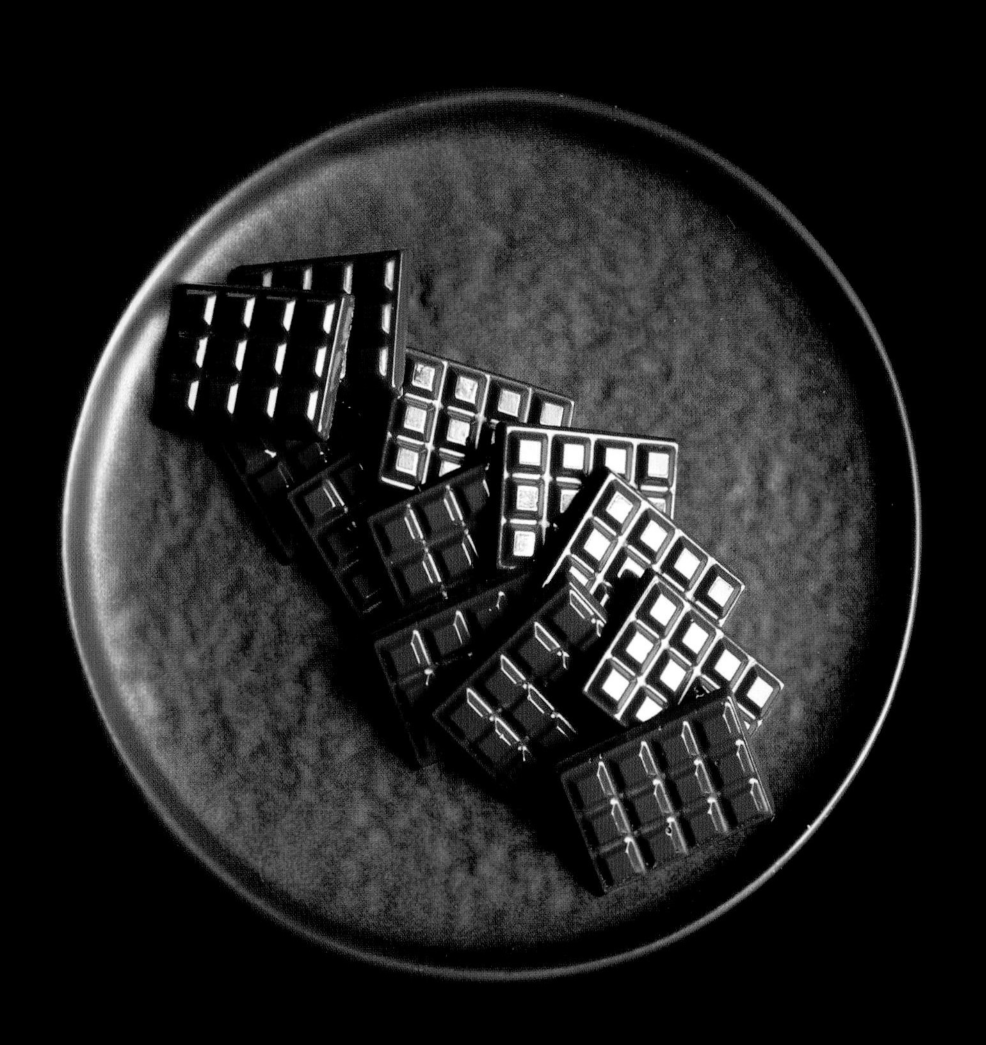

Pure Chocolate Bars

Makes one 7-oz. {200-g} chocolate bar
Prep: 10 minutes
Chill: 30 to 60 minutes

INGREDIENTS

7 oz. {200 g} dark chocolate {78% cacao}, preferably
Trinitario grand cru chocolate {Cuba}

Chop the chocolate with a knife. To ensure that your chocolate bar is glossy, temper it as follows:
- Over a hot water bath, heat the chocolate to 122°F {50°C}.
- Place over a cool water bath and cool to 82°F {28°C}.
- Reheat the chocolate to 90°F {32°C} over a hot water bath.

Pour it into a silicone mold and refrigerate only until set, which should take between 30 minutes and one hour, depending on the thickness of your bar.

Chef's note

Serve with fine rum or whiskey.

Crunchy Almond & Hazelnut Praline Bars

Makes five ¾ by 2¾-inch {2 by 7-cm} bars
Prep: 20 minutes
Chill: 1 hour

INGREDIENTS

⅔ oz. {10 g} cacao butter
1 oz. {25 g} *feuillantine* {see Note}
1 oz. {25 g} almond praline
1 oz. {25 g} ground Hazelnut Praline
{see recipe, page 122}
½ oz. {15 g} dark chocolate {78% cacao}, preferably Trinitario grand cru chocolate {Cuba}

Melt the cacao butter over a hot water bath. Its temperature should not exceed 95°F {35°C}. Stir in the *feuillantine* carefully: it must be thoroughly coated in cacao butter to prevent it from softening later.

Add the two types of praline and mix in well.

Melt the chocolate over a hot water bath. Its temperature, like that of the cacao butter, should not exceed 95°F {35°C}. Pour it into the *feuillantine*-praline mixture and mix well.

Pour into a silicone mold, if possible with cavities measuring ¾ by 2¾ inches {2 by 7 cm}.

Refrigerate for one hour. Unmold and decorate as you like.

Chef's note

Pailleté feuillantine is available online. You can substitute crushed Breton Gavottes® cookies or other fine, crisp cookies.

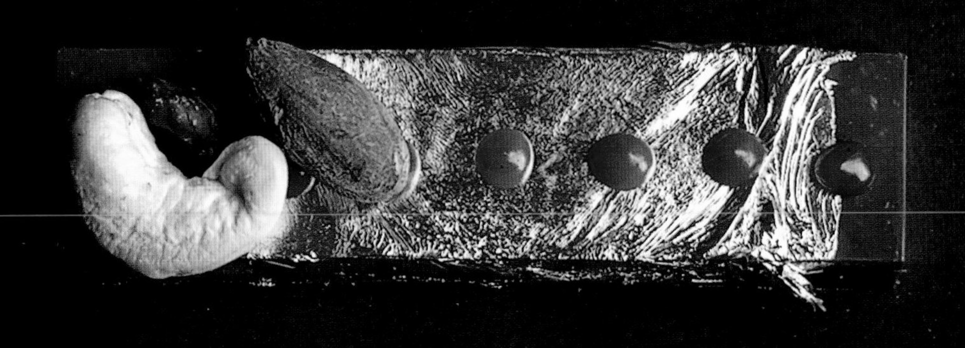

INGREDIENTS

4 bunches cherry tomatoes
1⅔ cups {400 ml} water
¼ cups {12½ oz. / 350 g} granulated sugar, divided
1 Tahitian vanilla bean, split, seeds scraped
Zest and juice of 1 unwaxed orange
Zest and juice of 1 unwaxed lemon
Zest and juice of 1 unwaxed lime
oz. {100 g} dark chocolate {78% cacao}, preferably Trinitario grand cru chocolate {Cuba}

Carefully wash and dry the tomatoes. Combine the water, 1 cup {7 oz. / 200 g} of the sugar, the vanilla bean and seeds, and the citrus zest and juice in a saucepan. Bring to a boil.

Reduce the heat to low and carefully place the cherry tomatoes in the syrup. Allow to simmer for 10 minutes. Add ¼ cup {1¾ oz. / 50 g} of the sugar and allow to simmer for a further 10 minutes. Repeat the procedure twice. Remove from the heat and allow the tomatoes to cool in the syrup.

Chop the chocolate with a knife. To ensure that your chocolate leaves are glossy, temper it as follows:
- Over a hot water bath, heat the chocolate to 122°F {50°C}.
- Place over a cool water bath and cool to 82°F {28°C}.
- Reheat the chocolate to 90°F {32°C} over a hot water bath.

Pour the chocolate onto a sheet of food-safe acetate and place a second sheet over it. Using a rolling pin, roll the chocolate as thinly as possible over the sheet. Cut out small disks of chocolate and refrigerate them for 20 minutes. Remove the acetate.

Pour a little of the syrup over the base of each serving plate. Arrange the candied tomatoes on the plate with a few leaves of chocolate.

Chef's note

You can use this candying method to candy the skins of your tomatoes too!

My Black Forest Cake

Serves 6
Prep: 40 minutes
Cook: 5 minutes
Chill: 30 minutes

INGREDIENTS

10½ oz. {300 g} dark chocolate {78% cacao}, preferably Trinitario grand cru chocolate {Cuba}
5 oz. {150 g} Flour-Free Chocolate Sponge Cake {see recipe, page 217}
8 oz. {240 g} whipped chocolate cream {see recipe for Layered Meringue & Chocolate Ganache Pastries, page 211}
18 black cherries, pitted

EQUIPMENT

Six 1¼-inch- {4-cm-} diameter cake rings, 1¼ {4 cm} inches high

Cut six 1¼ by 5½-inch {3 by 14-cm} rectangles in a sheet of food-safe acetate.

Chop the chocolate with a knife. To ensure that your rolled chocolate is glossy, temper the chocolate as follows:
- Over a hot water bath, heat the chocolate to 122°F {50°C}.
- Place over a cool water bath and cool to 82°F {28°C}.
- Reheat the chocolate to 90°F {32°C} over a hot water bath.

Using an offset spatula, spread the chocolate very thinly over the rectangles of acetate. When it begins to set {this should take about 3 minutes}, roll the strips of chocolate around the inside of the cake rings. Refrigerate until set, about 30 minutes. Remove the acetate.

While the chocolate is setting, cut small cubes of flour-free chocolate sponge and toast them in a 425°F {220°C} for 5 minutes, or sauté them in a skillet with a little butter.

Carefully remove the cake rings and acetate from the set chocolate and arrange the rounds on dessert places. Using a pastry bag fitted with a plain ⅓-inch {8-mm} tip, pipe out a dollop of whipped chocolate cream. Place 3 cherries on each plate, and garnish with crisp cubes of flour-free sponge cake.

Chef's note

You can add a dash of Profiterole Sauce {see recipe, page 288}.

Veal Trinitario

Cooked at Low Temperature

Serves 6
Prep: 45 minutes
Cook: 2 hours 30 minutes

INGREDIENTS

⅔ oz. {20 g} blanched almonds {about 2 tablespoons}
One 2¾ lb. {1. 2 kg} veal roast
3 bay leaves
1 tablespoon {20 g} unsalted butter

Chocolate Jus

⅔ oz. {20 g} dark chocolate {78% cacao}, preferably Trinitario grand cru chocolate {Cuba}
Scant ½ cup {100 ml} veal stock
1 pinch salt
A little freshly ground pepper
Finely grated zest of ¼ yuzu
⅔ oz {20 g} almond praline
⅓ oz. {10 g} black sesame seeds {about 1 tablespoon}

Preheat the oven to 325°F {160°F}. Spread the almonds on a baking sheet and roast for 10 minutes. When they are cool enough to handle, chop them with a knife.

Reduce the oven temperature to 140°F {60°C}. If you have a steam oven, set the moisture to 25%.

Slip the bay leaves beneath the twine encircling the veal roast. In a Dutch oven, heat the butter until it sizzles and brown the veal on all sides.

Cover and bake for 2 hours 30 minutes, basting the meat regularly.

Chop the chocolate with a knife. Heat the veal stock in a small saucepan. When it is simmering, add the chocolate and season with salt and pepper. Process with an immersion blender and add the yuzu zest.

Place a slice of veal on each of six plates. Make a few dots of praline, drizzle a little veal jus with chocolate on the plate, and decorate with the sesame seeds and chopped almonds.

Chef's note

Instead of yuzu zest, you might want to try mandarin orange zest.

Kendeng Lembu
State Plantation
{Perkelbunan Company}

Criollo Casse Clair Grand Cru Kendeng Lembu

{Java}

Rare white Criollo from Indonesia,
brought to Java by Dutch settlers.
Pronounced acidity.
Flavors: spicy aromas, pepper, and fruit.
Characterized by a smoky note.

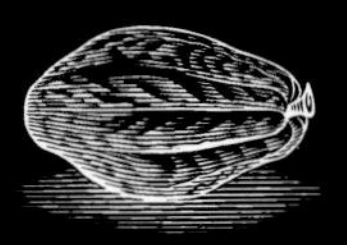

Spicy Chocolate and Orange Loaf

Makes four individual loaves
Prep: 25 minutes
Cook: 8 to 9 minutes

INGREDIENTS

1½ oz. {40 g} almond paste, room temperature
1 tablespoon {12 g} granulated sugar
1 egg
½ cup plus 1 tablespoon {7 oz. / 200 g} honey
¼ cup {60 ml} whole milk
1 cup {4 oz. / 120 g} chestnut flour
1 tablespoon {12 g} baking powder
3½ oz. {100 g} dark chocolate {78% cacao}, preferably Criollo casse claire grand cru chocolate {Java}
1 pinch cinnamon
1 pinch ground nutmeg
1 pinch ground aniseed
A few spoonfuls of orange marmalade

EQUIPMENT

Four 1¾-inch square molds, 4 inches {10 cm} deep

Preheat the oven to 350°F {180°C}. Grease the molds with butter and dust them lightly with flour. {Alternatively, line them with parchment paper.}

In the bowl of a mixer fitted with the paddle, combine the almond paste, sugar, and egg. Beat in the honey and milk. Transfer to a large bowl.

Sift the chestnut flour and baking powder together.

Melt the chocolate over a hot water bath, ensuring that the temperature does not exceed 95°F {35°C}.

Fold the sifted dry ingredients into the almond paste–milk mixture. Stir in the spices, and then the melted chocolate. When the batter is smooth, fill the prepared molds three-quarters full and bake for 8 to 9 minutes, until a cake tester inserted into the center of one of them comes out clean. Immediately unmold and allow to cool on a rack.

Serve the loaves with orange marmalade.

Chef's notes

This grand cru chocolate has heady notes of spices and a marvelous acidity.

If you prefer to bake one large cake, allow 30 minutes baking time.

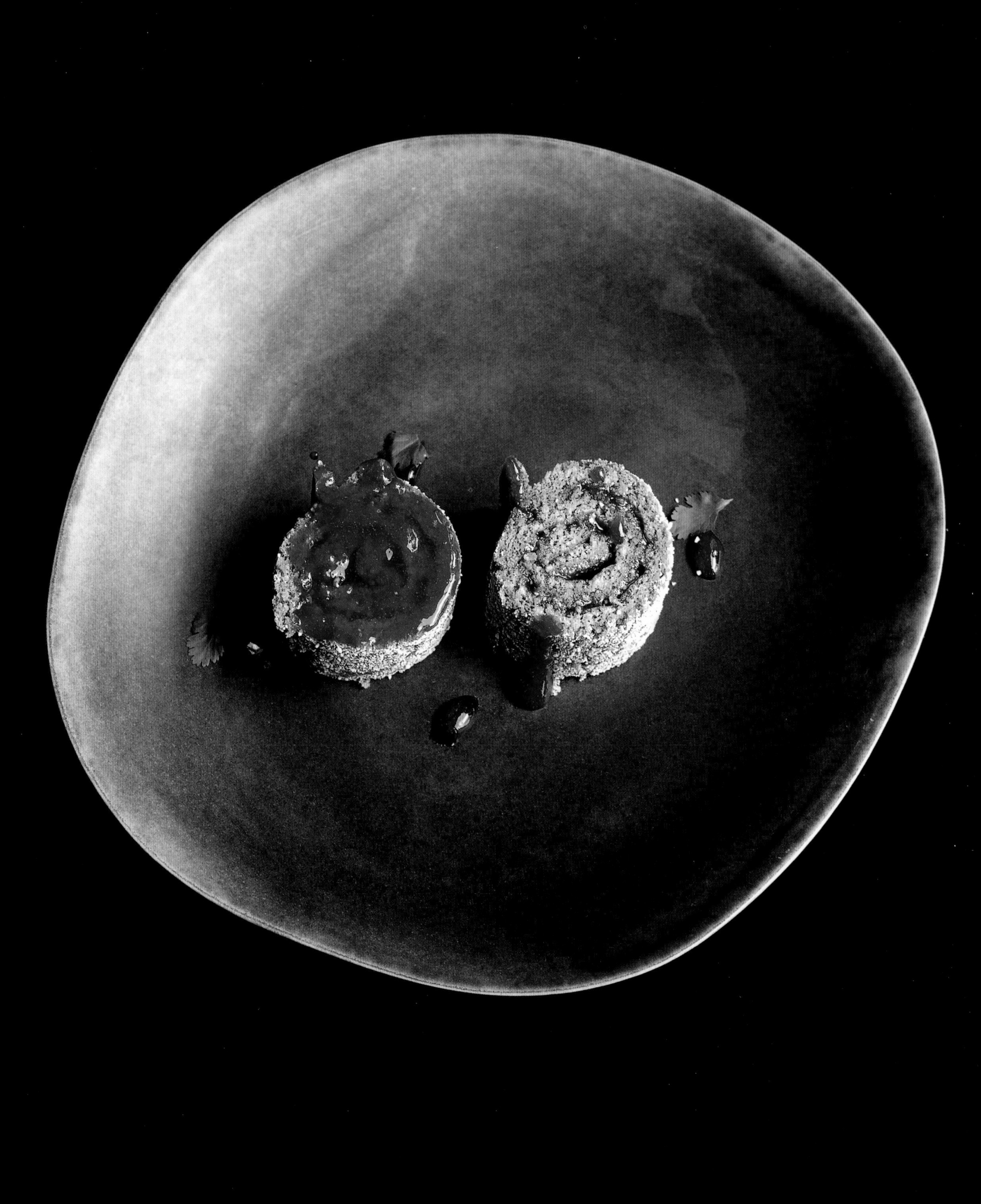

Chocolate-Raspberry Roulade

Serves 4
Prep: 30 minutes
Cook: 4 minutes
Chill: 1 hour

INGREDIENTS

⅔ oz. {20 g} dark chocolate {78% cacao}, preferably Criollo casse claire grand cru chocolate {Java}
1½ tablespoons {22 g} unsalted butter
1 cup {3½ oz. / 90 g} ground almonds
¾ cup {3½ oz. / 100 g} confectioners' sugar
6 eggs, plus 3 egg whites
7 tablespoons {2 oz. / 50 g} all-purpose flour, sifted
1½ tablespoons {18 g} granulated sugar
Raspberry jam to spread over the roulade
Fresh raspberries for decoration

Preheat the oven to 375°F {190°C}. Line a small baking sheet with parchment paper.

Melt the chocolate and butter over a hot water bath.

Whisk the ground almonds with the confectioners' sugar and pour into the bowl of a mixer fitted with the whisk. Add the 6 eggs. Whisk briskly until the mixture becomes pale and doubles in volume. Incorporate the flour.

Whisk the egg whites until they hold soft peaks, gradually adding the granulated sugar. With a flexible spatula, carefully fold the egg whites into the batter.

Pour the melted chocolate and butter mixture in a steady stream over the batter and stir to combine.

Pour the batter evenly over the prepared baking sheet and bake for 4 minutes. Allow to cool slightly, then carefully remove the baked sponge layer from the parchment paper. Spread the raspberry jam over it.

Using a sheet of parchment paper, roll the sponge layer up tightly. Refrigerate for 1 hour and cut into thin slices.

Garnish with a few fresh raspberries.

Chef's notes

Of course, you can use whatever type of jam you like best.

This sponge layer, a Joconde, is also suitable for making Christmas log cakes.

Chocolate Crème Caramel

Serves 6
Prep: 30 minutes
Chill: 3 hours

INGREDIENTS

1 sheet {2 g} gelatin
3 oz. {80 g} dark chocolate {78% cacao}, preferably Criollo casse claire grand cru chocolate {Java}
2 tablespoons {30 ml} water
¾ cup {5 oz. / 140 g} granulated sugar
¾ cup {200 ml} heavy cream {35% butterfat}
Scant ⅓ cup {70 ml} whole milk
½ teaspoon {2 g} fleur de sel
3 tablespoons {2 oz. / 50 g} unsalted butter, diced

Soften the gelatin in a bowl of very cold water for 10 minutes.

Chop the chocolate with a knife and place it in a mixing bowl.

Heat the water. In a saucepan over low heat, caramelize the sugar. When it is a pronounced yellow color {340°F / 170°C}, deglaze it with the hot water, taking care not to burn yourself—it will splatter—and stir. When the caramel is perfectly smooth, stir in the cream, milk, and fleur de sel. Heat the mixture and pour it over the chocolate, stirring to combine as if you were making a ganache.

Squeeze the water from the gelatin and stir it into the cream-chocolate mixture, then stir in the butter.

Process with an immersion blender and refrigerate for 3 hours.

Chef's note

You can heighten the caramel notes of this dessert by drizzling a little liquid caramel over each dessert.

Chocolate Bavarian Cream

& Caramelized Cherries

Serves 10
Prep: 30 minutes
Chill: 24 hours

INGREDIENTS

Chocolate Bavarian Cream

9 oz. {250 g} dark chocolate {78% cacao}, preferably Criollo casse claire grand cru chocolate {Java}
3¼ cups {800 ml} heavy cream {35% butterfat}, well chilled, divided
3 tablespoons {40 ml} whole milk
3 egg yolks
⅓ cup {2 oz. / 60 g} granulated sugar

Caramelized Cherries

5 oz. {150 g} pitted sour cherries
⅓ cup {2 oz. / 60 g} granulated sugar
2 tablespoons {25 g} unsalted butter

A day ahead, make a chocolate pouring custard:
Chop the chocolate and heat it to 113°F {45°C} over a hot water bath.

In a saucepan, bring one scant ½ cup {100 ml} of the cream to a boil with the milk.

In the bowl of a mixer fitted with the whisk, beat the egg yolks with the sugar until pale. Pour a little of the hot liquid over the egg yolk–sugar mixture to warm it slightly, beating as you pour, then pour in the remaining hot liquid. Beat to combine and return to the saucepan.

Stirring continuously, heat to 180°F {82°C}, at which stage the mixture coats the back of a spoon. Pour it over the chopped chocolate, process with an immersion blender until smooth, and allow to cool.

Whisk the remaining cream until it holds soft peaks. With a flexible spatula, fold it into the chocolate custard. Refrigerate, covered with plastic wrap, for 24 hours.

Just before serving, cut the cherries into halves. Melt the sugar over low heat. When it caramelizes, add the butter and cherry halves. Allow the cherries to caramelize and remove from the heat. You can serve them hot or cooled, as you prefer.

Place a portion of chocolate cream on each plate and arrange a few caramelized cherries around.

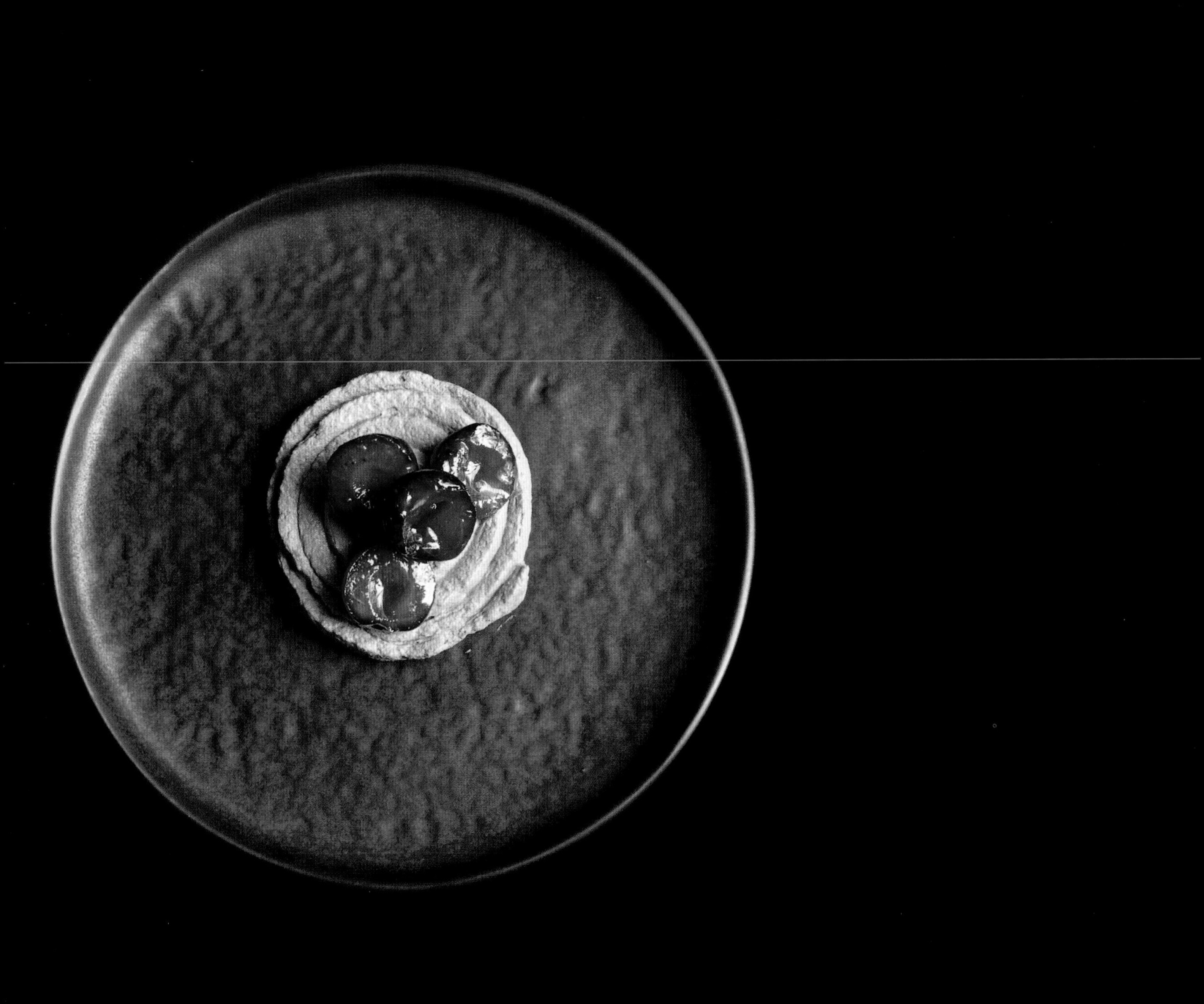

Chocolate Sauce
with Berries

Serves 8 to 10
Prep: 10 minutes

INGREDIENTS

5 oz. {150 g} dark chocolate {78% cacao}, preferably Criollo casse claire grand cru chocolate {Java}
½ cup {125 ml} heavy cream {35% butterfat}
8 oz. {250 g} berries {raspberries, red currants, and black currants}
⅓ cup {2 oz. / 60 g} granulated sugar
2 tablespoons {30 g} unsalted butter, diced

Chop the chocolate with a knife and place it in a mixing bowl.

Bring the cream to a boil with the berries and sugar. Remove from the heat and process with an immersion blender. Pour over the chocolate and stir in the butter.

Chef's note

This sauce is an excellent accompaniment for many desserts. You can garnish with whole berries.

Florentine Cookies

Makes 30 cookies
Prep: 30 minutes
Cook: 10 minutes
Chill: 10 to 15 minutes

INGREDIENTS

3 tablespoons {50 ml} whole milk
⅔ cup {4½ oz. / 125 g} granulated sugar, divided
7 tablespoons {3½ oz. / 100 g} butter
5 teaspoons {35 g} glucose syrup
0.1 oz. {3 g} pectin
3½ oz. {100 g} sliced almonds {about 1 cup}
2 oz. {50 g} assorted candied fruit,
such as apricots and cherries
3½ oz. {100 g} dark chocolate {78% cacao}, preferably
Criollo casse claire grand cru chocolate {Java}

Bring the milk to a boil with one scant ½ cup {3 oz. / 90 g} of the sugar, the butter, and glucose syrup. Combine the pectin with the remaining sugar. When the milk mixture comes to a boil, stir in the pectin and sugar. Then stir in the sliced almonds followed by the candied fruit.

Preheat the oven to 340°F {170°C}. With a soup spoon, place the mixture in silicone pans with 2-inch- {4 to 5-cm-} diameter cavities. The cookies should be no thicker than ¼ inch {5 mm}.

Bake for 10 minutes and allow to cool in the pans. When the cookies reach room temperature, turn them out of the pans.

Chop the chocolate with a knife. To ensure that the chocolate coating of the cookies is glossy, temper the chocolate as follows:
- Over a hot water bath, heat the chocolate to 122°F {50°C}.
- Place over a cool water bath and cool to 82°F {28°C}.
- Reheat the chocolate to 90°F {32°C} over a hot water bath.

Spoon the chocolate into a pastry bag. Snip the tip of the pastry bag off with a pair of scissors and pipe a small round of chocolate, about 1 inch {2.5 cm} in diameter, into the cavities. Immediately place the cookies into the cavities and place the pan in the refrigerator. Allow to set for 10 to 15 minutes.

Chef's note

If you are using an oven with convection heat, turn the pan around halfway through the baking.

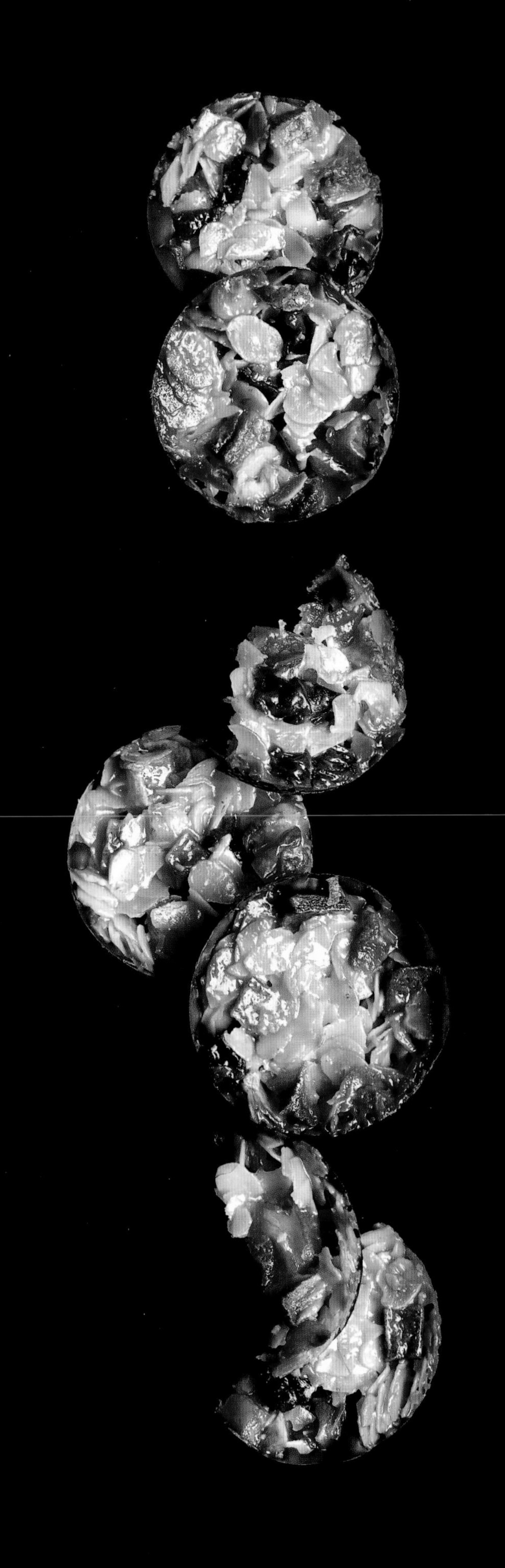

Crisp Chocolate-Coated Almonds

Makes 1 lb. 12 oz. {800 g} coated almonds
Prep: 30 minutes
Cook: 15 minutes

INGREDIENTS

1 lb. 2 oz. {500 g} blanched almonds
3 tablespoons {50 ml} water
½ cup {3½ oz. / 100 g} granulated sugar
7 oz. {200 g} dark chocolate {78% cacao}, preferably Criollo casse claire grand cru chocolate {Java}
7 tablespoons {2 oz. / 50 g} unsweetened cocoa powder

Preheat the oven to 325°F {160°C}. Line a baking sheet with parchment paper.

Spread the almonds over the prepared baking sheet and roast for 15 minutes, then allow to cool.

Combine the water and sugar in a saucepan and cook, over low heat, to 221°F {105°C}. Stir in the almonds and allow them to caramelize for a few minutes.

Pour the mixture over a silicone baking sheet and allow to cool.

Chop the chocolate and melt it over a hot water bath, heating it to 95°F {35°C}.

Pour the cocoa powder into a mixing bowl.

Wearing disposable gloves, dip the almonds in the melted chocolate. Drain briefly and roll in the cocoa powder to coat.

Chef's notes

You can make this recipe with other types of nuts, such as hazelnuts, pistachios, and cashew nuts.

These confections keep for up to one month in an airtight container.

Chocolate Financiers

Makes 12 to 15 financiers
Prep: 30 minutes
Cook: 14 minutes

INGREDIENTS

½ cup {4½ oz. / 125 g} egg whites {4 to 5 whites}
Scant cup {4½ oz. / 125 g} confectioners' sugar
1½ cups {4½ oz. / 125 g} ground almonds
1 stick plus 2 teaspoons {4 ½ oz. / 125 g} unsalted butter
2 tablespoons plus 1 teaspoon {22 g} chestnut flour, sifted
2 oz. {50 g} dark chocolate {78% cacao}, preferably Criollo casse claire grand cru chocolate {Java}

EQUIPMENT

Silicone pan with 1¾ by 2¾-inch {2 by 7-cm} cavities

Preheat the oven to 350°F {180°C}. Combine the egg whites, confectioner's sugar, and ground almonds.

Melt the butter in a saucepan until it browns and gives off the aroma of hazelnuts {this is called *beurre noisette*}. Strain it over the egg white–almond mixture and stir in. Fold in the chestnut flour.

Melt the chocolate over a hot water bath and stir it into the mixture. Transfer the batter to a saucepan.

Heat the batter over very low heat. When it reaches a temperature of 130°F {55°C}, divide it among the financier molds, stopping 1/16 inch {2 mm} short of the rim.

Bake for 4 minutes, then lower the oven temperature to 325°F {160°C} and bake for another 10 minutes. Allow to cool for 5 minutes and unmold. Allow to cool completely on a rack.

Chef's notes

To reduce the oven temperature rapidly, keep the door ajar.

Add an extra touch of sweetness to your financiers by inserting a few shards of caramel as soon as you remove them from the oven.

To make the caramel shards, caramelize ½ cup {3½ oz. / 100 g} of granulated sugar with the seeds of half a vanilla bean over low heat. When the sugar reaches a yellow color {340°F / 170°C}, spread it thinly over a silicone baking mat and allow to cool, then break into shards.

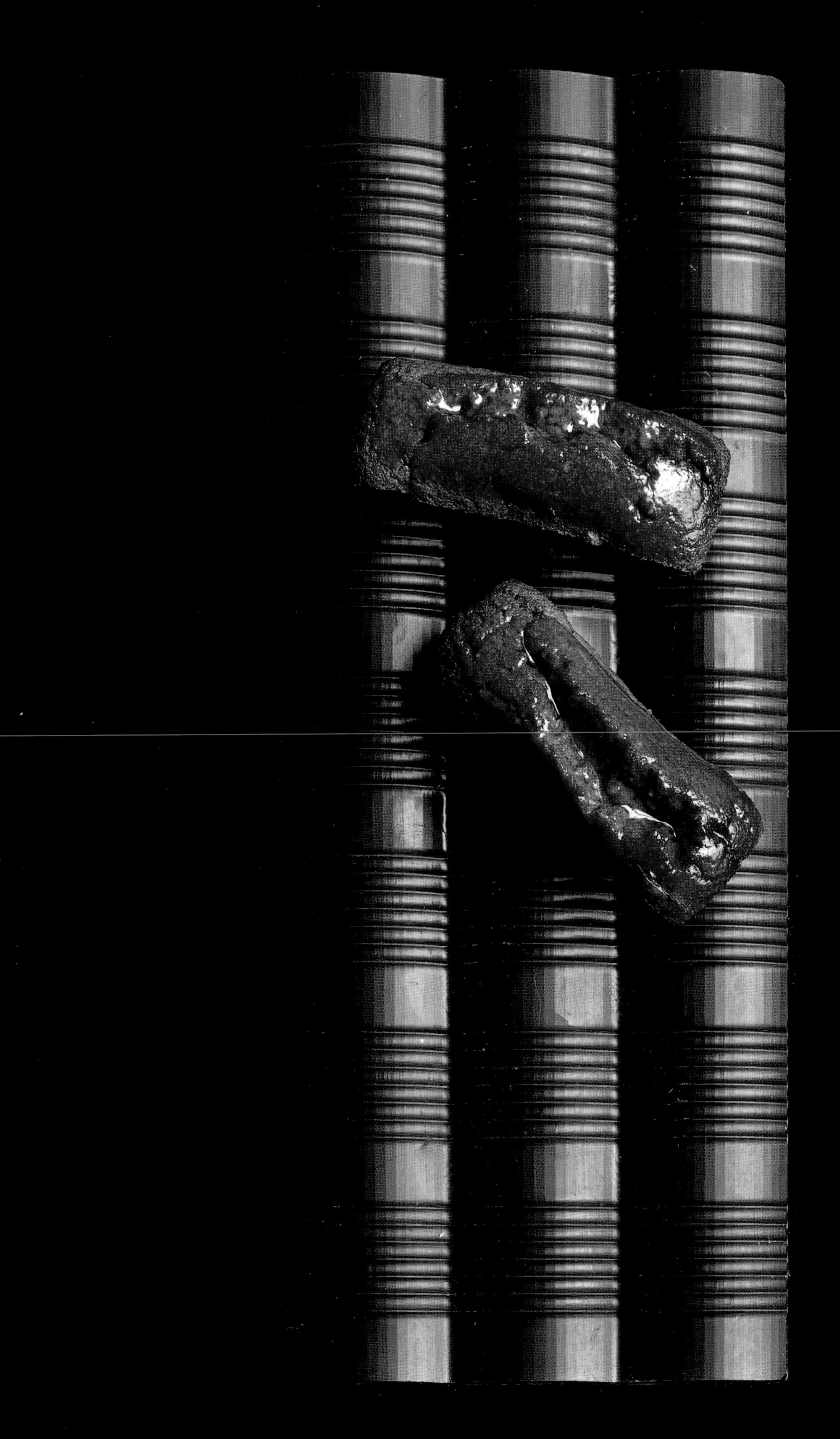

Chocolate Tubes

Makes 6 filled chocolate tubes
Prep: 30 minutes
Chill: 30 minutes

INGREDIENTS

10 oz. {300 g} dark chocolate {78% cacao}, preferably Criollo casse claire grand cru chocolate {Java}
9 oz. {250 g} Chocolate Bavarian Cream {see recipe, page 244}

Cut six 2½ by 4-inch {6 by 10-cm} rectangles of food-safe acetate.

Chop the chocolate with a knife. To ensure that the tubes are glossy, temper the chocolate as follows:
- Over a hot water bath, heat the chocolate to 122°F {50°C}.
- Place over a cool water bath and cool to 82°F {28°C}.
- Reheat the chocolate to 90°F {32°C} over a hot water bath.

Using an offset spatula, spread the chocolate thinly over the rectangles of acetate. When it begins to set {after about 5 minutes}, roll the rectangles into thin tubular shapes. Refrigerate for 30 minutes, until set.

Carefully remove the chocolate tube from the sheet of acetate. Spoon the chocolate Bavarian cream into a pastry bag and snip off the tip with scissors. Pipe the cream into each chocolate tube.

Chef's notes

To accentuate the chocolaty character of this dessert, sprinkle each plate with a few freshly roasted cacao nibs {see page 44 or 45}.

Candied Kumquats {see recipe, page 164} are delicious when served with the filled chocolate tubes.

Kendeng Lembu

Serves 8
Prep: 30 minutes
Cook: 20 minutes

INGREDIENTS

2 oz. {50 g} peeled hazelnuts {about 1/3 cup}
2 oz. {50 g} blanched almonds {about 1/3 cup}
5 oz. {140 g} liquid caramel deglazed with cream {see third paragraph of recipe, page 243}
11 oz. {320 g} Chocolate Bavarian Cream {see recipe, page 244}
16 slices Spicy Chocolate and Orange Loaf {see recipe, page 238}
6 oz. {180 g} fine leaves of dark chocolate {78% cacao}, preferably Criollo casse claire grand cru chocolate {Java} {see recipe, page 191}

Preheat the oven to 325°F {160°C}. Line a baking sheet with parchment paper.

Spread the hazelnuts and almonds over the prepared baking sheet and roast for 20 minutes, then allow to cool.

Coat the nuts in the caramel.

With a pastry bag fitted with a plain ¼-inch {6-mm} tip, pipe a log of Bavarian cream over each dessert plate. Arrange the slices of spicy chocolate and orange loaf and a thin leaf of tempered chocolate on each plate. To finish, scatter with the caramel-coated hazelnuts and almonds.

Chef's note

To add an original touch to your caramel, stir in a pinch each of freshly grated turmeric and ginger.

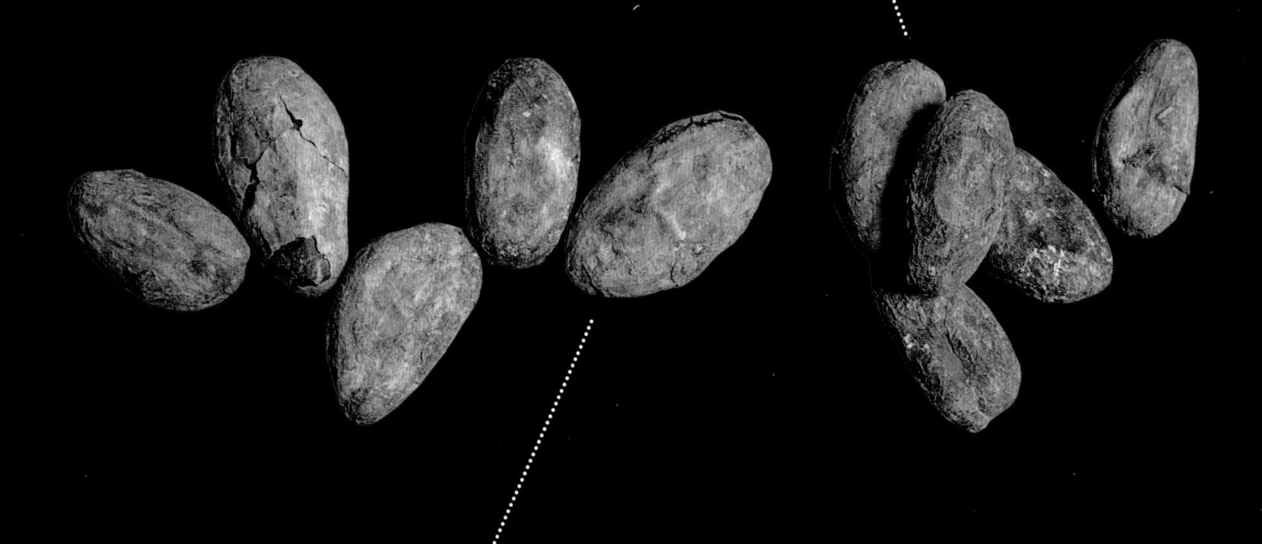
Aragua
Chuao Terroir

Pure Criollo Grand Cru Chuao Terroir

{Venezuela}

An exceptional cacao of a rare variety that has remained isolated for many centuries. A fine balance between acidity and bitterness. Flavors: delicate mouthfeel with a subtle violet freshness

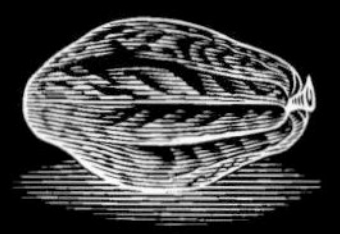

Chocolate Loaf

Serves 6 to 8
Prep: 20 minutes
Rest: 1 hour
Cook: 10 minutes

INGREDIENTS

2 cups {8½ oz. / 240 g} all-purpose flour, plus extra for the molds
¼ cup {1 oz. / 30 g} unsweetened cocoa powder
1½ teaspoons {6 g} baking powder
1½ oz. {40 g} dark chocolate (78% cacao), preferably Chuao grand cru chocolate {Venezuela}
7 tablespoons {3½ oz. / 100 g} unsalted butter, plus extra for the molds
6 eggs
1⅔ cups {11½ oz., 320 g} granulated sugar
½ cup {120 ml} heavy cream {35% butterfat}
1 pinch fleur de sel

EQUIPMENT

1¾-inch {4-cm} square molds 2 inches {5 cm} deep

Sift the flour, cocoa powder, and baking powder together.

Chop the chocolate with a knife and melt it over a hot water bath with the butter.

In the bowl of a mixer fitted with the whisk, beat the eggs and sugar until pale. Incorporate the cream and fleur de sel. Fold in the sifted dry ingredients by hand.

Stir in the melted chocolate and butter and allow to rest in the refrigerator for one hour.

Preheat the oven to 350°F {180°C}. Grease the molds with butter and dust them lightly with flour.

Pour the batter into the molds and bake for 10 minutes, until a cake tester inserted into the center of one of them comes out dry.

Chef's note

If you would prefer to make a single large cake, bake it for 35 minutes.

Chocolate Soil

Serves 6
Prep: 20 minutes
Cook: 24 minutes

INGREDIENTS

½ oz. {15 g} cacao nibs {see recipe, page 44 or 45}
4 tablespoons {2 oz. / 65 g} unsalted butter
⅓ cup {1½ oz. / 40 g} all-purpose flour
3 tablespoons plus 1¼ teaspoons {1½ oz. / 35 g} light brown sugar, divided
1½ oz. {45 g} dark chocolate (78% cacao), preferably Chuao grand cru chocolate {Venezuela}

Preheat the oven to 325°F {160°C}. Line a baking sheet with parchment paper.

In a small food processor, grind the cacao nibs to powder.

Combine the butter, flour, 3 tablespoons of the light brown sugar, and ground almonds. Spread on the prepared baking sheet and bake for 12 minutes, then allow the short pastry to cool for a few minutes.

Reduce the oven temperature to 300°F {150°C}.

Place the chocolate over a hot water bath and cook to 95°F {35°C}.

Finely crush the cooled short pastry. Stir in the ground cacao nibs, 1¼ teaspoons {5 g} of the light brown sugar, and the melted chocolate. Combine well.

Spread the mixture again over a baking sheet lined with parchment paper or a silicone baking mat and bake for 12 minutes. The texture should be like fine crumbs. Use to garnish an ice cream or chocolate mousse.

Chef's note

You can also eat this cacao soil with a black berry coulis or chocolate ice cream, or use it as a base for a dessert to provide a crisp texture.

Hazelnut Praline–Chocolate Mousse

Serves 4
Prep: 30 minutes
Chill: 12 hours

INGREDIENTS

7 oz. {200 g} dark chocolate (78% cacao), preferably Chuao grand cru chocolate {Venezuela}
3 tablespoons {50 g} unsalted butter, diced
5 eggs, separated, plus 5 egg whites
⅓ cup {2 oz. / 60 g} granulated sugar, divided
Scant ¾ cup {180 ml} heavy cream {35% butterfat}
⅔ oz. {20 g} peeled hazelnuts {about 2 tablespoons}
2 oz. {50 g} Hazelnut Praline {see recipe, page 122}

Chop the chocolate with a knife and melt it over a hot water bath. Add the butter and stir until completely smooth.

In the bowl of a mixer fitted with the whisk, beat the egg yolks with half of the sugar until pale. Pour the mixture into the melted chocolate–butter mixture and stir well.

Whisk the cream until it holds soft peaks and fold it carefully into the chocolate mixture with a flexible spatula.

Whisk the egg whites with the remaining sugar until they hold firm peaks. Gradually fold into the chocolate-cream mixture.

Pour into a large serving bowl, cover with plastic wrap, and refrigerate for 12 hours before serving.

Preheat the oven to 325°F {160°C}. Spread the hazelnuts on a baking sheet and roast for 15 minutes. When they are cool enough to handle, chop them with a knife.

Heat the hazelnut praline over a hot water bath until it is liquid. Draw lines of praline over the chocolate mousse with a spoon or fork and sprinkle with the chopped hazelnuts.

Chef's note

This mousse is best when it is made 24 to 48 hours ahead of time. Serve it at room temperature.

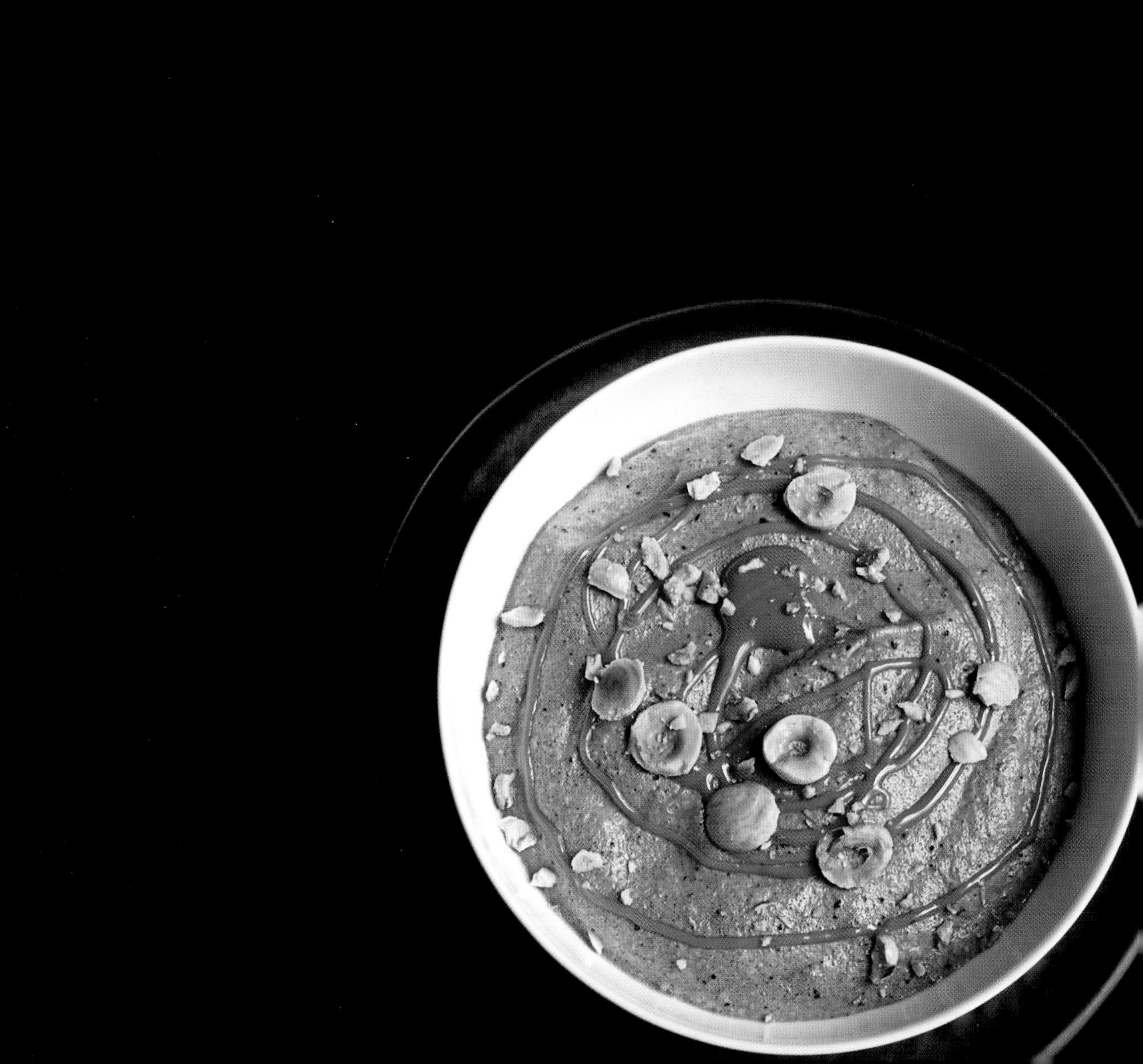

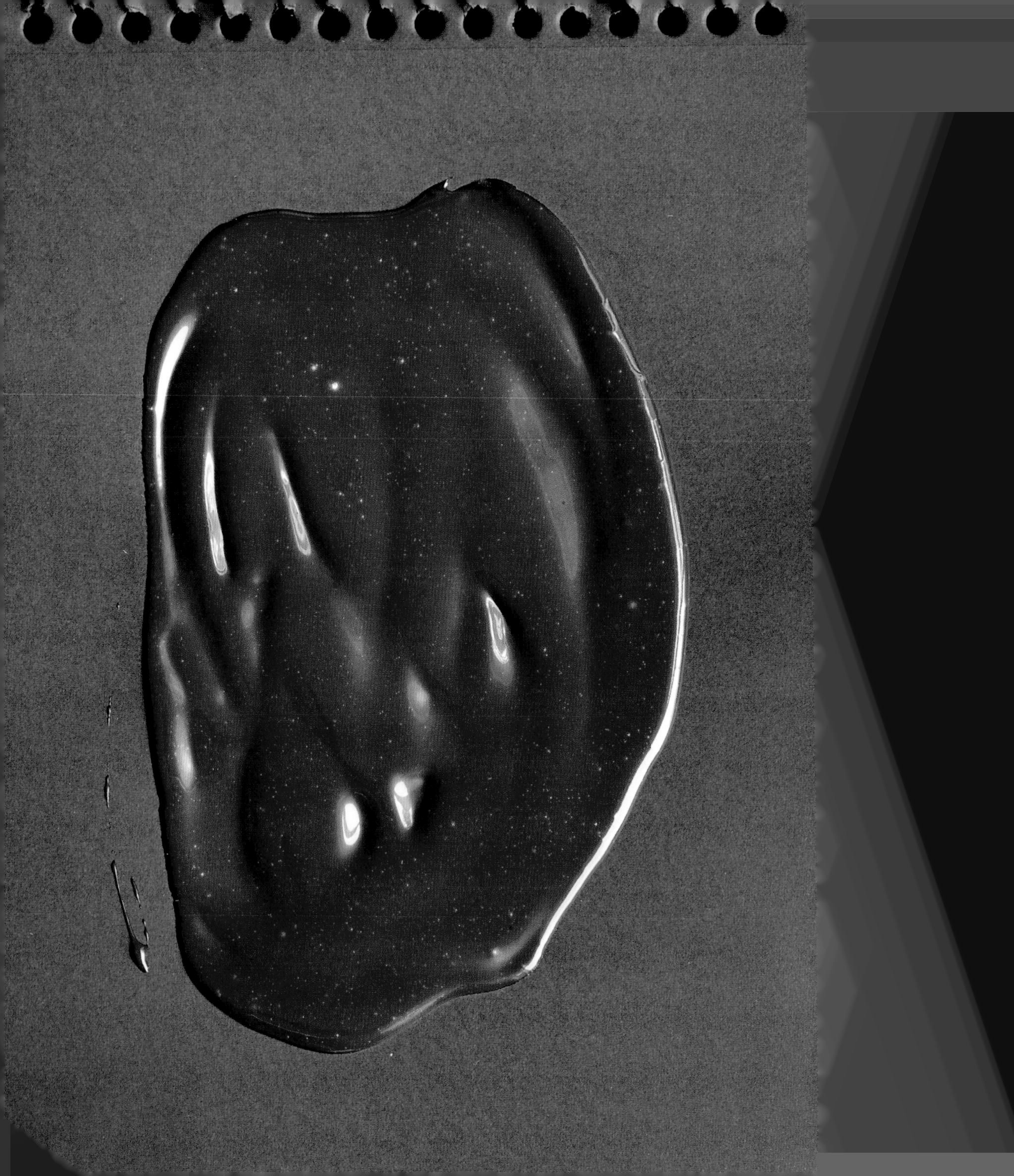

Chocolate Glaze

Serves 12
Prep: 25 minutes

INGREDIENTS

10 oz. {280 g} dark chocolate (78% cacao), preferably Chuao grand cru chocolate {Venezuela}
8½ sheets {17 g} gelatin
Scant ½ cup {100 ml} very cold water
plus ½ cup {125 ml} water
1¼ cups {9 oz. / 250 g} granulated sugar
¾ cup {9 oz. / 250 g} glucose syrup
Scant ¾ cup {200 g} unsweetened evaporated milk

Chop the chocolate with a knife.

Soften the gelatin sheets in a scant ½ cup of very cold water for 10 minutes.

In a saucepan, heat the remaining ½ cup {125 ml} of water, sugar, and glucose syrup to 217°F {103°C}. Off the heat stir in the evaporated milk. Squeeze the water from the gelatin sheets and stir in until completely dissolved.

Stir in the chocolate and process with an immersion blender for 30 seconds.

Heat the mixture again to 217°F {103°C}, until the glaze is shiny.

Chef's note

This glaze can be frozen. Use it to glaze loaf cakes and chocolate cakes, or as a shiny sauce over a banana split, a dame blanche {vanilla ice cream with whipped cream}, or profiteroles.

Chocolate Marshmallows

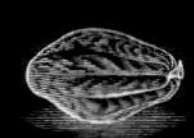

Makes 15 marshmallows
Prep: 30 minutes
Set: 30 minutes
Chill: 30 minutes

INGREDIENTS

15 sheets {30 g} gelatin
Scant ¼ cup {1 oz. / 30 g} confectioners' sugar
3 tablespoons {1 oz. / 30 g} cornstarch
¾ cup {200 ml} water
3¼ cups {1 lb. 6 oz. / 620 g} granulated sugar
1 vanilla bean, split, seeds scraped
Scant ½ cup {3½ oz. / 100 g} egg whites
{3 to 4 whites}
3½ oz. {100 g} dark chocolate (78% cacao),
preferably Chuao grand cru chocolate {Venezuela}

Soften the gelatin sheets in very cold water for 10 minutes. Line a 1¾-inch- {2-cm-} high confectionery frame set on a baking pan {or brownie pan} with parchment paper.

Sift the confectioners' sugar with the cornstarch.

Bring the water to a boil with the sugar and vanilla bean and seeds, keeping an eye on the temperature. When it reaches 230°F {110°C}, begin whisking the egg whites.

When the syrup reaches 250°F {121°C}, remove the vanilla bean and pour it over the whisked egg whites, continuing to whisk briskly.

Squeeze the water from the gelatin sheets and whisk them into the egg white–syrup mixture. Continue until the mixture has cooled.

Pour the marshmallow mixture into the prepared frame and allow to set at room temperature for 30 minutes.

Chop the chocolate. To ensure that the coating is glossy, temper the chocolate as follows:
- Over a hot water bath, heat the chocolate to 122°F {50°C}.
- Place over a cool water bath and cool to 82°F {28°C}.
- Reheat the chocolate to 90°F {32°C} over a hot water bath.

Remove the set marshmallow from the frame and pan with the parchment paper.

Cut into 1-inch {2-cm} cubes and sprinkle all the sides with the sifted confectioners' sugar and cornstarch.

Using a toothpick, dip the marshmallow cubes into the tempered chocolate and refrigerate until set, about 30 minutes.

Chocolate Macarons

Makes 20 macarons
Prep: 50 minutes
Cook: 20 minutes
Chill: 12 hours

INGREDIENTS

CHOCOLATE GANACHE

14 oz. {400 g} dark chocolate (78% cacao), preferably Chuao grand cru chocolate {Venezuela}
¾ cup {200 ml} heavy cream {35% butterfat}
1 Tahitian vanilla bean, split, seeds scraped
1 oz. {25 g} sorbitol
4½ oz. {130 g} fondant icing
2 sticks plus 1 tablespoon {9 oz. / 260 g} unsalted butter, diced

MACARON SHELLS

1¾ cup {5 oz. / 150 g} ground almonds
1 generous cup {5 oz. / 150 g} confectioners' sugar
4 egg whites
¾ cup {5 oz. / 150 g} granulated sugar
3½ tablespoons {1 oz. / 25 g} unsweetened cocoa powder
0.07 oz. {2 g} fat-soluble red food coloring {optional}

A day ahead, make the ganache:
Chop the chocolate and place it in a mixing bowl. Bring the cream to a boil with the vanilla bean and seeds, sorbitol, and fondant icing. Remove from the heat and cover with the lid. Allow to infuse for 10 minutes and strain.

Pour the hot infusion over the chocolate and stir well. When the ganache has cooled to 98°F {37°C}, stir in the butter. Transfer to an airtight container and store in a cool, dry place for 12 hours.

Make the macarons:
Preheat the oven to 300°F {150°C}. Line a baking sheet with parchment paper.

Combine the ground almonds with the confectioners' sugar and sift together.

Whisk the egg whites with the granulated sugar until they hold firm peaks. Gradually fold the ground almond–confectioners' sugar mixture into the beaten egg whites. Fold in the cocoa powder and then the food coloring, if using.

Using a pastry bag fitted with a plain ⅛-inch {3-mm} tip, pipe small balls onto the prepared baking sheet. Allow to rest at room temperature for 10 minutes, until a light crust has formed. Bake for 20 minutes and allow to cool on the baking sheet.

While the macaron shells are cooling, process the ganache in a blender to incorporate air bubbles into it.

Turn half of the macaron shells over and, using a pastry bag fitted with a plain ⅓-inch {8-mm} tip, pipe balls of ganache onto the smooth side of the turned macaron shells. Cover with the remaining shells.

Chef's note

Wrap the macarons well and refrigerate for several hours to ensure that the taste matures before you serve them.

Candied Carrots

with Chocolate

Makes 10 candied carrots
Prep: 20 minutes
Rest: 24 hours

INGREDIENTS

10 new carrots with their stalks
2 cups {500 ml} water
2¼ cups {15¼ oz. / 450 g} granulated sugar, divided
Zest and juice of 1 unwaxed lemon
1½ teaspoons {5 g} white peppercorns
A few sprigs cilantro
1 oz. {25 g} dark chocolate (78% cacao), preferably Chuao grand cru chocolate {Venezuela}
3 tablespoons {2 oz. / 50 g} mascarpone
3 tablespoons {2 oz. / 50 ml} heavy cream {35% butterfat}

Carefully scrape down the carrots and rinse them. Bring a pot of salted water to a boil and drop the carrots in, leaving them for a few seconds to blanch, then drain.

Candy the carrots:
Bring the 2 cups {500 ml} of water to a boil with 1½ cups {10 oz. / 300 g} of the sugar. Allow to simmer for 3 minutes to make a syrup. Add the lemon zest and juice, white peppercorns, and cilantro sprigs. Bring to a boil again and add the carrots.

Reduce the heat to low and allow to simmer for 10 minutes. Add ¼ cup {1¾ oz. / 50 g} of the sugar and boil again for 10 minutes. Repeat the procedure twice more.

Remove the pot from the heat and allow to cool. Leave the carrots in the syrup for 24 hours. Using a slotted spoon, remove the carrots and drain them. {You can reserve the syrup to make a glaze later.}

Chop the chocolate and melt it over a hot water bath.

In a mixing bowl, combine the mascarpone with the cream. Shape the mascarpone-cream mixture into oval scoops, placing one carefully on each of the serving dishes. Arrange the carrots on the plates and drizzle lines of melted chocolate over.

Chef's note

This dish will be even better if you use the syrup as a glaze.

One suggested presentation

Hazelnut Praline–Chocolate Mousse in Chocolate Cups

Serves 6 to 8
Prep: 30 minutes
Chill: 10 minutes

INGREDIENTS

10 oz. {300 g} dark chocolate (78% cacao), preferably Chuao grand cru chocolate {Venezuela}
12 oz. {350 g} Hazelnut Praline–Chocolate Mousse {see recipe, page 264}

DECORATION

Fresh raspberries
Chocolate Loaf Cake {see recipe, page 261}, for garnish
Cacao Soil {see recipe, page 262}, for garnish

EQUIPMENT

Silicone muffin molds

Chop the chocolate with a knife. To ensure that the cups are glossy, temper the chocolate as follows:
- Over a hot water bath, heat the chocolate to 122°F {50°C}.
- Place over a cool water bath and cool to 82°F {28°C}.
- Reheat the chocolate to 90°F {32°C} over a hot water bath.

With a pastry brush, carefully coat the muffin molds with the melted chocolate. Ensure that there is not too much chocolate around the rim. {If you wish, you can trim the rim with a pair of scissors so that the cups are neat.} Allow to cool slightly.

Coat the silicone molds a second time, and even a third if the chocolate seems to thin. Refrigerate for 10 minutes.

As soon as you take them out of the refrigerator, unmold the chocolate shells.

Pour the mousse into a pastry bag fitted with a fluted tip and fill the chocolate cups.

Garnish with fresh raspberries and pieces of chocolate loaf cake and/or sprinkle with some cacao soil.

Chef's notes

The chocolate loaf cake can also be placed at the bottom of the chocolate cup, before you fill it with mousse. If you like kirsch or maraschino, use some to moisten the pieces of loaf cake.

Candied Celery
& Chocolate Sorbet

Serves 6
Prep: 40 minutes
Chill: 24 hours

INGREDIENTS

10 celery sticks
2 cups {500 ml} water
2 cups {15¼ oz. / 450 g} granulated sugar, divided
10 oz. {300 g} Chocolate Sorbet
{see recipe, page 311}

Separate the celery sticks and remove the outer fibers with a vegetable peeler. Rinse them well.

Bring a pot of salted water to a boil and drop the celery stalks in, leaving them for a few seconds to blanch, then drain.

Bring the 2 cups {500 ml} of water to a boil with 1¼ cups {10 oz. / 300 g} of the sugar. Allow to boil for 3 minutes to make a syrup. Add the celery stalks.

Reduce the heat to low and allow to simmer for 10 minutes. Add ¼ cup {1¾ oz. / 50 g} of the sugar and boil again for 10 minutes. Repeat the procedure twice more.

Remove from the heat. Refrigerate the celery stalks in their syrup for 24 hours. Remove them from the pot with a slotted spoon and drain.

Cut the celery into thin sticks and serve with a scoop of chocolate sorbet.

Chef's note

You can use the candying syrup as a sauce to drizzle over this dessert.

Tuna Chuao

Serves 6
Prep: 30 minutes
Cook: 5 minutes

INGREDIENTS

3 tablespoons {50 g} unsalted butter
10 oz. {300 g} tuna steak, room temperature
Salt and freshly ground pepper
2 oz. {50 g} dark chocolate (78% cacao), preferably Chuao grand cru chocolate {Venezuela}
1 egg yolk
1 teaspoon French mustard
3 tablespoons {50 ml} sunflower seed oil
1 tonka bean

DECORATION

6 leaves shiso

Heat the butter in a skillet until it foams. Season the tuna with salt and pepper. Sear it on one side for 3 minutes and on the other side for 1 minute. Remove it from the skillet and allow to rest in a warm place.

Chop the chocolate and place it over a hot water bath. Heat it to 86°F {30°C}.

Make a mayonnaise:
In a high-sided bowl, place the egg yolk, French mustard, salt, and pepper. Use an immersion blender to whip the mayonnaise, gradually drizzling in the sunflower seed oil.

When the mayonnaise is emulsified, incorporate the melted chocolate. With a fine grater, grate in a little tonka bean, flavoring the mayonnaise well.

Place a shiso leaf on each plate and set a piece of the tuna on it. Dot mayonnaise over the plate and, to finish, grate a little more tonka bean over.

Chef's note

You can also drizzle a line of soy sauce on the plate.

Sambirano
Domaine of
Ambanja

Trinitario Sambirano Grand Cru

{Madagascar}

From the Valley of Sambirano,
an exceptional Trinitario,
a rarity among the cacaos of Africa.

It has the agreeable acidity specific to fine cacaos.

Flavors: yellow and red berries {cherry},
and floral notes.

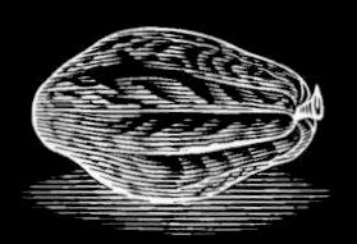

Chocolate Crackers

Makes 15 crackers
Prep: 15 minutes
Chill: 1 hour
Cook: 10 minutes

INGREDIENTS

1 oz. {30 g} dark chocolate {78% cacao}, preferably Trinitario grand cru chocolate {Madagascar}
1 stick plus 2 tablespoons {5 oz. / 150 g} unsalted butter, room temperature
¾ cup {5 oz. / 150 g} granulated sugar
1 cup plus 2 tablespoons {5 oz. / 150 g} all-purpose flour
1 teaspoon {4 g} fleur de sel

Chop the chocolate with a knife and place it over a hot water bath to heat to 86°F {30°C}.

Beat the butter with the sugar. Beat in the flour and fleur de sel. Lastly, incorporate the melted chocolate. Cover with plastic wrap and refrigerate for one hour.

Preheat the oven to 325°F {160°C}.

Working between two sheets of parchment paper, roll the dough to a thickness of 1/16 inch {2 to 3 mm}. Cut out about 15 rough rectangles or squares of the dough.

Bake for 10 minutes; the dough should be very lightly colored. Allow to cool on a rack.

Chef's notes

A few drops of orange flower water add a delicious flavor to these crackers.

If you want to make perfectly shaped rectangles or squares, place the dough in the freezer for 30 minutes before cutting it.

Breton Shortbread Cookies

Makes 30 to 40 cookies
Prep: 30 minutes
Chill: 12 hours
Cook: 28 minutes

INGREDIENTS

1⅔ cups {7 oz. / 200 g} all-purpose flour
1½ teaspoons {6 g} baking powder
¾ teaspoon {3 g} fine salt
1 stick plus 2 tablespoons {5 oz. / 150 g} unsalted butter
Generous ⅔ cup {4½ oz. / 130 g} granulated sugar
3 egg yolks
5 oz. {150 g} dark chocolate {78% cacao}, preferably Trinitario grand cru chocolate {Madagascar}

Sift the flour with the baking powder and whisk in the salt.

In the bowl of a stand mixer fitted with the paddle, combine the butter and sugar until the texture of sand.

Beat in the egg yolks, one by one, and then incorporate the sifted dry ingredients.

Roll the dough to a thickness of ¾ inch {2 cm}. Place it on a baking sheet, cover with parchment paper, and refrigerate for 12 hours.

Preheat the oven to 325°F {160°C}. Bake the dough for 25 minutes. As soon as you remove it from the oven, cut it into 1 by 3½-inch {4 by 9-cm} rectangles. Return them to the oven for 2 to 3 minutes, until very crisp. Allow to cool on a rack.

Chop the chocolate with a knife and melt it over a hot water bath. Dip one-third of each cookie in the melted chocolate.

Place on a sheet of parchment paper and allow to set.

Chef's note

These cookies make an excellent base for a dessert. Place a cookie on a plate with a dollop of Chantilly cream and a few fresh raspberries.

HAY-SCENTED PASTRY CREAM

Serves 8
Prep: 30 minutes
Rest and chill: 2 hours 12 minutes

INGREDIENTS

INFUSED MILK

2 cups {500 ml} whole milk
1 oz. {25 g} hay

PASTRY CREAM

1¼ oz. {35 g} dark chocolate {78% cacao}, preferably Trinitario grand cru chocolate {Madagascar}
1 tablespoon {20 g} unsalted butter
1⅔ cups {400 ml} infused milk {add extra whole milk if the hay has absorbed too much}
4 egg yolks
⅓ cup {2½ oz. / 70 g} granulated sugar
3 tablespoons {1 oz. / 30 g} cornstarch

Bring the milk to a boil. Off the heat, place the hay in the milk, ensuring that it is completely covered. Cover with plastic wrap so that none of the flavors escape. Allow to infuse for 12 minutes, then strain.

Melt the chocolate and butter over a hot water bath.

Bring the infused milk to a boil. Whisk the egg yolks with the sugar and cornstarch until pale. Pour a little of the hot milk over the egg yolk-sugar mixture to warm it up slightly. Then place the diluted egg yolk-sugar mixture in the saucepan with the remaining milk and stir well.

Whisking continuously, bring to a boil. Pour the pastry cream over the melted chocolate and butter. Process with an immersion blender until smooth and refrigerate for two hours.

Chef's note

If you would like the taste of hay to be more pronounced, infuse it in the milk in the refrigerator for 24 hours.

Airy Chocolate Cream

Serves 5
Prep: 25 minutes
Chill: 24 hours

INGREDIENTS

1½ oz. {40 g} dark chocolate {78% cacao}, preferably Trinitario grand cru chocolate {Madagascar}
¾ cup {200 ml} heavy cream {35% butterfat}
3½ tablespoons {1½ oz. / 40 g} granulated sugar
½ Madagascar vanilla bean, split, seeds scraped

Chop the chocolate with a knife and place it in a bowl.

Bring the cream to a boil with the sugar and vanilla bean and seeds. Remove the vanilla bean, cover the saucepan with a lid, and allow to infuse for 10 minutes off the heat.

Pour the hot cream over the chocolate and stir well. Process with an immersion blender until smooth and refrigerate for 24 hours.

Place the chocolate cream in the bowl of a mixer fitted with the whisk and whip until very airy. Return to the refrigerator until needed.

Chef's note

You can use this cream to fill éclairs.

Profiterole Sauce

Makes enough sauce for 6 to 8 servings
of profiteroles
Prep: 10 minutes

INGREDIENTS

1 cup {250 ml} whole milk
10 oz. {300 g} dark chocolate {78% cacao}, preferably Trinitario grand cru chocolate {Madagascar}, chopped
½ cup {125 ml} heavy cream {35% butterfat}
2 tablespoons {30 g} unsalted butter
2½ teaspoons {10 g} sugar

Combine all the ingredients in a saucepan and bring to a boil. Remove from the heat and process with an immersion blender until smooth and shiny.

Chef's notes

This sauce keeps for up to one week in the refrigerator. Reheat it over a hot water bath and process with an immersion blender just before serving.

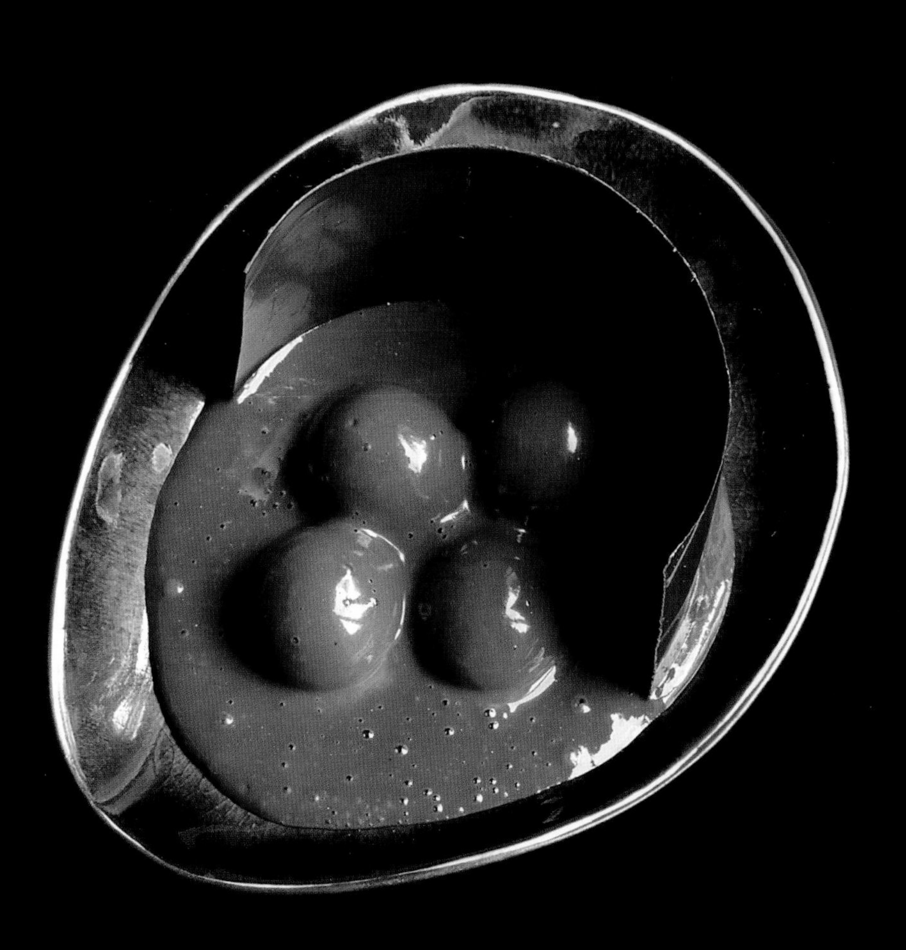

Vanilla-scented Hot Chocolate

Serves 2
Prep: 10 minutes

INGREDIENTS

3 oz. {90 g} dark chocolate {78% cacao}, preferably Trinitario grand cru chocolate {Madagascar}
1 cup {250 ml} whole milk
1 Madagascar vanilla bean, split, seeds scraped

Chop the chocolate with a knife and place it in a bowl.

Heat the milk with the vanilla bean and seeds and bring to a boil. Remove from the heat and allow to infuse for 10 minutes. Remove the vanilla bean and pour the hot milk over the chocolate.

Process with an immersion blender until very smooth and foamy.

Chef's note

This is an excellent drink to serve with a brioche.

Cacao Meringues

Makes 6 to 8 large meringues
Prep: 15 minutes
Cook: 2 hours

INGREDIENTS

¾ cup {3½ oz. / 100 g} confectioners' sugar
1 tablespoon plus 2 teaspoons {12 g} unsweetened cocoa powder
Scant ½ cup {3½ oz. / 100 g} egg whites {3 to 4 whites}
½ cup {3½ oz. / 100 g} granulated sugar
⅓ oz. {10 g} cacao nibs {see recipe, page 44 or 45}

Preheat the oven to 200°F {100°C}. Line a baking sheet with parchment paper.

Sift the confectioners' sugar with the cocoa powder.

Whisk the egg whites, gradually incorporating the sugar, until they hold soft peaks.

With a flexible spatula, fold in the sifted dry ingredients. Scatter the cacao nibs over the mixture.

Shape large meringues on the prepared baking sheet. Bake for two hours, and allow to cool on a rack.

Chef's note

If you prefer your meringues very crisp, leave them in the oven for a few hours after you have turned it off.

Fresh Truffles

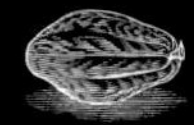

Makes 60 truffles
Prep: 30 minutes
Chill: 12 hours plus 1 hour

INGREDIENTS

9 oz. {260 g} dark chocolate {78% cacao}, preferably Trinitario grand cru chocolate {Madagascar}, divided
Scant ½ cup {100 ml} heavy cream {35% butterfat}
Scant ½ cup {100 ml} whole milk
⅓ cup {2 oz. / 60 g} granulated sugar
4½ tablespoons {2½ oz. / 70 g} unsalted butter, diced
Generous ⅓ cup {1½ oz. / 40 g} unsweetened cocoa powder

A day ahead, make a ganache:
Chop 5½ oz. {160 g} of the chocolate with a knife and place it in a bowl.

Bring the cream, milk, and sugar to a boil in a saucepan. Pour the hot liquid in a steady stream over the chocolate, whisking constantly. Then process with an immersion blender until smooth.

Allow to cool and stir in the diced butter. Process again with the immersion blender to thoroughly combine.

Scoop the ganache into an airtight container and refrigerate for 12 hours.

Melt the remaining chocolate over a hot water bath. Using two teaspoons, shape the ganache into balls. Holding the balls on the tines of a fork, dip them into the melted chocolate to coat. Roll them in the cocoa powder and refrigerate for one hour.

Chef's note

The simplest way to coat the truffles is to wear disposable gloves. Pour a little melted chocolate into the palm of one hand, and then roll the truffles in the cocoa powder.

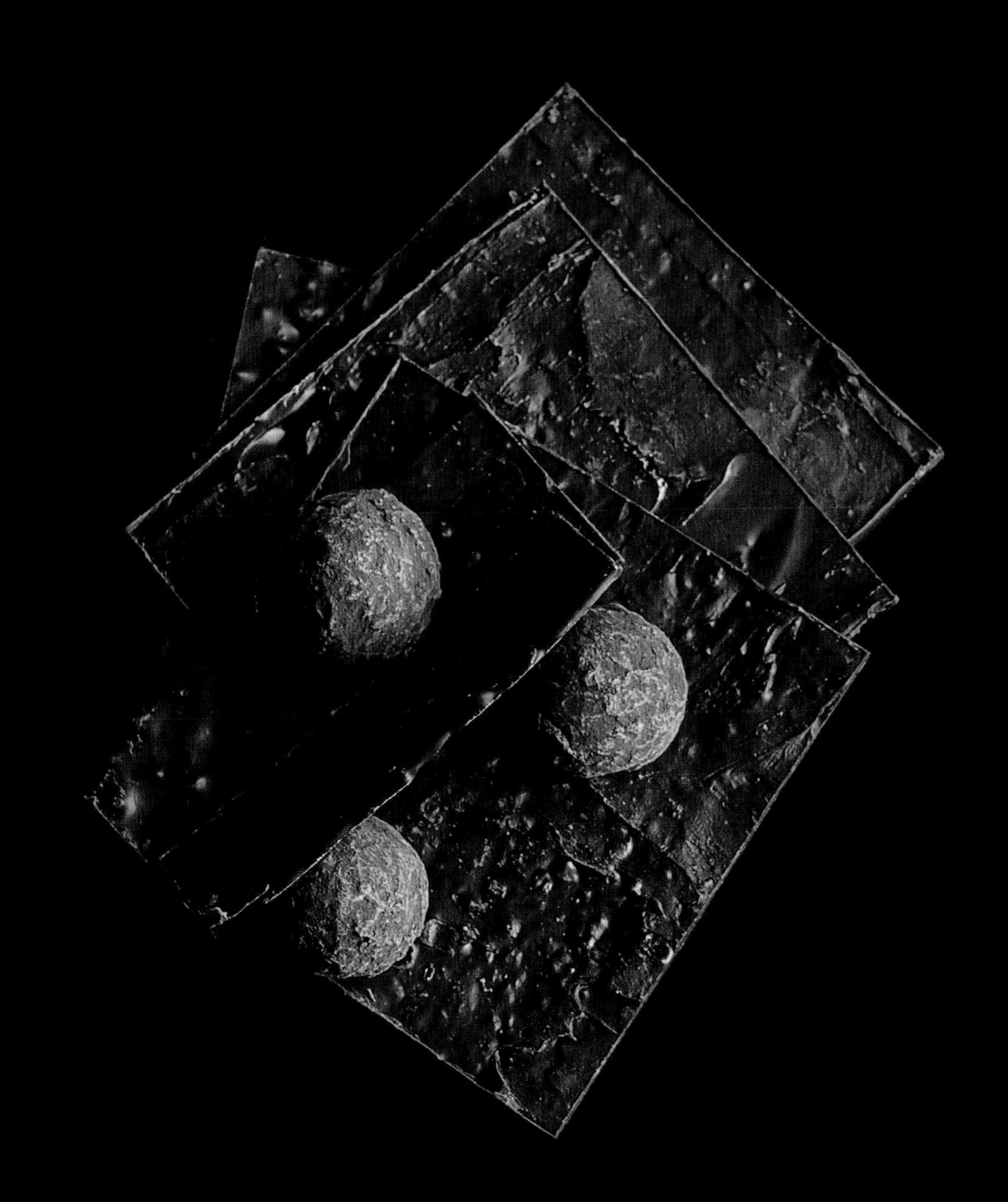

Scallops
with Chocolate & Cacao Nibs

Serves 4
Prep: 30 minutes
Cook: 27 minutes

INGREDIENTS

4 large scallops
1 tablespoon {10 g} all-purpose flour
3 tablespoons {2 oz. / 50 g} unsalted butter, plus extra to cook the scallops
2 tablespoons {25 g} granulated sugar
2 Belgian endives
Juice and grated zest of 1 unwaxed orange
Salt and freshly ground pepper
3½ oz. {100 g} Cacao Nib Nougatine {see recipe, page 314}
0.17 oz. {5 g} dark chocolate {78% cacao}, preferably Trinitario grand cru chocolate {Madagascar}

Dust the scallops with the flour on one side and leave them at room temperature.

Melt the butter with the sugar in a skillet. Cut the Belgian endives in half lengthwise. Place them, cut side down, in the skillet to caramelize. Cover with a lid and braise them over medium heat for 15 minutes without turning them. Deglaze the skillet with the orange juice and zest. Season with salt and pepper and set aside, keeping warm.

In another skillet over high heat, melt a little butter and place the scallops, floured side down, in it. Cook for no more than 2 minutes on each side.

Preheat the oven to 325°F {160°C}. Spread the cacao nib nougatine between two sheets of parchment paper and bake for 10 minutes.

As soon as you remove the sheet of nougatine from the oven, cut out disks the size of the scallops with a cookie cutter. Set them aside.

Melt the chocolate over a hot water bath. Incorporate the melted chocolate into the cooking juices of the Belgian endives, mixing well.

To plate, place a Belgian endive half, caramelized side down, on each plate. Place a scallop on each plate and drizzle with the cooking juices. To finish, place the nougatine disks over the scallops.

Chef's note

Instead of scallops, you might like to try large shrimp.

Layered Chocolate Crackers & Cream

Serves 6
Prep: 20 minutes

INGREDIENTS

1 lb. 2 oz. {500 g} Chocolate Crackers
{see recipe, page 282},
cut into 1½ by 3½-inch {4 by 9-cm} rectangles
9 oz. {250 g} Chocolate Pastry Cream
{see recipe, page 221}

To assemble this dessert, proceed as you would to make a napoleon: Start with one chocolate cracker sheet and cover it with a layer of pastry cream {you can pipe this out with a pastry bag fitted with a plain ⅓-inch {8-mm} tip}. Repeat twice to make three layers of covered crackers. To finish, place a fourth cracker {attractively broken} over the top, to give it some volume.

Chef's note

This crisp base simply cries out for vanilla-scented Chantilly cream and strawberries—a magnificent combination.

SAMBIRANO

Serves 6
Prep: 20 minutes

INGREDIENTS

6 large Cacao Meringues {see recipe, page 292}
10 oz. {300 g} Airy Chocolate Cream {see recipe, page 287}
20 Caramelized Cherries {see recipe, page 244}

Using a fine grater, grate the tops of the meringues to flatten them. Reserve the meringue powder.

Place the meringues on the serving plates. Top each meringue with an oval scoop of chocolate cream.

Arrange the caramelized cherries over the plate and dust with a little meringue powder.

Chef's note

If you prefer, you can replace the chocolate cream with a chocolate ice cream or sorbet.

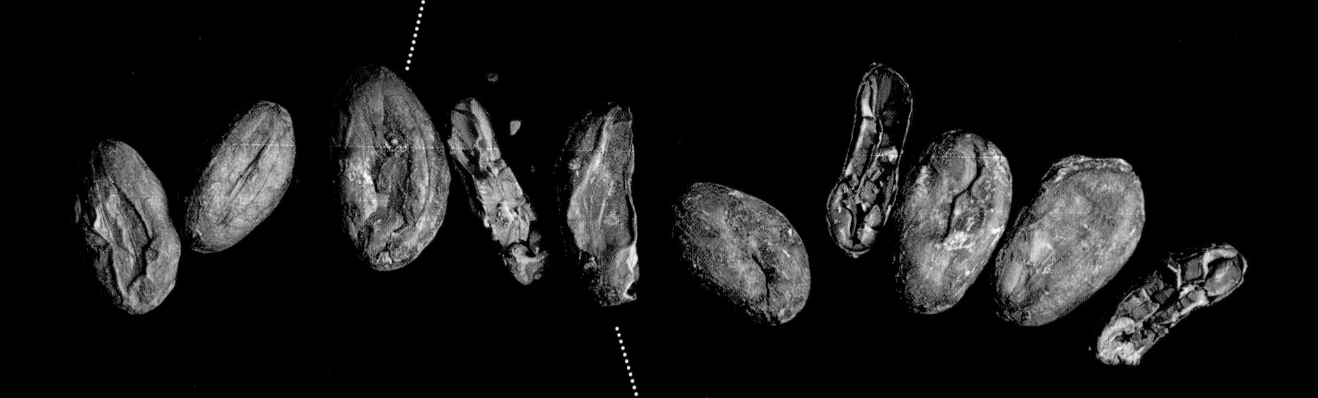
Alto Piura
Las Pampas Plantation

Criollo Alto Piura Grand Cru

{Peru}

From the heart of the terroir that is home to most of Peru's Criollos, a voluptuous, elegant, and well-balanced cacao.

Flavors: citrus, with a fine cacao presence and fermented taste

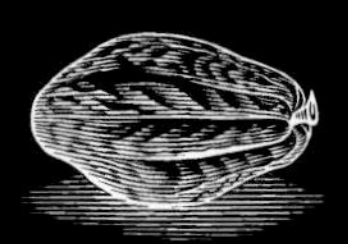

Chocolate Streusel

Prep: 15 minutes
Chill: 2 hours
Cook: 15 minutes

INGREDIENTS

½ oz. {15 g} dark chocolate {85% cacao}, preferably Alto Piura grand cru chocolate {Peru}
1 stick plus 2 tablespoons {5 oz. / 150 g} unsalted butter, room temperature
¾ cup {5 oz. / 150 g} light brown sugar
1¾ cup {5 oz. / 150 g} ground almonds
¾ cup plus 2 tablespoons {4 oz. / 115 g} all-purpose flour
½ teaspoon {2 g} fleur de sel

Melt the chocolate over a hot water bath.

In a mixing bowl, combine the butter and light brown sugar. Beat in the ground almonds, flour, and fleur de sel. Lastly, stir in the melted chocolate. Refrigerate for 2 hours.

Preheat the oven to 325°F {160°C}. Line a baking sheet with parchment paper.

When you remove the dough from the refrigerator, you can either spread it out thinly or shape it into small balls. Place on the prepared baking sheet and bake for 15 minutes, until crisp.

Allow to cool on a rack before serving: the streusel can be eaten as a snack {just use your fingers!}, or served with a creamy dessert to make for a delightful contrast between crisp and creamy textures.

Chef's note

Well wrapped, this dough freezes well. You can also use it as a crisp base for a dessert.

Chocolate Sponge Cakes

with Mango

Makes 6 individual cakes
Prep: 30 minutes
Cook: 9 minutes

INGREDIENTS

1½ oz. {40 g} dark chocolate {85% cacao}, preferably Alto Piura grand cru chocolate {Peru}
1 cup {8½ oz. / 240 g} eggs {4 to 5}
¾ cup {5 oz. / 150 g} granulated sugar
½ cup {4 oz. / 130 ml} heavy cream {35% butterfat}
1¼ cups {5½ oz. / 160 g} all-purpose flour
½ teaspoon {2 g} fleur de sel
1½ teaspoons {6 g} baking powder
6 tablespoons {95 g} clarified butter
{made from 1 stick plus 1 tablespoon (130 g) butter}
A few cubes of fresh mango
Mango jam

EQUIPMENT

Individual molds of the shape of your choice

Preheat the oven to 300°F {150°C}. Grease the molds with butter and dust them lightly with sugar.

Melt the chocolate over a hot water bath.

In the bowl of a mixer fitted with the whisk, beat the eggs with the sugar until pale, then add the cream.

Sift the flour and whisk in the fleur de sel and baking powder. Using a flexible spatula, fold the dry ingredients into the egg-sugar mixture. Lastly, stir in the melted chocolate and clarified butter.

Pour the batter into the prepared molds and bake for 9 minutes, until a cake tester inserted into the center of one comes out clean. Transfer to a rack to cool.

Just before serving, spoon over a few cubes of mango and serve with a little mango jam.

Chef's note

When apricots are in season, you can use them in place of mango.

Chocolate Sorbet

Serves 6
Prep: 20 minutes
Chill: 12 hours

INGREDIENTS

2½ oz. {70 g} dark chocolate {85% cacao}, preferably Alto Piura grand cru chocolate {Peru}
3 cups {720 ml} whole milk
½ cup plus 2 tablespoons {4 oz. / 115 g} granulated sugar
2½ tablespoons {2 oz. / 50 g} glucose syrup
¼ cup {1 oz. / 30 g} unsweetened cocoa powder

Chop the chocolate with a knife.

In a saucepan, bring the milk to a boil with the sugar and glucose syrup. As soon as it comes to a boil, remove from the heat and stir in the chocolate and cocoa powder.

Process the mixture with an immersion blender and refrigerate for 12 hours.

Then follow the manufacturer's directions to churn the sorbet in an ice cream maker.

Iced Chocolate Parfait

Serves 6
Prep: 30 minutes
Freeze: 5 hours

INGREDIENTS

3½ oz. {100 g} dark chocolate {85% cacao}, preferably Alto Piura grand cru chocolate {Peru}
1 cup {250 ml} whole milk
7 egg yolks
½ cup {3½ oz. / 100 g} granulated sugar
1⅔ cups {400 ml} heavy cream {35% butterfat}

Make a chocolate custard:
Chop the chocolate with a knife. Bring the milk to a boil in a saucepan.

In the bowl of a mixer fitted with the whisk, beat the egg yolks with the sugar until pale. Pour a little of the hot milk over the egg yolk–sugar mixture to warm it slightly. Then pour in the remaining hot milk, beating constantly.

Return the mixture to the saucepan and, stirring constantly, heat to 180°F {82°C}, at which stage it has thickened and coats the back of a spoon. Allow to cool, keeping an eye on the temperature.

When it has cooled to 122°F {50°C}, add the chocolate and process with an immersion blender. Allow to cool completely.

Whisk the cream until it holds very soft peaks, then fold it carefully into the custard-chocolate mixture. Stir well. Pour into silicone molds and freeze for five hours.

Turn out of the molds and serve like an ice cream.

Chef's note

This parfait is simpler to make than an ice cream and, what's more, it does not require an ice cream maker.

Jasmine-scented Chocolate Drink

Serves 2
Prep: 20 minutes

INGREDIENTS

1 oz. {25 g} dark chocolate {85% cacao}, preferably Alto Piura grand cru chocolate {Peru}
3 tablespoons {50 ml} whole milk
Scant ½ cup {100 ml} water
A few jasmine flowers

Chop the chocolate with a knife and place it in a bowl. Heat the milk and water in a small saucepan. When the liquid reaches 176°F {80°C}, remove from the heat, add the jasmine flowers, and cover with the lid. Allow to infuse for 10 minutes, then strain and pour over the chocolate.

Process with an immersion blender.

Chef's note

You can serve this recipe as a cool drink or to accompany a dessert.

お茶がほしい
「想ひそめし」京都 小倉山荘 × 「やぶきた強火仕上」静岡県産

Cacao Nib Nougatine

Makes about 2 lbs. {900 g} nougatine
Prep: 30 minutes
Cook: 12 minutes

INGREDIENTS

Scant ½ cup {100 ml} whole milk
1¼ cups {9 oz. / 250 g} granulated sugar, divided
3½ tablespoons {2½ oz. / 75 g} glucose syrup
1¾ sticks {7 oz. / 200 g} unsalted butter
0.18 oz. {5 g} pectin
9 oz. {250 g} cacao nibs
{see recipe, page 44 or 45}
2½ tablespoons {25 g} black sesame seeds

Preheat the oven to 340°F {170°C}.

Bring the milk to a boil with three-quarters of the sugar, the glucose, and butter.

Combine the pectin with the remaining sugar and incorporate it into the boiling liquid.
Stir in the cacao nibs and black sesame seeds.

Spread the mixture over a sheet of parchment paper and cover with another sheet. With a rolling pin, roll it as thinly as possible.

Transfer to a baking sheet and bake for 12 minutes. Allow to cool on a rack.

Chef's note

Instead of black sesame seeds, use chopped nuts of your choice.

Old-fashioned Chocolate-coated Orange Quarters

Makes 24 coated strips
Prep: 30 minutes
Chill and rest: 12 hours plus 2 hours

INGREDIENTS

3 large, thick-skinned unwaxed oranges
2 cups {500 ml} water
2 cups {15¼ oz. / 450 g} granulated sugar, divided
½ Tahitian vanilla bean, split, seeds scraped
1 clove
1 pinch nutmeg
¼ cup {1 oz. / 30 g} unsweetened cocoa powder
7 oz. {200 g} dark chocolate {85% cacao}, preferably Alto Piura grand cru chocolate {Peru}

Rinse the oranges and cut them into quarters. Blanch the quarters in salted boiling water for a few seconds and allow to drain.

To candy the oranges, make a syrup:
Combine the 2 cups {500 ml} water with 1¼ cups {10 oz. / 300 g} of the sugar. Add the vanilla bean and seeds, the clove, and nutmeg. Bring to a boil. Add the orange quarters. Simmer over low heat for 10 minutes. Then add ¼ cup {1¾ oz. / 50 g} of the sugar and boil again for 10 minutes. Repeat the procedure twice.

Remove the orange quarters from the syrup and drain them. Coat them in the cocoa powder and refrigerate for 12 hours.

The next day, chop the chocolate with a knife. To ensure that the chocolate coating is glossy, temper it as follows:
- Over a hot water bath, heat the chocolate to 122°F {50°C}.
- Place over a cool water bath and cool to 82°F {28°C}.
- Reheat the chocolate to 90°F {32°C} over a hot water bath.

Cut the orange quarters roughly and coat the pieces in the tempered chocolate. Allow to drain for two hours before serving.

Chocolate Ice Cream

with Candied Fennel

Serves 6
Prep: 25 minutes
Chill: 12 hours plus 1 hour

INGREDIENTS

CHOCOLATE ICE CREAM

4 oz. {110 g} dark chocolate {85% cacao}, preferably Alto Piura grand cru chocolate {Peru}
2 cups {500 ml} whole milk
¾ cup {200 ml} heavy cream {35% butterfat}
¼ cup plus 2½ teaspoons {33 g} powdered skim milk
2 tablespoons {1½ oz. / 45 g} invert sugar
2 egg yolks
¾ cup {5 oz. / 140 g} granulated sugar

CANDIED FENNEL

6 new fennel
2 cups {500 ml} water
2 cups {15¼ oz. / 450 g} granulated sugar, divided
1 Madagascar vanilla bean, split, seeds scraped

Make a chocolate pouring custard:
Chop the chocolate and place it in a mixing bowl.

Bring the milk and cream to a boil in a saucepan with the powdered skim milk and invert sugar.

In the bowl of a mixer fitted with the whisk, beat the egg yolks with the sugar until pale. Pour in a little of the hot liquid to warm the egg yolk–sugar mixture slightly, beating as you pour. Pour in the remaining hot liquid, beating constantly. Return to the saucepan and, stirring constantly, heat to 180°F {82°C}, at which stage the mixture coats the back of a spoon.

Pour the custard over the chocolate and process with an immersion blender until smooth. Refrigerate, covered with plastic wrap, for 12 hours.

Pour the chilled custard into an ice cream maker and proceed according to the manufacturer's directions to make an ice cream.

Make the candied fennel:
Cut the fennel bulbs in half and blanch them for a few seconds in salted boiling water.

Now make a syrup: Combine the 2 cups {500 ml} water with 1¼ cups {10 oz. / 300 g} of the sugar. Add the vanilla bean and seeds and bring to a boil. Add the fennel and simmer over low heat for 10 minutes.

Add ¼ cup {1¾ oz. / 50 g} of the sugar and simmer for a further 10 minutes. Repeat the procedure twice. Refrigerate for one hour, until chilled.

To plate, place an oval scoop of chocolate ice cream on each plate and add a few strips of candied fennel.

Chef's note

To accentuate the taste of the fennel, sprinkle the plate with a few fennel seeds.

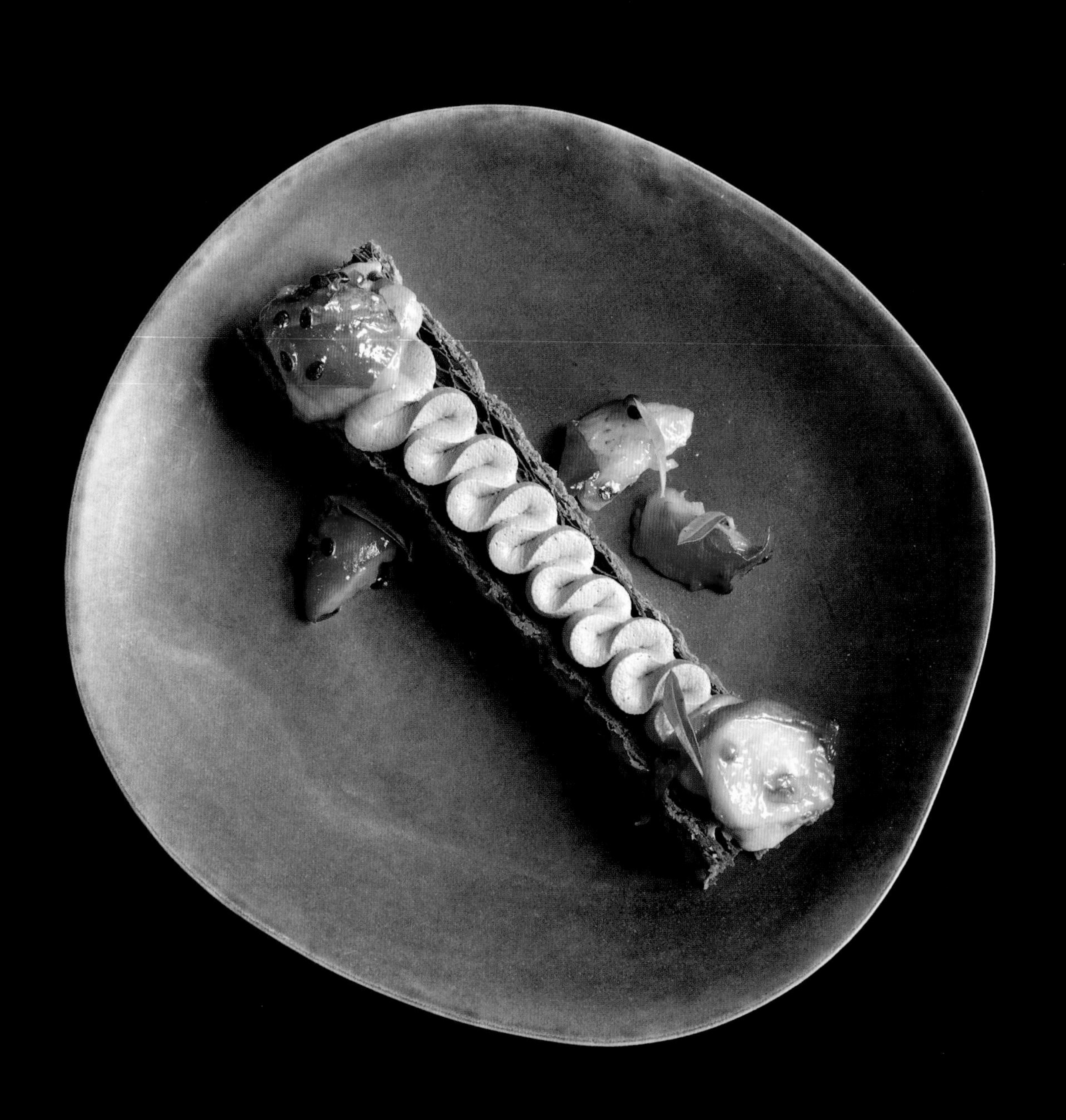

Chocolate Napoleon

Serves 6
Prep: 30 minutes
Chill: 2 hours
Cook: 30 minutes

INGREDIENTS

10 oz. {300 g} Chocolate Puff Pastry {see recipe, page 329}
2 white peaches
¼ cup {2 oz. / 50 g} granulated sugar
3 tablespoons {2 oz. / 50 g} unsalted butter
Pulp of 1 passion fruit
10 oz. {300 g} Chocolate Chantilly Cream {make a day ahead, see recipe, page 348}

Roll the puff pastry to a thickness of about ⅛ inch {3 to 4 mm}. Place it on a baking sheet lined with parchment paper. Prick with the tines of a fork and refrigerate for two hours.

Preheat the oven to 340°F {170°C}. Bake the puff pastry for 30 minutes. As soon as you remove it from the oven, cut it into 1¼ by 5-inch {3 by 12-cm} rectangles and place on a rack.

Remove the pits from the peaches and cut them into quarters without peeling them.

Place the sugar in a saucepan and cook over low heat until it caramelizes. Add the butter and peaches. Allow the peaches to caramelize and then remove from the heat. Stir in the passion fruit pulp, pour off the juice, reserving it, and allow to cool.

While the fruit and juice are cooling, whisk the chocolate Chantilly cream.

To plate, place two rectangles of puff pastry on their sides on the plate. With a pastry bag fitted with a Saint Honoré tip, pipe the Chantilly cream between the rectangles of puff pastry and over the top of the pastry. To finish, arrange a few pieces of caramelized peach on each plate.

Chef's note

To give a more intense note of chocolate to this dessert, add a few fine shards of chocolate.

Alto Piura

Serves 6
Prep: 30 minutes
Chill: 20 minutes

INGREDIENTS

7 oz. {200 g} dark chocolate {85% cacao}, preferably Alto Piura grand cru chocolate {Peru}
10 oz. {300 g} Chocolate Sponge Cake {see recipe, page 307}
3 very moist Medjool dates, cut into halves
3½ oz. {100 g} Chocolate Streusel {see recipe, page 304}
5 oz. {150 g} Chocolate Sorbet {see recipe, page 311}
3½ oz. {100 g} Jasmine-Scented Chocolate Drink {see recipe, page 312}

Chop the chocolate with a knife. To ensure that your chocolate shards are glossy, temper the chocolate as follows:
- Over a hot water bath, heat the chocolate to 122°F {50°C}.
- Place over a cool water bath and cool to 82°F {28°C}.
- Reheat the chocolate to 90°F {32°C} over a hot water bath.

Pour the tempered chocolate over a sheet of food-safe acetate and place another sheet over it. With a rolling pin, roll the chocolate out very thinly. Refrigerate for 20 minutes.

Cut the Chocolate Sponge Cake into 2-inch {5-cm} squares just under ½ inch {1 cm} thick.

Break the tempered chocolate into uneven shards.

On each plate, place a square of sponge standing upright with a chocolate shard. Place a half date on each plate {if you like, you can coat them in edible gold leaf}, then sprinkle with a little streusel, and finish with an oval scoop of chocolate sorbet. Dot the plate with a few drops of jasmine-scented chocolate drink.

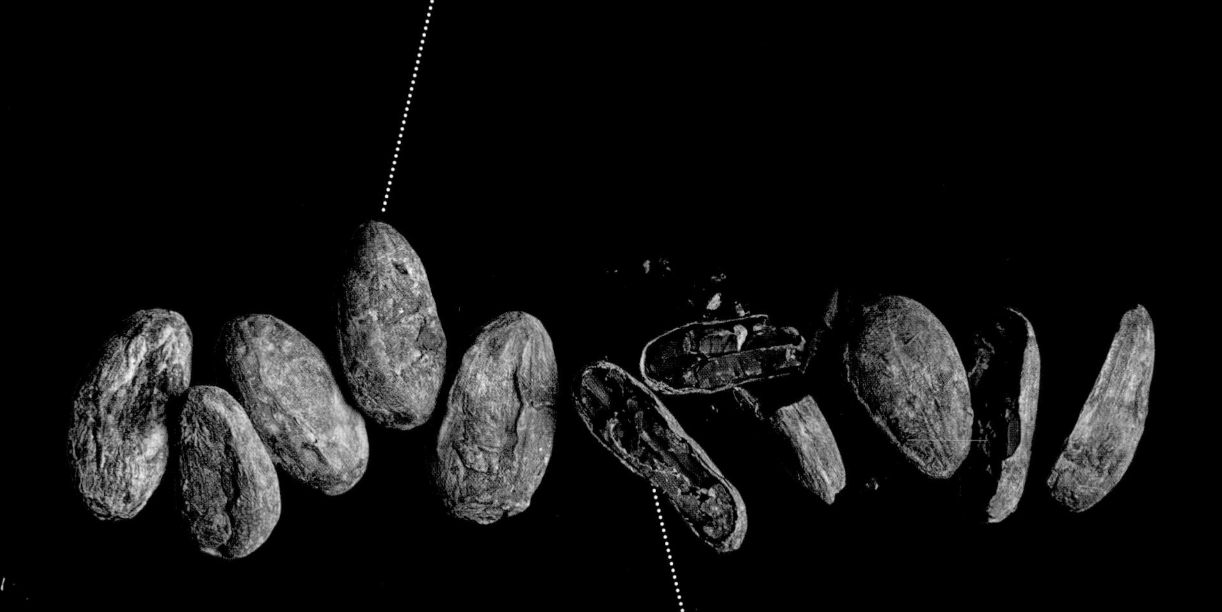
Upper Penja
Dark Mungo Plantation

Forastero Grand Cru, Upper Penja

{Cameroon}

A magnificent Forastero that grows on a rich volcanic terroir.

Barely acidic with pronounced bitterness.

Flavors: earthy with citrus and basil

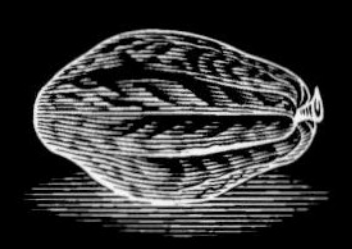

Strawberry Brownies

Serves 8
Prep: 40 minutes
Cook: 20 minutes

INGREDIENTS

5 eggs
2 cups {14 oz. / 400 g} granulated sugar
6½ oz. {180 g} dark chocolate {78% cacao}, preferably Upper Penja Forastero grand cru {Cameroon}
2 sticks {8½ oz. / 240 g} unsalted butter
1 cup {4 oz. / 120 g} all-purpose flour, sifted
7 oz. {200 g} strawberries or wild strawberries

EQUIPMENT

Eight 3-inch {7-cm} molds, 1¼ inches {3 cm} high

Preheat the oven to 325°F {160°C}. Grease the molds with butter and dust them lightly with flour. {Alternatively, line them with parchment paper.}

In the bowl of a mixer fitted with the whisk, beat the eggs with the sugar until pale.

Melt the chocolate and butter over a hot water bath, ensuring that the temperature of the melted mixture does not exceed 104°F {40°C}.

Carefully stir the melted chocolate and butter into the egg-sugar mixture, then gradually fold in the flour with a flexible spatula.

Slice the strawberries. Pour the batter into the prepared molds and arrange the strawberry slices over the top. Bake for 20 minutes.

Chef's note

Raspberries are a fine substitution for the strawberries.

If you want to make one larger cake, bake for 40 minutes.

Chocolate Puff Pastry

Prep: 45 minutes
Chill: 5 hours 30 minutes
Cook: 20 minutes

INGREDIENTS

6⅔ sticks {1 lb. 10 oz. / 750 g} unsalted butter, divided
1 heaping tablespoon {18 g} fine salt
5⅔ cups {1 lb. 8 oz. / 700 g} all-purpose flour
7 tablespoons {1¾ oz./ 50 g} unsweetened cocoa powder
2 teaspoons {10 ml} white vinegar

In the bowl of a stand mixer fitted with the paddle, beat 2 sticks {9 oz. / 250 g} of the butter with the salt.

Sift the flour and cocoa powder together, then beat them into the creamed butter. Beat in the vinegar, and continue until the ingredients form a smooth ball of dough.

Lightly dust the work surface with flour and roll the dough to a thickness of just under ½ inch {1 cm}. Shape the remaining butter into a square the same shape. Place it in a diamond shape over the dough. Fold the corners of the dough over the butter.

Make 6 "turns": Roll the dough into a long rectangle and fold it in three. Repeat this operation six times, rolling the dough in the opposite direction of the previous fold. Refrigerate the dough for one hour between each turn.

Roll the dough on a sheet of parchment paper to a thickness of ¼ inch {5 mm} and prick it with a fork. Refrigerate once again, for 30 minutes.

Preheat the oven to 325°C {160°C}. Slide the parchment paper and dough onto a baking sheet and bake for 20 minutes.

Chef's note

If you are using convection heat, turn the baking sheet around halfway through the baking.

Chocolate Custard

Scented with Fresh Thyme

Serves 6
Prep: 25 minutes
Rest: 10 minutes
Chill: 26 hours

INGREDIENTS

⅔ cup {150 ml} whole milk
2 cups {480 ml} heavy cream {35% butterfat}, divided
{2 g} fresh thyme, plus a little for decoration
3 tablespoons {2 oz. / 50 g} egg yolks {2 to 3 yolks}
3½ tablespoons {1½ oz. / 40 g} granulated sugar
9 oz. {250 g} dark chocolate {78% cacao}, preferably Upper Penja Forastero grand cru {Cameroon}

Make a pouring custard:
Bring the milk and one scant ½ cup {100 ml} of the cream to a boil in a saucepan. Off the heat, stir in the fresh thyme, cover with a lid, and allow to infuse for 10 minutes.

In the bowl of a mixer fitted with the whisk, beat the egg yolks with the sugar until pale. Pour a little of the hot liquid over the egg yolk–sugar mixture and beat to warm it slightly. Then pour in the remaining hot liquid, beating constantly.

Over a hot water bath, heat the chocolate to 113°F {45°C}.

Strain the custard mixture and stir in the melted chocolate.

Transfer to the saucepan and, stirring constantly, heat to 180°F {82°C}, at which stage it has thickened and coats the back of a spoon. Refrigerate for two hours, until cooled.

Whisk the remaining cream until it holds soft peaks.

Process the chilled custard with an immersion blender for 1 minute.

Using a flexible spatula, carefully fold the whipped cream into the chocolate custard mixture. Refrigerate for 24 hours, covered with plastic wrap.

To serve, place oval scoops on the dessert plates and scatter with a few leaves of fresh thyme.

Chef's note

You can use rosemary instead of thyme.

Citrus-scented Chocolate Sauce

Serves 6
Prep: 25 minutes

INGREDIENTS

6 oz. {180 g} dark chocolate {78% cacao}, preferably Upper Penja Forastero grand cru {Cameroon}
2 cups {500 ml} water
½ cup {3½ oz. / 100 g} granulated sugar
Finely grated zest of 1 unwaxed orange
Finely grated zest of ½ unwaxed lemon
Finely grated zest of ½ unwaxed lime

Chop the chocolate with a knife and place it in a bowl.

In a saucepan, bring the water to a boil with the sugar and citrus zest. Pour it over the chocolate and process with an immersion blender.

Serve the chocolate sauce hot.

Chef's note

This sauce can be served on its own, poured over orange segments, or as an accompaniment to a dessert such as ice cream.

COFFEE-CHOCOLATE TRUFFLES

Makes 40 truffles
Prep: 30 minutes
Rest: 10 minutes
Chill: 12 hours

INGREDIENTS

7 oz. {200 g} dark chocolate {78% cacao}, preferably Upper Penja Forastero grand cru {Cameroon}
⅔ cup {150 ml} heavy cream {35% butterfat}
2½ tablespoons {1 oz. / 30 g} granulated sugar
1 oz. {30 g} roasted coffee beans, crushed with a rolling pin
1 tablespoon {20 g} unsalted butter, diced

Chop the chocolate with a knife and place it in a bowl. In a saucepan, bring the cream to a boil with the sugar and crushed coffee beans. When it begins to simmer, remove from the heat and allow to infuse for 10 minutes.

Strain and pour over the chocolate. Stir well and process with an immersion blender.

When the ganache has cooled to nearly 95°F {35°C}, stir in the butter. Refrigerate for 12 hours.

Using two spoons, shape the ganache into truffles. Dipping the spoons into hot water first helps to shape the truffles attractively.

M
A
R
C

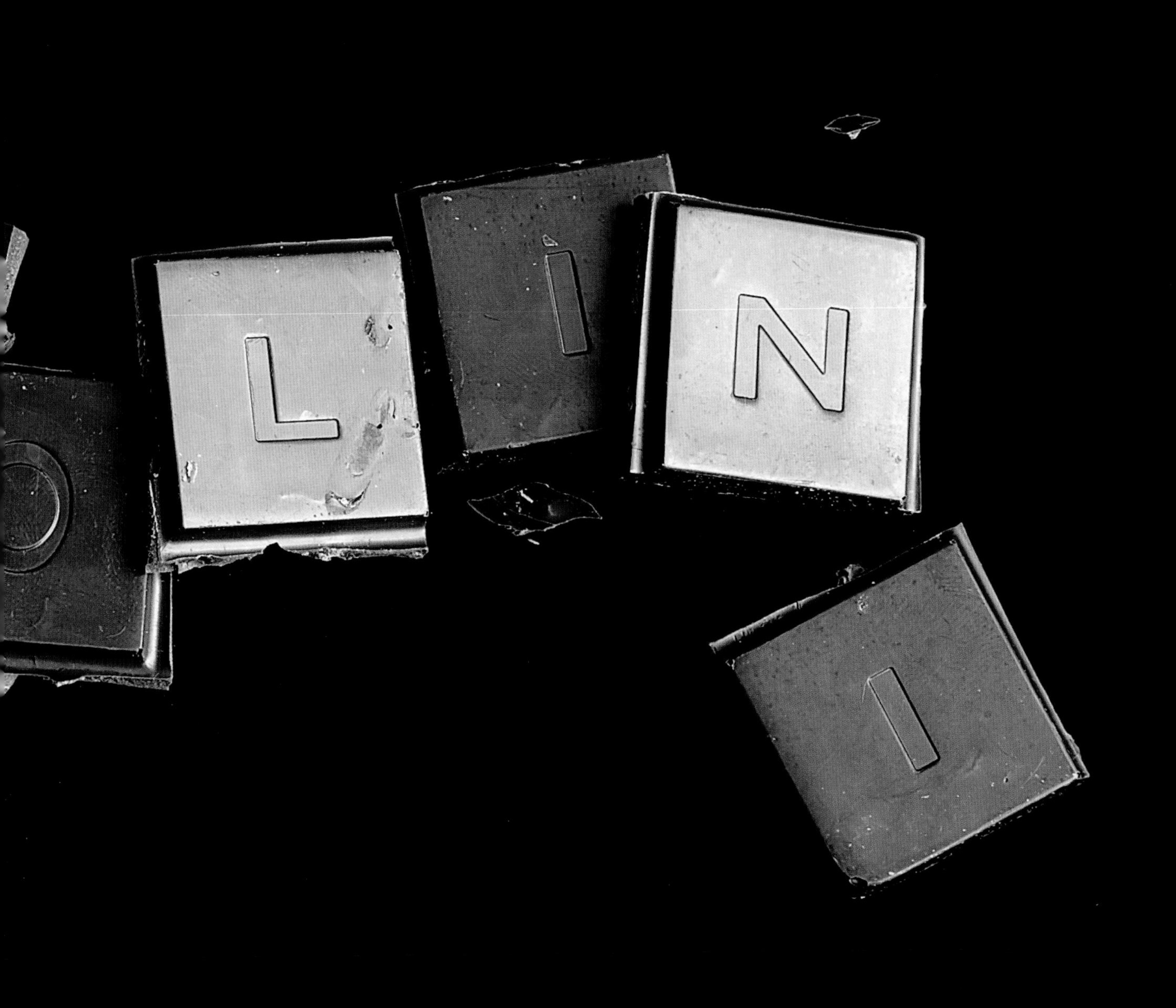
L
I
N
I

Cameroon Chocolate Bar

Makes one 12-oz. {350-g} bar of chocolate
Prep: 25 minutes
Chill: From 30 minutes to 1 hour

INGREDIENTS

10½ oz. {300 g} dark chocolate {78% cacao}, preferably Upper Penja Forastero grand cru {Cameroon}
2 oz. {50 g} cacao nibs
{see recipe, page 44 or 45}

Chop the chocolate with a knife. To ensure that the chocolate bar is glossy and snaps cleanly, temper it as follows:
- Over a hot water bath, heat the chocolate to 122°F {50°C}.
- Place over a cool water bath and cool to 82°F {28°C}.
- Reheat the chocolate to 90°F {32°C} over a hot water bath.

Combine the tempered chocolate with the cacao nibs. Pour into a silicone mold and refrigerate until set, 30 minutes to one hour, depending on the thickness of the bar. Turn out of the mold.

Chef's note

Instead of cacao nibs, use the same amount of nuts of your choice.

M A R
C O L
I N I

Chocolate Meringue Dessert, Montélimar Style

Makes 6 pastries
Prep: 30 minutes
Cook: 2 hours 20 minutes

INGREDIENTS

⅔ oz. {20 g} unsalted pistachios {about 3 tablespoons}
⅔ oz. {20 g} blanched almonds {about 3 tablespoons}
¾ cup {3½ oz. / 100 g} confectioners' sugar
1 tablespoon plus 2 teaspoons {12 g} unsweetened cocoa powder
Scant ½ cup {3½ oz. / 100 g} egg whites {3 to 4 whites}
½ cup {3½ oz. / 100 g} granulated sugar
12 oz. {350 g} Chocolate Chantilly Cream {see recipe, page 348}

Preheat the oven to 325°F {160°C}. Spread the pistachios and almonds over a baking sheet and roast for 20 minutes. Set aside a few whole nuts for decoration and, when the others are cool enough to handle, chop them with a knife.

Sift the confectioners' sugar and cocoa powder together. Whisk the egg whites, gradually adding the sugar. When they reach a meringue texture, carefully fold in the sifted confectioners' sugar and cocoa powder with a flexible spatula. Fold in the chopped nuts.

Set the oven temperature to 200°F {100°C}. Line a baking sheet with parchment paper.

Spoon the meringue batter into a pastry bag fitted with a plain ⅓-inch {8-mm} tip. Pipe six 5-inch {12-cm} lines onto the prepared baking sheet and bake for two hours. Transfer to a rack and allow to cool.

To plate, place a meringue tube on each dessert dish. Fill a pastry bag fitted with a ¼-inch {6-mm} tip with the chocolate Chantilly cream and pipe the Chantilly over the meringue. Decorate with the reserved whole almonds and nuts.

Chef's note

For an elegant presentation, decorate the plates with triangles of edible rice paper.

Upper Penja

Serves 6
Prep: 30 minutes

INGREDIENTS

10 oz. {300 g} Citrus-Scented Chocolate Sauce
{see recipe, page 333}
10 oz. {300 g} Chocolate Custard
Scented with Fresh Thyme
{see recipe, page 330}
6 caramelized apricots
{see recipe for Caramelized Cherries, page 244}
10 oz. {300 g} Chocolate Puff Pastry,
cut into ½ by 2½-inch {1 by 6-cm} sticks
{see recipe, page 329}

Drizzle a little chocolate sauce onto each place. Place an oval scoop of chocolate custard on one side with two caramelized apricot halves. Arrange the sticks of puff pastry attractively around the plate.

Chef's note

For a variation, replace the apricots with peaches.

Mekong Delta
Ben Tre Island
Cooperative

Trinitario Grand Cru, Ben Tre Island

{Vietnam}

With a fine balance
between bitterness and acidity,
a Trinitario from the Mekong Delta.

Flavors: red wine,
nuts, cacao

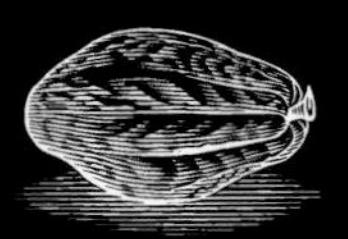

CHOCOLATE SAVARIN

Makes about 20 savarin cakes
Prep: 20 minutes
Rise: 45 minutes to 1 hour 30 minutes
Cook: 10 to 12 minutes

INGREDIENTS

3 tablespoons {50 ml} whole milk, warmed
½ cake {⅓ oz. / 10 g} fresh yeast
1⅔ cups {7 oz. / 210 g} all-purpose flour
½ oz. {15 g} dark chocolate {78% cacao}, preferably Trinitario grand cru chocolate {Vietnam}
3 eggs
3 tablespoons {2 oz. / 50 g} unsalted butter, slightly softened
1½ tablespoons {⅔ oz. / 20 g} granulated sugar
1 teaspoon {5 g} fine salt

Pour the milk into the bowl of a mixer and dilute the yeast in it. Gradually add the sugar, kneading with the dough hook at low speed until combined. Allow to rest until doubled in volume.

Melt the chocolate over a hot water bath and incorporate it into the dough with the dough hook. Then knead in the eggs, one at a time, followed by the butter. Lastly, incorporate the sugar and salt. Continue kneading until the dough pulls away from the sides of the bowl.

Cover with a clean cloth and allow to rise for between 45 minutes and 1 hour 30 minutes, depending on the temperature, until doubled in volume.

Preheat the oven to 350°F {180°C}. With a pastry bag fitted with a plain ½-inch {10-mm} tip, fill 1 by 4-inch {2 by 10-cm} molds, cutting the dough with a pair of scissors each time you have filled one. Bake for 10 to 12 minutes, until light brown and well risen.

Chocolate Chantilly Cream

Serves 6
Prep: 15 minutes
Chill: 12 hours

INGREDIENTS

2 oz. {60 g} dark chocolate {78% cacao}, preferably Trinitario grand cru chocolate {Vietnam}
1 cup plus 2 tablespoons {280 ml} heavy cream {35% butterfat}

Chop the chocolate with a knife and place it in a bowl.

Bring the cream to a boil and pour it over the chocolate, mixing well. When combined, refrigerate, covered with plastic wrap, for 12 hours.

Whisk the cream at medium speed until it holds between the loops of the whisk.

Chef's note

To add interesting flavors to the Chantilly cream, use spices of your choice.

Light Chocolate Mousse

with Blueberries

Serves 8
Prep: 25 minutes
Chill: 2 hours

INGREDIENTS

3 oz. {80 g} dark chocolate {78% cacao}, preferably Trinitario grand cru chocolate {Vietnam}
⅓ cup plus 2 teaspoons {90 ml} heavy cream {35% butterfat}
⅓ cup plus 2 teaspoons {90 ml} whole milk
⅓ cup {3 oz. / 90 g} egg yolks {4 to 5 yolks}

SWISS MERINGUE

3 tablespoons {1½ oz. / 40 g} egg whites {the white of 1 extra-large egg}
Scant ½ cup {3 oz. / 80 g} granulated sugar

GARNISH

3½ oz. {100 g} blueberries

Make a chocolate pouring custard:
Chop the chocolate with a knife and heat it over a hot water bath to 113°F {45°C}.

Bring the cream and milk to a boil in a saucepan.

In the bowl of a mixer fitted with the whisk, lightly beat the egg yolks. Pour a little of the hot liquid over them to warm them, whisking as you pour. Pour in the remaining liquid, whisk, then return to the saucepan. Stirring constantly, heat to 180°F {82°C}, at which stage the custard should coat the back of a spoon. Incorporate the melted chocolate and process with an immersion blender. Refrigerate, covered with plastic wrap, for 2 hours.

While the custard is chilling, make a Swiss meringue. Pour the egg white into a heat-resistant mixing bowl and place it over a hot water bath. Whisk briskly until the white is foamy. Incorporate the sugar and whisk until the mixture forms a smooth, glossy meringue. Remove from the heat and whisk until completely cooled.

Using a flexible spatula, carefully fold in nine-tenths of the Swiss meringue into the chocolate pouring custard.

To plate, spoon the light chocolate mousse into the base of a glass, add a few berries, and top with a scoop of the remaining Swiss meringue.

Chef's note

Make some foamy milk {just like for a cappuccino} to top the blueberries with. If you opt for this topping, incorporate all of the Swiss meringue into the chocolate custard.

Iced Chocolate

Serves 4
Prep: 10 minutes
Chill: 2 hours

INGREDIENTS

⅔ cup {150 ml} whole milk
Scant ½ cup {100 ml} water
2 teaspoons {10 g} granulated sugar
3 oz. {80 g} dark chocolate {78% cacao}, preferably Trinitario grand cru chocolate {Vietnam}

In a saucepan, bring the milk and water to a boil with the sugar.

Chop the chocolate and melt it over a hot water bath. Pour the hot milk mixture over the melted chocolate and stir well. Process with an immersion blender until perfectly smooth.

Refrigerate for 2 hours. Place in a blender with crushed ice, process briefly, and serve immediately.

Chef's note

Instead of crushed ice, add a touch of luxury with a scoop of chocolate ice cream.

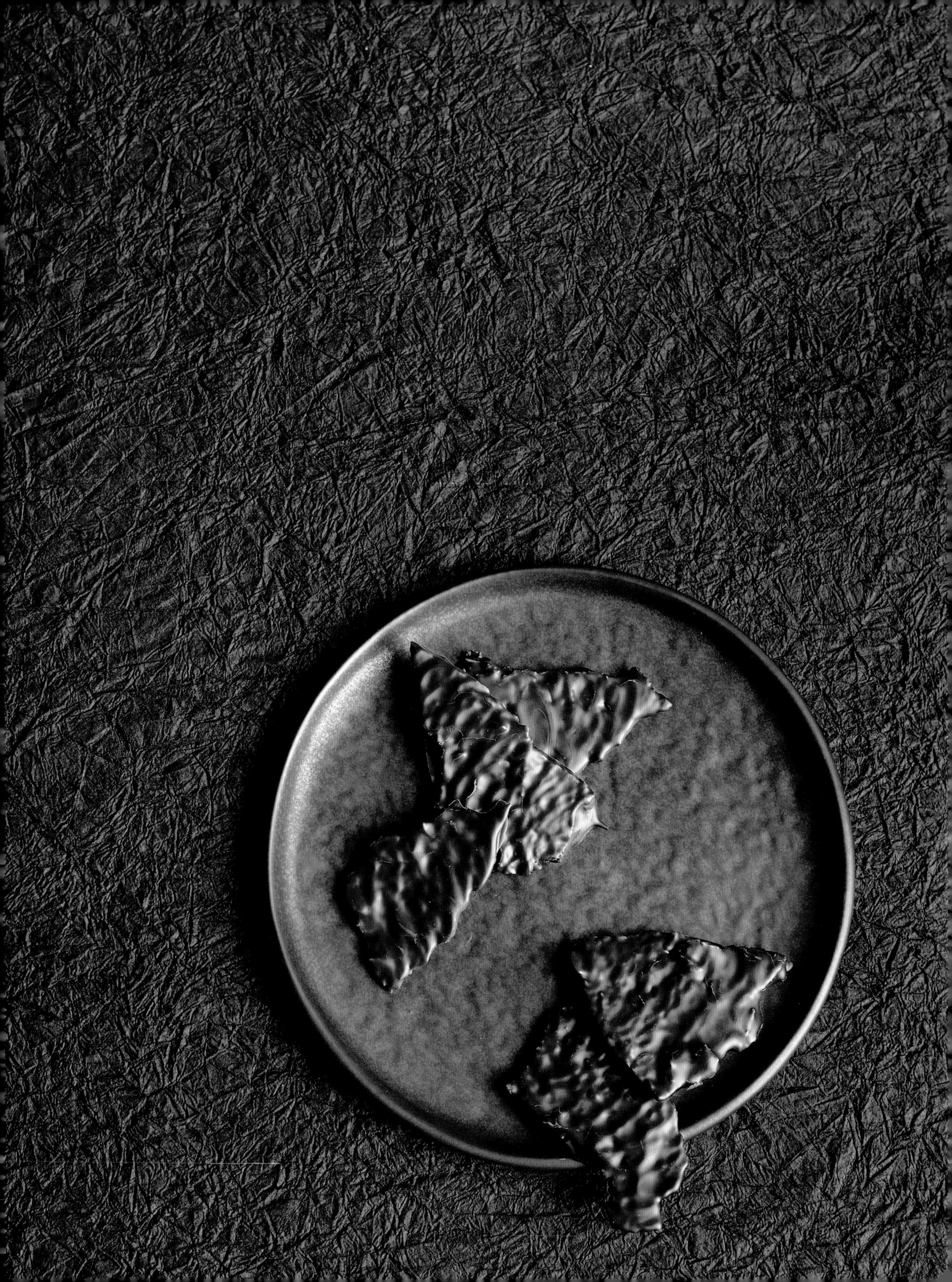

Chocolate-coated Almond Nougatine

Prep: 30 minutes
Cook: 12 minutes
Rest: 40 minutes
Set: 1 hour

INGREDIENTS

Scant ½ cup {100 ml} whole milk
1¼ cups {9 oz. / 250 g} granulated sugar, divided
3½ tablespoons {2½ oz. / 75 g} glucose syrup
1¾ sticks {7 oz. / 200 g} butter
0.17 oz. {5 g} pectin
7 oz. {200 g} sliced almonds {about 2 cups}
5 oz. {150 g} dark chocolate {78% cacao}, preferably Trinitario grand cru chocolate {Vietnam}

In a saucepan, bring the milk to a boil with three quarters of the sugar, the glucose syrup, and butter. Combine the pectin with the remaining sugar and stir into the boiling liquid. Carefully stir in the sliced almonds.

Preheat the oven to 340°F {170°C}. Working between two sheets of parchment paper, spread the mixture as thinly as possible with a rolling pin.

Bake for 12 minutes, then allow to cool for 40 minutes.

Chop the chocolate with a knife. To ensure that the chocolate coating is glossy, temper it as follows:
- Over a hot water bath, heat the chocolate to 122°F {50°C}.
- Place over a cool water bath and cool to 82°F {28°C}.
- Reheat the chocolate to 90°F {32°C} over a hot water bath.

Break the sheet of almond nougatine into pieces and coat in the tempered chocolate. Allow to set at room temperature for one hour on a sheet of parchment paper.

Chef's note

The unbaked nougatine mixture keeps very well in the freezer. You can break off pieces and bake and coat them as needed.

Sesame Praline Chocolate Candies

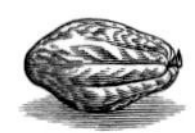

Makes 60 chocolates
Prep: 60 minutes
Cook: 15 minutes
Chill: 4 hours 10 minutes

INGREDIENTS

⅓ cup {2 oz. / 55 g} white sesame seeds
¾ teaspoon {6 g} glucose syrup
3 tablespoons {2 oz. / 60 g} acacia honey {or multi-floral honey}
⅓ cup {2 oz. / 60 g} sugar
6½ oz. {170 g} milk chocolate
1¼ oz. {35 g} cacao butter
7 oz. {200 g} dark chocolate {78% cacao}, preferably Trinitario grand cru chocolate {Vietnam}

Preheat the oven to 325°F {160°C}. Spread the sesame seeds on a baking sheet lined with parchment paper and roast for 15 minutes.

In a saucepan over medium heat, make a caramel with the glucose syrup, honey, and sugar. When the mixture reaches 330°F {165°C}, add the sesame seeds and stir well to combine.

Spread the caramel mixture over a silicone baking mat and allow to cool.

Over a hot water bath, heat the milk chocolate and cacao butter to 104°F {40°C}.

Grind the cooled caramel mixture in a food processor and combine it with the melted milk chocolate and cacao butter. Refrigerate the sesame praline for one to two hours, until set.

When it is set, chop the grand cru chocolate with a knife. To ensure that the coating of the candies is glossy, temper the chocolate as follows:
- Over a hot water bath, heat the chocolate to 122°F {50°C}.
- Place over a cool water bath and cool to 82°F {28°C}.
- Reheat the chocolate to 90°F {32°C} over a hot water bath.

Fill a candy mold with the tempered chocolate and turn it upside down over a bowl to make a thin coat—the shell of the candies. Refrigerate for 30 minutes.

Repeat the procedure once more to make a second coat.

Fill the shells with the sesame praline. Place the filled shells in the refrigerator and chill for 30 minutes. Cover with the remaining tempered chocolate. Allow to set for 40 minutes, then turn out of the molds.

Chef's note

When you have mastered the technique of molding filled chocolates, try your hand with a ganache or other creamy filling.

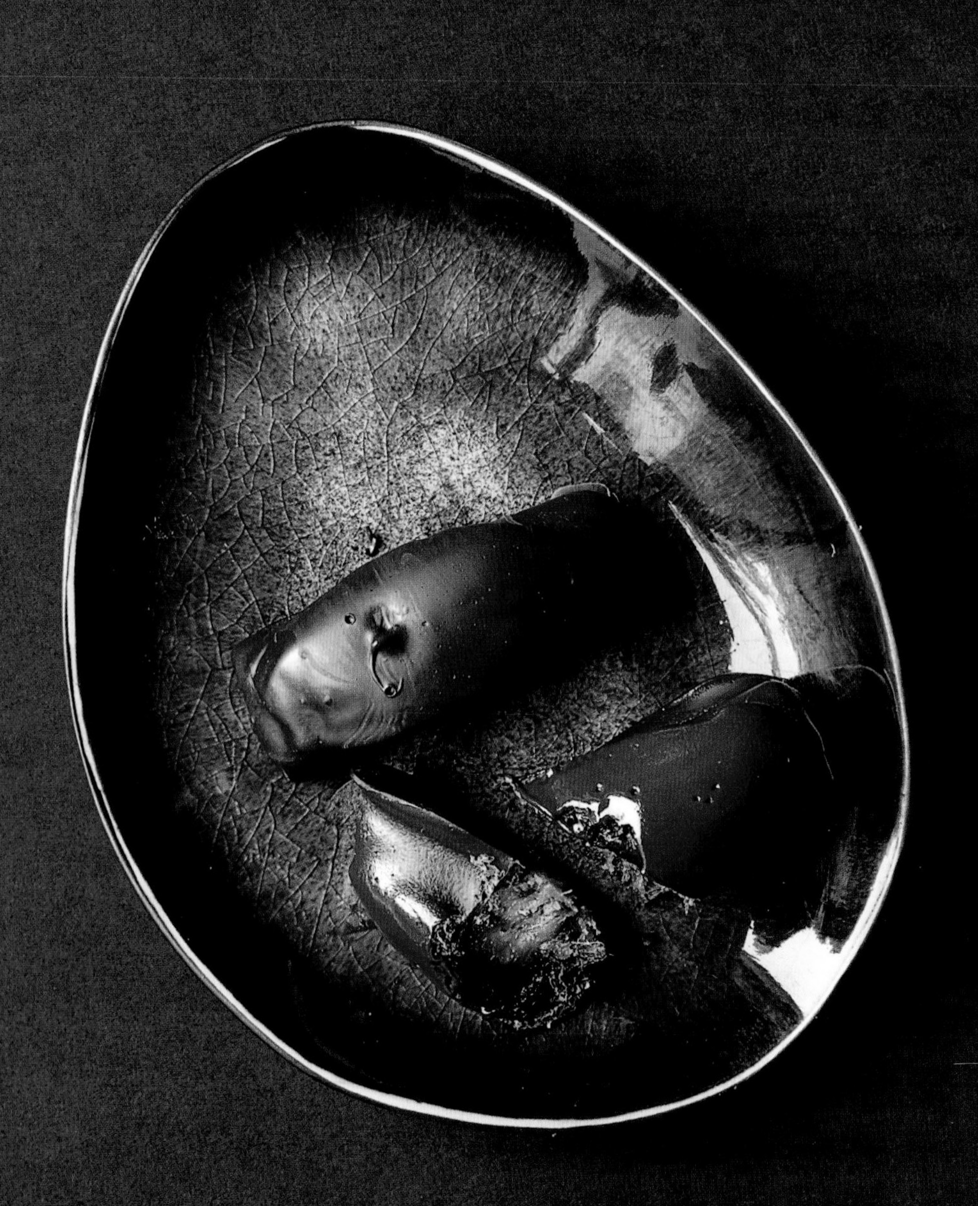

Chocolate-coated Dates

with Almond-Pistachio Paste

Makes 20 coated dates
Prep: 30 minutes
Chill: 30 minutes

INGREDIENTS

5 oz. {150 g} almond paste, room temperature
2 teaspoons {½ oz. / 15 g} acacia honey {or multi-floral honey}
1 oz. {30 g} unsalted pistachios {about ¼ cup}
5 pitted Medjool dates
7 oz. {200 g} dark chocolate {78% cacao}, preferably Trinitario grand cru chocolate {Vietnam}

In a mixing bowl, soften the almond paste and honey with a spatula or wooden spoon. Chop the pistachios and incorporate them into the almond paste–honey mixture. Shape into a log just under ½ inch {1 cm} in diameter and cut it into pieces the length of the dates.

Quarter the dates lengthwise and place each quarter on a piece of the almond-pistachio paste.

Chop the chocolate with a knife. To ensure that the coating is glossy, temper the chocolate as follows:
- Over a hot water bath, heat the chocolate to 122°F {50°C}.
- Place over a cool water bath and cool to 82°F {28°C}.
- Reheat the chocolate to 90°F {32°C} over a hot water bath.

Holding the date pieces with the almond-pistachio paste on the tines of a fork, dip into the tempered chocolate to coat. Place on a sheet of parchment paper and refrigerate for 30 minutes to set.

Chef's note

You can replace the dates with dried figs.

Praline Hearts

Makes 40 praline candies
Prep: 45 minutes
Chill: 2 hours

INGREDIENTS

1 lb. 2 oz. {500 g} dark chocolate {78% cacao}, preferably Trinitario grand cru chocolate {Vietnam}
⅔ oz. {20 g} cacao butter
2 oz. {55 g} crushed *feuillantine* {see Chef's note}
7 oz. {200 g} Pistachio Praline {see recipe, page 131}
6 oz. {175 g} white chocolate
1¼ oz. {35 g} chopped unsalted pistachios
A pinch of fine salt

EQUIPMENT

Heart-shaped candy molds

Chop the grand cru chocolate with a knife. To ensure that the candies are glossy, temper the chocolate as follows:
- Over a hot water bath, heat the chocolate to 122°F {50°C}.
- Place over a cool water bath and cool to 82°F {28°C}.
- Reheat the chocolate to 90°F {32°C} over a hot water bath.

Fill a mold with heart-shaped cavities with the tempered chocolate and turn it upside down to drain. This makes the shell of the candies. Refrigerate for 30 minutes.

Heat the cacao butter to a maximum of 95°F {35°C}. Stir in the feuillantine, mixing well so that it is coated in cacao butter to prevent it from softening later. Stir in the praline.

Melt the white chocolate, ensuring that the temperature does not exceed 95°F {35°C}. Stir it into the feuillantine-praline mixture until completely incorporated. Lastly, stir in the chopped pistachios and salt.

Fill the molds with the praline mixture and refrigerate for one hour, until set. Pour the remaining tempered chocolate over the top to encase the praline mixture. Return to the refrigerator for 30 minutes, until set, and then turn out of the molds.

Chef's note

Pailleté feuillantine is available online. You can substitute crushed Breton Gavottes® cookies or other thin, crisp cookies.

You can replace the pistachios with chopped unsalted cashew nuts.

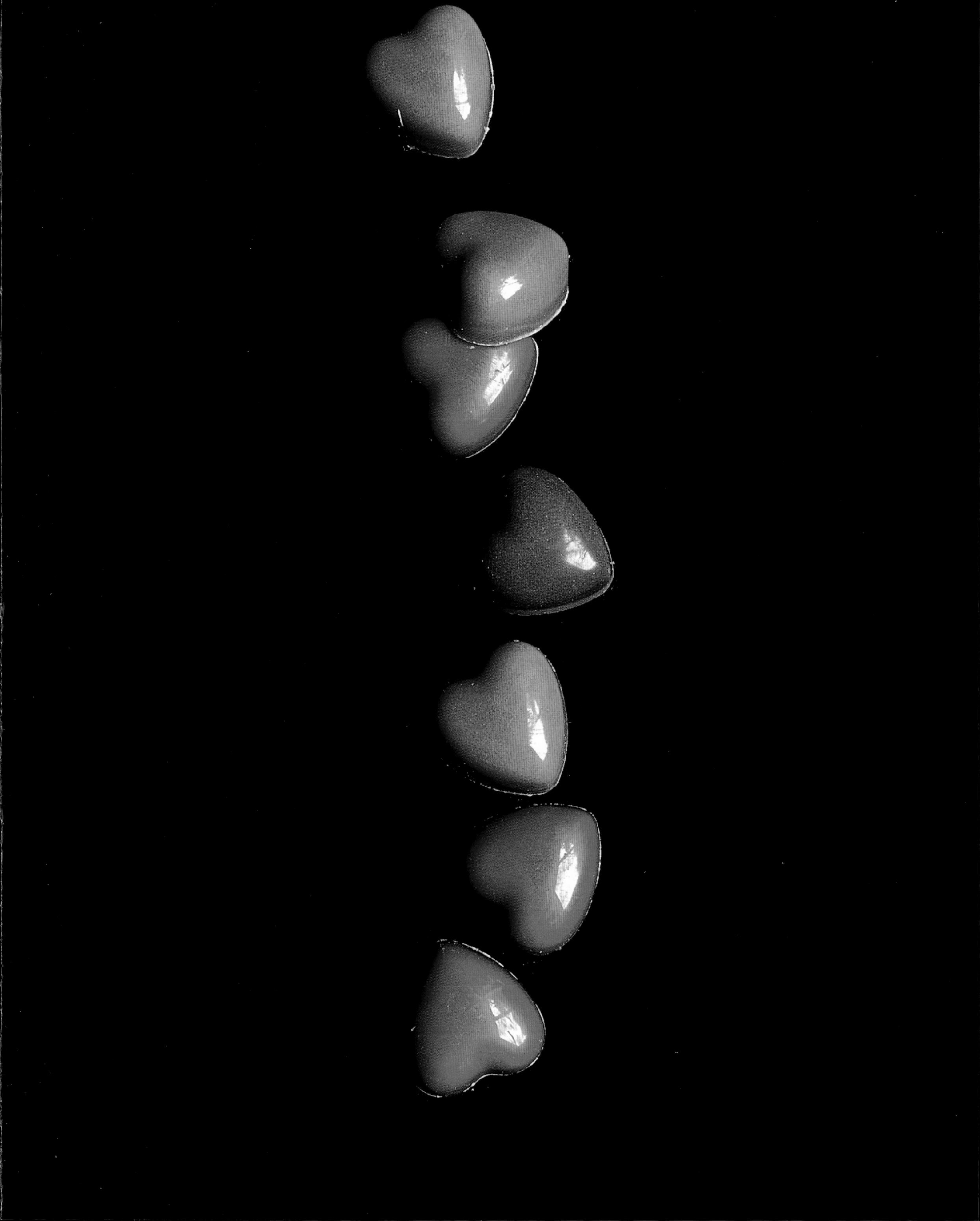

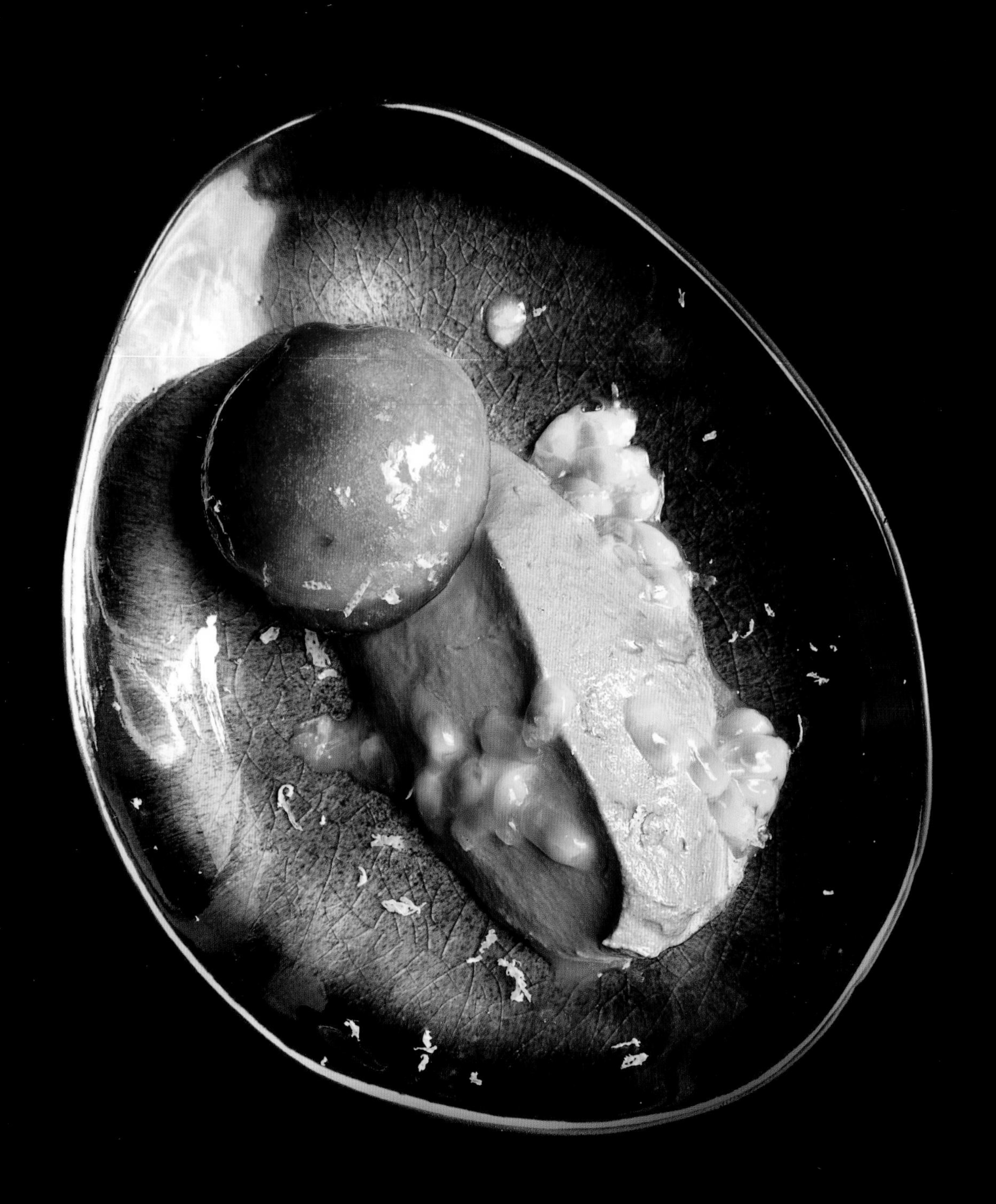

Chocolate Babas

with Exotic Fruit

Makes 6 individual babas
Prep: 30 minutes
Cook: 12 minutes

INGREDIENTS

10 oz. {300 g} Chocolate Savarin dough
{see recipe, page 346}
4 passion fruit
Juice and finely grated zest of an unwaxed lime, plus finely grated zest of an unwaxed lime for decoration
Juice and finely grated zest of an unwaxed orange
1 Madagascar vanilla bean, split, seeds scraped
1¾ cups {12½ oz. / 350 g} granulated sugar
10½ oz. {300 g} Chocolate Chantilly Cream
{see recipe, page 348}

EQUIPMENT

Hemispherical silicone mold with 6 cavities

Make the chocolate babas:
Preheat the oven to 350°F {180°C}. Place the savarin dough in the molds and bake for 10 to 12 minutes, until well risen and nicely colored. Immediately turn out of the molds and place on a rack. {They should be warm when you moisten them with the syrup.}

Meanwhile, make the syrup: In a saucepan, combine the pulp of three of the passion fruit, the lime juice and zest, the orange juice and zest, the vanilla bean and seeds, and the sugar. You will need 2 cups {500 ml} of syrup, so it may be necessary to add some water. Bring all these ingredients to a boil and allow to cool to lukewarm for 10 minutes. Remove the vanilla bean.

Place the warm babas on a rack set over a rimmed baking sheet. With a spoon, moisten them with the warm syrup. Allow to drain and then moisten once again with the syrup. The texture of the babas should be moist yet light. Allow them to cool.

Whip the chocolate Chantilly cream until light.

To plate, place a baba on each plate with an oval scoop of Chantilly cream. Decorate with a few passion fruit seeds from the remaining passion fruit and the grated lime zest.

Chef's note

Purists will want to serve a fine rum with this dessert.

Ben Tre

Serves 6
Prep: 25 minutes
Chill: 20 minutes

INGREDIENTS

5 oz. {150 g} dark chocolate {78% cacao}, preferably Trinitario grand cru chocolate {Vietnam}
7 oz. {200 g} assorted berries {raspberries, black currants, blueberries, and red currants}
1 tablespoon {20 g} acacia honey {or multi-floral honey}
7 oz. {200 g} Light Chocolate Mousse {see recipe, page 351}
7 oz. {200 g} Almond Nougatine, uncoated {see recipe, page 355}

Chop the chocolate with a knife. To ensure that the chocolate is glossy, temper as follows:
- Over a hot water bath, heat the chocolate to 122°F {50°C}.
- Place over a cool water bath and cool to 82°F {28°C}.
- Reheat the chocolate to 90°F {32°C} over a hot water bath.

Pour the chocolate over a sheet of food-safe acetate and place another sheet over it. With a rolling pin, spread the chocolate very thinly. Refrigerate for 20 minutes. Break the chocolate into shards.

Meanwhile, cook the berries with the honey to make a compote. Allow the mixture to simmer for a few minutes over medium heat, until slightly caramelized.

To plate, spoon out a line of softened berries. Next to that, arrange a few oval scoops of light chocolate mousse. Scatter broken bits of almond nougatine over the plate and add a few shards of chocolate.

Chef's note

Instead of the berries, try a rhubarb compote.

Annexes

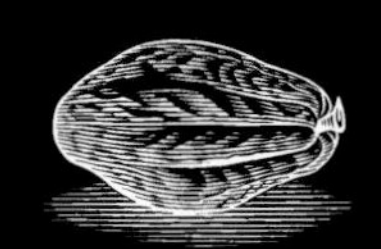

A Tasting
Session

Biting into a square of chocolate is more than a mere pleasurable act; it's one that awakens all our senses. Here are some of the fundamentals of chocolate tasting so that you can maximize your enjoyment, whether you share the ritual with others or simply indulge yourself.

Order

"Crescendo" is the watchword: Begin a tasting session with a delicate chocolate, such as a Criollo. Continue with a Trinitario and finish off with the most powerful variety. Whatever your selection, keep in mind that after five or six varieties of chocolate, your taste buds will have reached a threshold after which they are no longer receptive.

Temperature

For aromas to reveal themselves at their best, chocolate must be tasted at room temperature, between 64 and 72°F {18 and 22°C}.

Use your eyes

To tempt the amateur, the chocolate must be smooth and glossy, signs that the conching has been carried out correctly and that the right crystallization has been achieved. Colors are warm, ranging from brown through auburn to mahogany.

As well as your nose

Before you bite into it, inhale the odor of the chocolate. Beyond the deep cacao odor, you should be able to capture a number of volatile substances, such as notes of fruit, plants, and flowers, as well as animal, peppery, or roasted notes. However, the aromas that are contained in the cacao butter develop more intensely through retronasal olfaction.

And listen carefully

The noise of chocolate snapping prefigures the enjoyment of tasting. Chocolate should break easily and clearly with a nice snap. If the sound is soft, muffled, or subdued, the chocolate is probably too fatty or too warm.

In your mouth

Taste your chocolate slowly, small piece by small piece. Allow it to melt for a few seconds for your taste buds to be imbued; they will capture the primary tastes: sweet, salty, sour, and bitter. The thicker the chocolate, the more time it will need to come to the right temperature.

An attack with a subtle acidity, followed by bitterness without harshness, bodes well for what is to follow.

Bite several times, rubbing the chocolate gently against the palate, to reveal the secondary aromas: red or yellow fruit, spices, and flowers. When you breathe out, new aromatic components will enrich the profile of the chocolate through retronasal olfaction. Lastly, a lasting mouthfeel is the fitting end to the tasting of a quality chocolate.

Storage Advice & Tips

The basic principles for best preserving the qualities of chocolate can be summed up easily: a dry place, protected from moisture, light, and heat. But there's more to it.

Wrap it carefully. Chocolate absorbs smells; in addition, its aromas are volatile. Wrap chocolate in aluminum foil or store it in an airtight container. Cardboard gives off an unpleasant smell and should be avoided.

Store chocolate at room temperature, between 64 and 72°F {18 and 22°C}. The refrigerator is too cold. When the weather is very hot, store your chocolate—carefully wrapped, of course—in a wine cellar or in the vegetable crisper drawer. When you use this storage method, remember to bring the chocolate back to room temperature for one hour before serving. Leave it in the wrapping to prevent any risk of condensation.

Bloom. If chocolate is exposed to sudden heat or a drop in temperature, the cacao butter rises to the surface and solidifies, leaving a white veil. Although this detracts from its appearance, the taste will not be altered. If the surface of your chocolate looks uneven, that's probably because it was stored in a place with too much moisture.

Shelf life. Wine and chocolate have many commonalities in terms of enjoyment and pleasure, but long life is not one of them. Although chocolate does not perish rapidly, neither does it improve with age. Bittersweet chocolate keeps longer than milk chocolate, and milk chocolate longer than white. Chocolate-based confections are even more fragile, and you should check the expiration dates given by the chocolate maker.

Waste not, want not. Any chocolate that no longer looks attractive can still be used in cakes or other pastries.

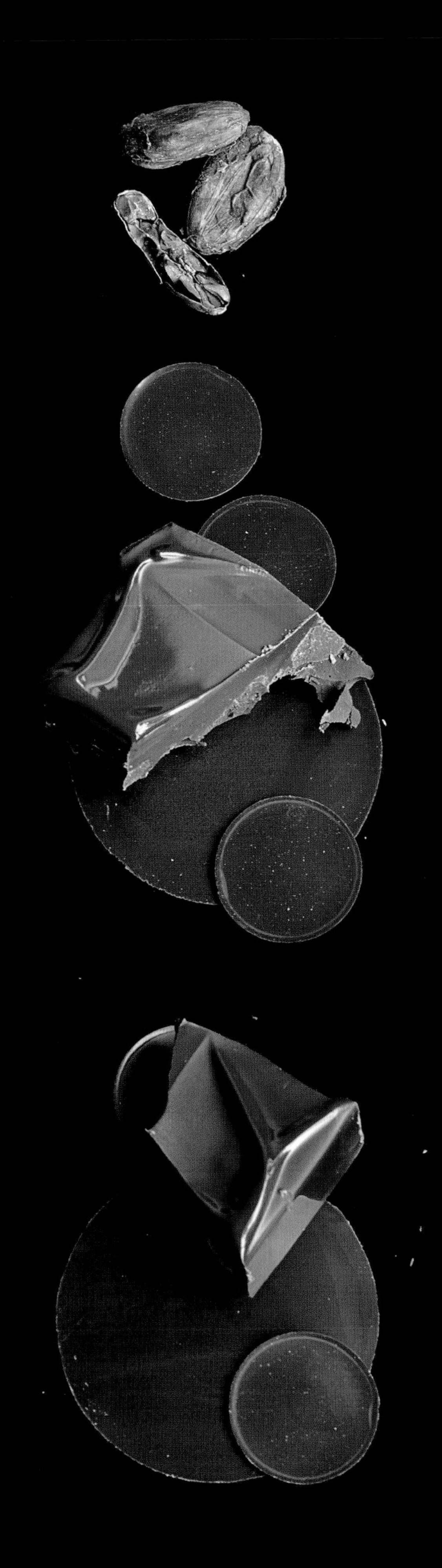

BARS, DISKS, SQUARES & TWISTS

BEVERAGES

BROWNIES

CACAO BEANS & NIBS

CAKES & LOAVES

CANDIES & TRUFFLES

COMPOSED DESSERTS

Where to Find Cacao Beans and Nibs

A Selection of Pierre Marcolini boutiques:

Belgium

Sablon
Rue des Minimes 1
1000 Bruxelles
+32 2 514.12.06
sablon@marcolini.be

France

Scribe
3, rue Scribe
75009 Paris
+33 1 44 71 03 74
paris-scribe@marcolini.fr

UK

Marylebone
37 Marylebone High Street
W1U 4QE London
+44 2 074 867 196
marylebone@marcolini.com

A list of all Pierre Marcolini boutiques can be found on www.marcolini.com.
Beans can also be purchased here.

On The Internet :

US

Kalustyan's: kalustyans.com
Nuts: nuts.com
Terrasoul Superfoods: terrasoul.com
Thrive Market: thrivemarket.com
Z Natural Foods: znaturalfoods.com

UK

Buy Whole Foods Online:
buywholefoodsonline.co.uk
Detox Trading: detoxtrading.co.uk
Goji King: gojiking.co.uk
Healthy Supplies: healthysupplies.co.uk
Real Foods: realfoods.co.uk

Acknowledgments

I would like to thank
All the members of my team, without whom this book would not have come into being;
My anonymous clients, who have placed their trust in me for 20 years;
Nicolette, who tirelessly seeks out the finest cacao beans and who has helped me make sense of the vast world;
The members of the team at La Martinière, and Florence in particular, for showing me their confidence;
Marie-Pierre, for her exquisite photos;
Chae Rin, for translating the language of professionals into everyday language;
Laure, for her meticulous work and her re-reading;
Laurence, for her outstanding graphic work;
Clémence and David, for their precious help in putting this book together;
My friends who work in restaurants, tightrope-walking on a daily basis;
My three musketeers and lifetime companions;
Neo, who has just joined me in this adventure;
Valérie, Sacha,
and last but not least, la Mama, a wonderful woman.

Photography Credits:
Xavier Harcq: p. 4, 9, 10–11, 17, 20, 22, 23, 24, 25, 27, 382–383